The Botanical Kitchen

For Caroline Stenner, as
proof that I eat more than
just cheese sandwiches.

And Jack Van Praag, for
inspiring a journey that
ensured it was so.

Elly McCausland

The Botanical Kitchen

Cooking with
fruits, flowers,
leaves & seeds

BLOOMSBURY ABSOLUTE
LONDON · OXFORD · NEW YORK · NEW DELHI · SYDNEY

Contents

Introduction   6

Orchard Fruits   14
Apples, cherries, peaches, pears, plums, quince

Mediterranean Fruits   50
Apricots, bergamots, dates, figs, lemons, oranges

Tropical Fruits   90
Bananas, grapefruits, lychees, mangos, papayas,
persimmons, pineapples, pomelos

Leaves   130
Banana leaves, blackcurrant leaves, herbs,
kaffir lime leaves, tea leaves

Flowers   170
Chamomile, elderflower, lavender, rose, saffron, vanilla

Seeds   202
Cardamom, nutmeg, poppy seeds, sesame seeds

Berries & Currants   228
Blackberries, blackcurrants, blueberries, gooseberries,
raspberries, redcurrants, strawberries

Stockists & Index   260

About the Author & Acknowledgements   269

Introduction

botanical, n. /bəˈtænɪk(ə)l/

Of or relating to botany, or the biological characteristics
and attributes of the plants with which it is concerned.

THIS BOOK begins with a nutmeg.

A nutmeg is a fairly indistinguishable object. At a passing glance, it could be a wooden bead, a trinket, an anonymous nut in a Christmas box. Its surface is unpromising, weathered with wrinkles and more reminiscent of furniture than food. Yet apply a little pressure with a sharp grater, start to mine the nutmeg for its contents, and something rather magical happens. That tough surface begins to give way to a yielding, creamy interior, criss-crossed with dark rivulets like the veins of a leaf, or a scan of a human brain. As tiny furls of nutmeg fall softly from the grater like sawdust, you start to detect a warming, spicy woodiness, redolent of the inside of a camphor chest or a sandalwood box; a slightly medicinal tang; a hint of butter and cream. The scent of the nutmeg is comforting, familiar, exotic and alluring all at once – no surprise, perhaps, for a botanical whose Latin name is *Myristica fragrans*. This spice was once believed to ward off the plague, was once more valuable than gold, and is often cited as possessing hallucinatory powers. It is just as at home simmered into Malaysian and Indonesian sweets as folded into the cosseting white sauce for a fish pie or the buttery rubble that will top an apple crumble. The nutmeg is unassuming, inexpensive and compact, yet a few strokes with a grater brings it to life and adds an essential spicy warmth to a whole host of dishes.

The nutmeg, staple of kitchen cupboards and cauliflower cheeses everywhere, also has perhaps the bloodiest history of any ingredient. When you add its russet shavings to your dinner or dessert, you are following in a long line of consumers for whom the nutmeg was a desirable seasoning – so desirable, in fact, that it was at the heart of Dutch colonialism in the islands of Indonesia and prompted a series of atrocities that decimated the indigenous population of the Banda islands, where nutmeg grows native. Prior to this, nutmeg was traded by the Arabs during the Middle Ages and sold to the Venetians for high prices because the sailors refused to divulge the source of their supply. It was prized in medieval cuisine, where it made pease pudding – a type of gruel made from dried pulses – more appealing, and improved the flavour of ale. Used medicinally since at least the seventh century, including as an aphrodisiac, the psychoactive effects of nutmeg rendered the spice notorious during the nineteenth century. Following the Napoleonic Wars, the British took nutmeg trees to Sri Lanka, Penang and Singapore, then to other colonial strongholds in the Caribbean and West Africa. Today, nutmeg is widely used in Malaysian and Caribbean cuisine.

On a trip to Penang in 2013, I found myself strolling wide-eyed round a bustling grocery market. Between the piles of coconuts, the wriggling fish in buckets and the baskets of powdered spices lay the humble nutmeg in more manifestations than I had ever considered possible. Whole nutmegs, at least twice as large as any I had ever acquired back home, dark and glossy like horse chestnuts; candied nutmeg, shredded and sugared for use as a topping on *ais kacang*, a sweet shaved ice dessert; nutmeg rind, to be boiled and served as iced juice; nutmeg pods, candied and sold in syrup of various colours and fragrances; golden, spiky mace, the coating – or 'aril' – that forms around the nutmeg seed inside its shell, for simmering in curries, soups and stews; nutmeg oil, to treat stomach pain and nausea; nutmeg balm, which turned out to be the best treatment for insect bites I have ever laid my hands on. I took home a bag of candied nutmeg, some of which was folded into an apple and blueberry tea bread for breakfast back in my Yorkshire kitchen, and some of which was baked into pumpkin muffins.

That a once-mysterious and highly prized spice from the Far East is now almost as common in kitchens the world over as salt and pepper fascinates me. How did all these different countries find such diverse uses for its woody fragrance? Why do we Brits tend to pair nutmeg with cream, cauliflower or potatoes, while other cultures partner it with beef, pumpkin or rum? To what other innovative uses might we put it in the kitchen? And, going further, what great potential is there for the other fruits, flowers, leaves, seeds and spices we tend to keep in our cupboards? What were the historical journeys of these natural treasures? Such questions were at the heart of the food blog I started in 2010, named 'Nutmegs, seven' after a quotation from Shakespeare's *Winter's Tale*. Many years later, those same questions are at the heart of this book, too.'

Although they have formed the backbone of cuisines the world over for centuries, botanical ingredients – fruits, flowers, leaves, seeds and spices – have a tendency to shy away from the limelight, letting more boisterous flavours take centre stage. That is, to an extent, their purpose: to coax out other flavours while remaining subtle, bringing a sense of completion to a dish. Consider an apple crumble without a whisper of cinnamon, or a roast leg of lamb without the resinous tang of rosemary. Yet there is also something luxuriant about using these ingredients in cooking: they are rarely vital, but rather a way to add complex layers of flavour, new twists and aromatic surprises. This book explores some of that magic, aiming to place botanicals back in the limelight and to appreciate them for their unique qualities, history and potency.

We have recently begun to pay more attention to these 'supporting acts' in the kitchen. Increasingly exotic botanicals are appearing in the supermarkets every day: the presence of kaffir lime leaves, edible flowers and Thai basil on our shelves caters to the growing number of cooks embracing new flavours, while our burgeoning love of cuisines from the Middle East encourages creative ways with spices, rose petals and saffron. Drawing on the bounty of nature's botanicals is a wonderful way to tap into the vibrant cuisine of other cultures: stir a few shredded kaffir lime leaves into a pan of simmering coconut milk, and you could be slurping *tom kha gai* on a bustling street corner in Bangkok; top a syrupy yoghurt cake with rose petals for dessert and you've crossed continents to the frenetic bazaars of Morocco. Understanding the provenance, history and potential of botanical ingredients is both useful and rewarding, a pleasure for both the committed cook and for those interested in the way food shapes culture, myth and history, and vice versa.

We are also quickly becoming more aware of the benefits of a plant-based diet: whether you're a hardcore vegan or simply exploring the possibilities of flexitarianism, including more botanical ingredients in your everyday eating is a way to make the most of nature's bounty, particularly if you can find a small patch of land – or even a sunny windowsill – on which to grow your own. Contemplating the magic and provenance of individual botanicals is a way to reconnect food to the natural world, something that is of growing importance in an age where we are so far removed from the realities of agriculture and food production. This book offers recipes for my favourite fruits, flowers, leaves and seeds, but will also – I hope – inspire creativity with these types of ingredients, illustrating how botanicals can form a flavoursome backbone to the most quotidian cooking, as well as the experimental and adventurous. Cooking this way doesn't have to be expensive, or require multiple trips to esoteric delis or markets: you'll find many of these ingredients in supermarkets, and easily source many of the more unusual botanicals – a lemon verbena plant, for example, or a box of frozen lime leaves that will last for years. Failing that, many of the recipes have suggestions for alternatives that are more readily available and will enhance your dishes in equally interesting ways.

The food in this book exists at a series of intersections: between the exotic and the familiar, the necessary and the frivolous, the sweet and the savoury. It draws inspiration from classic British tastes and recipes, blending these with the techniques and aromas of some of the most inspirational food destinations: Scandinavia, the Mediterranean, the Middle East and southeast Asia. It explores tantalising marriages of tastes and textures. Above all, it places botanical ingredients at the fore, emphasising the power of a few small, often inexpensive, ingredients to transform and enhance your food.

Just like the nutmeg.

Elly McCausland
2020, Oslo

A note on botanicals

All ingredients derived from plants are, of course, botanicals. This book, however, is interested in plant-based ingredients that enhance flavour, shifting and developing the character of a dish. For that reason, it does not cover vegetables, which often form the bulk of a recipe. Instead, the focus is on fruits, flowers, leaves and seeds, often used in small quantities as supporting acts. While all spices are botanicals, helpful guides to the world of spices already exist, so this book focuses specifically on other categories (where spices are also, for example, seeds – such as nutmeg – they are included).

A note on the recipes

* All butter is unsalted, unless otherwise specified.

* All eggs are large, and free-range if possible.

* All salt is fine grain, unless coarse/flaky sea salt is specified.

* Unless specified, all milk is whatever you have in your fridge (whole, semi-skimmed, skimmed, and so on).

* For the best possible results, I highly recommend using a digital temperature probe to test for when cakes, custards, meat and fish are done. They are fairly inexpensive now and will make a world of difference to your cooking. I recommend Thermapen.

* I recommend using organic fruit, vegetables, eggs, meat and dairy produce. It really does make a difference, particularly when there are few other flavours to hide behind (as in, for example, ice cream). Try to use the best-quality meat and fish you can afford, and source the latter sustainably.

* Where a recipe contains two different botanicals (for example, both flowers and orchard fruits), it is categorised in terms of which flavour is the focal point of the dish. A quick look through the index will guide you to all the recipes for a particular ingredient.

Orchard Fruits

And still she slept an azure-lidded sleep/In blanched linen, smooth and lavendered/While he from forth the closet brought a heap/Of candied apple, quince, and plum, and gourd.

~ John Keats, 'The Eve of St. Agnes'

T HE ORCHARD has traditionally been a place where magic happens. The mythical land of Avalon, legendary resting place of King Arthur, possibly derives its name from the Old Cornish for 'apple tree', and is often depicted as a land of abundant orchards. Pomona, goddess of plenty and harvest in ancient Roman mythology, takes her name from the Latin *pomum*, meaning orchard fruit. In Celtic myth, passage to the Otherworld is granted only to bearers of a magical silver apple branch. Golden apples from Hera's mystical Garden of the Hesperides feature in several ancient Greek legends, associated with love and desire. Keats's Porphyro woos the innocent Madeline on the mysterious Eve of St. Agnes by presenting her with baskets of succulent orchard fruit, 'filling the chilly room with perfume light'. It works: the lovers elope together into the storm, never to be seen or heard from again.

Few fruits hold more luscious promise than those of the orchard. The golden spritz of citrus or the musky perfume of tropical mangoes and pineapples have their place, but it is the orchard fruits that beg, most of all, to be coaxed to full flavour with the darker, richer sweeteners: muscovado sugar, thick honey, maple syrup. 'Orchard', of course, refers to a space in which we can grow myriad fruits – including the vibrant specimens of the Mediterranean – but in this chapter I am thinking specifically of those fruits that we associate with the British summer and early autumn: pears, apples, peaches, quinces, plums and cherries. Of course, many of these are Roman or Eastern imports (domestication of apples is thought to have begun in Anatolia, and quinces originate from the foothills of the Caucasus mountains), but we have come to think of them as our own. These are the fruits that soften most deliciously and pleasingly under the crust of a homely pie, or the buttery rubble of a crumble. They will often give you the most reward when you apply a little heat: translucent pears become butter-soft bubbled in caramel or spiced red wine; cherries plump and darken in their own juices; plums, which can be disappointingly woolly or unnervingly gelatinous when raw, collapse into a thick compote when roasted or poached, taking on some of the sticky, red-wine notes of their dried relatives, prunes.

No fruit embodies this lesson more than the **quince**. I have long had a soft spot for this esoteric specimen, with its apple/pear appearance and coating of baby-soft fuzz that belies the rock-hard sourness within. The culinary heyday of the quince in Britain was the medieval period, a hedonistic era of stuffed fantasy animal sculptures and roast swans, when the line between sweet and savoury was deliciously blurred in a sugary, spicy, rosewatery haze. During this time, the down from the fruit's skin was mixed with wax and spread on the head as a 'cure' for baldness, but nowadays we tend to just rub it off with a cloth before cooking – what a waste! Dubious medical applications aside, it is also a fruit of romance: quince trees were said to spring up wherever the goddess Aphrodite walked, Greek wedding ceremonies often featured quinces baked in a cake with honey and sesame seeds, and women were advised to eat quince to sweeten their breath before entering the bridal chamber. It is also, of course, the fruit that the Owl and the Pussycat enjoy as part of their wedding dinner (eaten with a runcible spoon) in Edward Lear's famous poem. Some venture that the original fruit of knowledge in the garden of Eden was a quince, rather than an apple, which would certainly explain the catastrophic results of Eve's temptation: only bad things can come of biting into a raw quince, whether or not one is urged on by a serpent. Anaemic, tough and slightly gritty when raw, quinces mellow into beautiful glowing tenderness when gently simmered in liquid. The flesh deepens in colour to a luscious red and the fruit's perfumed aromas come to the fore. As the Vietnamese writer Monique Truong put it, 'watch their dry, bone-coloured flesh soak up the heat, coating itself in an opulent orange, not of the sunrises that you never see but of the insides of tree-ripened papayas, a colour you can taste'. Or, put rather more bluntly, the quince before cooking has 'the colour of an impassioned and scrawny lover', according to a Spanish poem from the tenth century. Somewhere between a fragrant apple and a succulent, sweet pear, the quince also has a slight citrus note to it. It works well with rich meats and cheeses, for this reason: in a classic lamb and quince tagine, perhaps, or a thick slab of honey-coloured *membrillo* with sharp manchego cheese. It is most at home when accompanied by other Eastern spices and flavours, sits well alongside its relatives, apples and pears, and is particularly gorgeous when partnered with dark sugar or caramel.

'Do I dare to eat a **peach**?' asks T. S. Eliot's J. Alfred Prufrock, famously, in his eponymous poem from 1915. Were he to ask this question today, I might be tempted to answer in the negative. Peaches (and their close relations, nectarines) are notoriously unreliable, particularly those purchased from the supermarket. Sometimes they fail to ripen altogether, remaining astringent and hard, and sometimes they 'ripen' into distastefully spongy specimens that even cooking cannot salvage. As legendary food writer Jane Grigson put it, 'you are gambling rather than choosing' when you select peaches for purchase: 'All you can do is make sure your horse is not lame or blind, by refusing peaches that are bruised or soft'. I find a good strategy is to smell them – promising, ripening fruit will have a heady, sweet aroma. If your fruit is fine texturally but a little more sour than you would like, it is an excellent contender for the peach recipes in this book, which put the fruit to savoury uses and so benefit from that extra tartness.

At one point when I lived in Denmark, I was given a bag of **apples** from a friend's garden. Until I took that bag in my hands, I would probably have argued that raw apples have no smell. Yet this plastic bag, crammed with blushing apples in all shapes and sizes, was redolent with a crisp, heady perfume. Hints of rose, orange and honey mingled in a glorious waft of pure apple essence that was still strong even after the apples had spent a week in my fridge. One sniff and I was walking through an orchard in late summer, or strolling through the storehouse of a cider press. You would never find such apples in the supermarket, and they were probably of some obscure variety that has long since died out commercially. Straight from the tree, they were the best apples I have ever tasted in my life, and made me wonder: what other wonderful fruit epiphanies – what *smells*? – are we missing out on through having our tastes governed by commercial convenience? What excitement, discovery and experimentation?

The horrible truth is that farmers are forced to throw away wonky carrots, wrinkly tomatoes and improperly curved bananas because the supermarkets, conscious of an apparent consumer desire for perfection, will not sell them. It is somewhat bizarre that certain chains offer bags of 'weather-blemished' apples and pears, priced slightly lower than their other orchard offerings – which, presumably, have had zero contact with any form of weather and are grown in some kind of vacuum pod lined with bubble wrap under light simulators. If we have to be reminded that some of our fruit and veg may be less than beauty-pageant-worthy because it has been besmirched by the hands of Mother Nature, something is very wrong indeed.

Some of the best **pears** I have ever tasted were from a crate generously left outside the front garden of one of the houses I pass every day on my way to work. I have absolutely no idea what variety they were, and the garden owners probably didn't know either. The modern pear unfortunately seems to suffer an even worse fate than the apple, with supermarkets largely confining their stocks to the sturdy Conference variety. I have nothing bad to say about this reliable stalwart, but would we content ourselves with only ever eating a single type of meat, fish, cheese or bread? Exactly. First cultivated by the Romans, the pear is thought to have originated in western China, and you will sometimes spy the Asian or Nashi pear for sale in supermarkets. There are thousands of varieties out there, but the fragility of a quality pear means that very few make it to our shelves. Although lacking the useful tartness of the apple, the pear has a greater complexity of fragrance and texture, making it doubly rewarding if you stumble across an unusual variety. I have been known to sit down for a few precious moments with just a perfectly ripe pear, a plate and a knife – something I have never found myself doing with an apple. The glassy flesh, brimming with delicately floral juice and perhaps a whisper of bracing tannin, is a genuine treat, particularly if you look outside the generically-branded supermarket box (the musky Comice, sinfully juicy Williams and russet-coloured Bosc are some of my favourites).

You can buy **plums** almost year-round in cheap supermarket punnets, where they tend to resemble indigo golf balls, both in appearance and in hardness (the cheery 'ripen at home' label is used to excuse all manner of supermarket sins). Unnaturally uniform in shape and shine, they look like they have gone through some kind of polishing process. I avoid eating these raw, as they tend to have a nasty woolly texture and very little flavour to speak of beyond unpleasant tannin. However, they can be rescued with the application of a little sugar and heat – roast plums with orange, brown sugar and star anise is one of my favourite breakfasts, and forms the basis of my ultimate crumble recipe (on page 49). When the first British plums – the Victoria, Czar and Opal varieties being among the most widespread – start appearing in the markets, though, it's a whole different story. Quivering, gelatinous, often festooned with a halo of wasps, these are plums to remind you of what plums actually *taste* like. They are a far cry from what the supermarkets would have us believe plums are. Oddly shaped and mottled in colour, their skins often sport a slight dusky bloom.

Greengages, when you find them, glow like swollen jade pearls; it is no accident that their French name is the regal *Reine Claude*, in honour of the medieval queen Claude, Duchess of Brittany. This pleasing idiosyncrasy cannot be cultivated on a supermarket scale, so seek out markets and independent grocers for an autumnal feast. While these can and should be enjoyed raw, they also make very fine desserts, and there are few things more delicious than a pan of greengages briefly simmered with vanilla and a delicious local honey.

Moving away from the seductive lure of sugar, orchard fruits have a plethora of savoury uses. A safe rule of thumb is to add salty cheese, greens and toasted nuts to make a variety of seasonal salads: apples with kale, walnuts and blue cheese, for example, or plums with feta, rocket and pine nuts. I have never understood the lure of the **cherry** for desserts, finding the fruit curiously bland and lacking in complexity – and for me it conjures up all sorts of artificially sweet American confections – but their sharpness and glamorous crimson colouring render them surprisingly wonderful in savoury applications, particularly when lightly pickled to serve alongside sharp cheeses. In Wisconsin a law was once passed banning the consumption of apple pie without cheese, and your dentist would probably thank you for adhering to this rule of thumb: a piece of cheese helps to mitigate the tooth-damaging acidity of the apple. Luckily, it also works

from a flavour point of view. Enjoy a crisp Cox apple or tender, ripe plum with a crumbly slice of Wensleydale. Tuck slivers of orchard fruits alongside roasting or pan-fried meat, particularly pork and chicken. Simmer gluts into compotes and use them to top porridge, ice cream, yoghurt or granola, or to form the basis for an upside-down cake or crumble tart. It is tempting to think of these fruits as quotidian (literally – we are, after all, encouraged to eat 'an apple a day') perhaps because they grow so abundantly in British climes, but this is also cause for celebration and experimentation.

However, our orchards are under threat. Despite Britain once producing over two thousand varieties of apple, supermarkets now stock only a handful of types, seventy per cent of which are imported and many of which were originally foreign cultivars. Over the past fifty years, ninety per cent of cherry orchards in Britain have disappeared, with foreign imports constituting a shocking ninety-five per cent of all fruit sold. It's a depressing fate for a fruit that has existed in Britain since Roman times (it is famously said that you can locate old Roman roads by the wild cherry trees growing alongside them, which sprang from the stones spat out by marching soldiers). Two thirds of our total orchards have been lost since 1960, to housing projects or cereal agriculture, and with them have disappeared hundreds of unusual, unique fruit varieties – many of which are highly regional, such as the Kentish Quarrenden apple or the Black Worcester pear – and the knowledge of how to cultivate them. Supermarkets, which choose fruit for appearance, longevity and consistency rather than flavour (the 'Knobby Russet' apple is never going to win any beauty pageants) now dictate our tastes. As Hugh Fearnley-Whittingstall puts it, 'such apples are the horticultural equivalent of intensively farmed chicken: mass produced to uniform standards, dosed with protective chemicals, harvested too early and shipped too far. In the end they leave a taste in the mouth that, if not actively nasty, is certainly on the dull side. We can do better.'

While these recipes will work with any orchard fruits, try to seek out local or unusual specimens where possible, in order to support small orchards and the cultivation of historic fruit varieties. Farmers markets are good locations, and many growers are now offering their unique produce online. Friends with trees or allotments are even better. There is much joy to be had in discovering a new variety that will awaken your taste buds from the homogeneity of supermarket offerings, and in choosing recipes to showcase its unique flavours and qualities.

Let us try not to lose the magic of the orchard: a quiet, ancient space of plenty and poetry that has so captivated the mythological and culinary imagination over the centuries.

Tips & tricks

* The core of a quince is solid, gritty and unpleasant, even after long, slow cooking. With apples and pears you can get away with leaving a little bit of the core on the fruit, but be sure to remove every trace of it from a quince.

* If poaching quinces, put the peelings and cores in a muslin bag and add to the poaching liquid – they contain a surprising amount of flavour, and important pectin that helps thicken the syrup (which also makes quinces excellent for jams and jellies).

* William Lawson, writing in the seventeenth century, advised against storing quinces near other fruit, 'for the scent is offensive both to the other fruit, and to those that keep the fruit or come amongst them'. While we can probably agree that he is wrong about the scent – quinces in a bowl give off a beautiful perfume – he was in fact correct about storage. Quinces can keep for weeks in a bowl and months in the fridge, but you should not store them touching one another or other fruit, as this can cause everything to overripen and rot. You can also freeze them whole or in slices, and you can of course freeze them in cooked form (like the compote on page 198) for cakes or breakfast.

* Quince trees take up little space, have gloriously fragrant blossom and are relatively easy to care for. For an excellent overview of growing, harvesting and cooking quinces, I direct you to the wonderful book *Quinces: Growing and Cooking* by Jane McMorland Hunter and Sue Dunster.

* The word 'marmalade' was originally used for a preserve made from quinces (the Portuguese for quince is *marmelo*), and modern-day *membrillo*, cut into small cubes or slices, is a great substitute for fresh quince in savoury pies and tarts.

* Sixteenth-century medical writers urged pregnant women to eat quince in order to have more intelligent children. If true, mine will be prodigies.

* Some apple varieties collapse completely when heated. Establish whether your chosen variety will hold its shape before attempting something like a *tarte tatin*, where the integrity of the fruit is quite important.

* I find the best way to test the ripeness of a pear is to press it gently with a fingernail where the bulbous lower half starts to taper into the slender stalk end. If it yields, it's ready; if you have to press harder, it's probably not. Remember, though, that some varieties of pear stay quite hard even when ripe, such as the Packham or Anjou.

* If you have an apple tree, gluts of the fruit freeze well for later cooking. Simply peel, core and chop the apples into chunks, then freeze in bags. Use them for jams, compotes or crumbles at a later date. You can also simmer peeled, cored and chopped apples into a purée with a little water, then freeze this in bags for later – it works well as a base for homemade granola, or as a substitute for some of the butter or oil in cake recipes.

* When roasting, poaching or baking plums or greengages, leave the skins on. The tannin in the skin contributes colour and flavour to their pellucid flesh. You can always remove the skins later, if desired.

Halloumi flatbreads
with spicy chipotle peach & basil salsa

Serves 4

As with strawberries, the sweetness of peach pairs beautifully with the sharp aniseed tang of basil. In this recipe, peaches are combined in a riotous, smoky–sweet salsa that is perfect alongside the squeaky richness of grilled halloumi. This is a fun, messy, do-it-yourself dinner. You can make it even quicker and easier by buying flatbreads, if you don't fancy making your own – I recommend hunting down a Middle Eastern grocer for some *khobez*.

**For the peach &
basil salsa**

juice and finely grated
zest of 1 lime
½ red onion, very
finely chopped
¼ teaspoon caster sugar
4 ripe but firm peaches,
stoned and cut into
rough 1cm dice
1 teaspoon chipotle
paste
25g basil leaves,
shredded
½ cucumber, deseeded
and chopped into
1cm dice
salt and freshly ground
black pepper

For the flatbreads

300g strong white flour
200g wholemeal flour
2 teaspoons salt
7g fast-action dried yeast
2 tablespoons sesame
seeds, nigella seeds or
linseeds (optional)
3 tablespoons olive oil

For the filling

500g halloumi, cut into
1cm slices
Greek yoghurt or soured
cream, to serve
chopped avocado,
to serve

For the salsa, put the lime zest and juice in a bowl and add the onion and sugar and a good grinding of salt. Mix well, then leave for 15 minutes or so while you get the flatbreads going.

For the flatbreads, put the flours in the bowl of an electric mixer fitted with a dough hook, or a large bowl if you plan to make the breads by hand. Add the salt to one side of the flour mixture in the bowl and the yeast to the other, then add the seeds, if using, and the olive oil and 280ml of water. Knead well using the dough hook or your hands for 10 minutes, or until you have a soft but not sticky dough. Cover the bowl with a clean tea towel and leave the dough to rise for about 1 hour, until doubled in size.

Continue with the salsa while the dough is rising. Add the peaches, chipotle paste and half the basil to the bowl with the lime and red onion mixture and stir well to combine. Set aside.

When the dough has risen, divide it into 8 equal pieces. Heat a large frying pan over a high heat. On a floured work surface, roll out each piece of dough to a circle of about 15cm in diameter and 5mm thick. Put 1 circle of dough in the frying pan and cook it for a couple of minutes, then flip it over and cook it for another couple of minutes on the other side, until both sides are lightly golden and slightly puffy and blackened in places. Repeat with the remaining pieces of dough, stacking them onto a plate under a clean tea towel (or placing them in a large plastic container with the lid on) as you cook them – this helps keep them soft and pliable by steaming them slightly.

Once the breads are cooked, use the same frying pan, over a high heat, to fry the halloumi slices for a couple of minutes on each side, until golden and slightly crispy all over. While the halloumi is cooking, add the remaining basil and the cucumber dice to the peach salsa. Stir well to combine and season to taste.

To serve, put a couple of pieces of halloumi inside a warm flatbread, top with the salsa and a dollop of yoghurt or soured cream, then a little chopped avocado. Serve immediately. Provide napkins – it gets messy.

Blue cheese risotto
with toasted pine nuts & sweet balsamic pears

Serves 4

Putting sweet, caramelised pears with a deeply savoury risotto might sound odd, but in fact it lifts the creamy starch of the rice and balances out the flavours perfectly. Blue cheese and pears work so wonderfully in any context, and this is no exception, but the toasted pine nuts and slight aniseed hint of the fennel in the risotto lift it to a new level.

For the risotto
2 litres chicken or
  vegetable stock
1 tablespoon rapeseed
  or olive oil
1 onion, finely chopped
1 fennel bulb, finely
  diced
1 tablespoon finely
  chopped rosemary
  needles
40g butter
350g risotto rice
150ml white wine
150g blue cheese
  (Stilton, Gorgonzola
  or Danish blue
  works well)
70g rocket leaves
4 tablespoons pine
  nuts, toasted
salt and freshly ground
  black pepper

For the pears
20g butter
4 ripe but firm pears
  (Conference are best),
  each cored and sliced
  lengthways into 8
1 tablespoon
  runny honey
1 tablespoon balsamic
  vinegar

Put the stock in a large saucepan and bring it to the boil over a high heat. Lower the heat to a very gentle simmer while you make the risotto – the stock needs to be hot so it doesn't stop the cooking process.

In a large, high-sided frying pan or saucepan, heat the oil over a medium heat. Add the onion and fennel, and sauté for about 10–15 minutes, until soft and golden. Don't rush this stage and don't allow the vegetables to brown – they should be very soft and sweet. Add the rosemary and butter and cook until the butter melts, then add the risotto rice. Cook for 2–3 minutes, stirring to coat the rice in the butter, then pour in the white wine. Stir the rice constantly until the wine has been absorbed, then add a ladleful of the hot stock. Stir the rice frequently until the stock has been completely absorbed, then add another ladleful. Repeat this process until the rice is just al dente (you may not need all the stock) – it should take 20–25 minutes.

Meanwhile, prepare the pears. Melt the butter in a large frying pan over a high heat, then add the pears. Allow them to cook without stirring or turning for 4–5 minutes, so they caramelise on one edge, then flip them over and allow them to caramelise on the other side. Once they are golden and burnished, lower the heat slightly and add the honey and balsamic vinegar. Stir to coat the pears in the syrupy liquid, then set them aside until the risotto is finished.

Once the risotto rice is ready, add a final ladleful of stock and the blue cheese, and stir vigorously until the cheese has melted and the liquid has been absorbed. Season to taste – cheese and stock are both salty, so you may not need much salt.

Divide the risotto equally between four plates or bowls. Top each plate with a handful of rocket leaves, 1 tablespoon of the toasted pine nuts, and a quarter of the balsamic pear slices. Serve immediately.

Apple, goat's cheese, honey & hazelnut tarts

Makes 12

This is one of the most versatile dishes in the book. These tarts work as a quick snack, starter or main course (with a salad), and you can vary the fruit, cheese, nuts and herbs to suit your taste or what you have in the kitchen already – just keep the quantities roughly the same. Pears, Stilton and walnuts/figs, ricotta and almonds/peaches, Gorgonzola and pecans – try experimenting to make these your own. I see these as a savoury recipe, but they so wonderfully bridge the savoury–sweet divide that you could easily add more honey and serve them as a dessert, or even instead of a cheese course.

320g ready-rolled
  puff pastry
1 egg, beaten, to glaze
300g soft goat's
  cheese log, sliced
  into 1cm rounds
3 teaspoons thyme or
  lemon thyme leaves,
  or 1 heaped teaspoon
  dried thyme
30g hazelnuts,
  finely chopped
4 apples or pears, cored
  and cut lengthways
  into 5mm slices
5 teaspoons runny
  honey

Pre-heat the oven to 220°C/200°C fan/gas mark 7. Line two baking sheets with baking parchment.

Lay the pastry out on a worktop. Cut it into 12 equal squares (about 8 x 8cm). Using a sharp knife, lightly score a border around each square, about 1.5cm in from the edges, without cutting completely through the pastry. Lightly brush the borders of the squares with beaten egg.

Place the pastry squares on the prepared baking sheets, with at least 5cm between each square.

Lay the goat's cheese slices over the pastry squares, avoiding the borders. The squares don't have to be completely covered in cheese, but you probably want about 3–4 slices per pastry square – enough to not leave any big gaps. Scatter half the thyme and half the hazelnuts over the cheese.

Place the apple or pear slices in a bowl with 3 teaspoons of the honey and toss well.

Lay the apple or pear slices over the top of the cheese – 2–4 slices per pastry square, depending on the size of your fruit.

Sprinkle the remaining thyme leaves and hazelnuts over the pastries, trying to keep them off the borders. Drizzle the pastries with the remaining honey.

Bake the tarts for 20–25 minutes, until the pastry has puffed up and turned golden, the cheese is bubbling and the fruit is starting to become golden and burnished. Leave to cool for a couple of minutes before serving.

Honeyed quince & sweet cheese pastries

Makes 14–16

Vaguely based on a Cretan pastry (and approved, much to my relief, by my Greek friend Vana), these sumptuous little pies showcase the versatility and honeyed sweetness of quince. Historically, quince has made a perfect partner for cheese (think of *membrillo*), and here it nestles perfectly on a cloud-like bed of feta and ricotta. I love to eat these for breakfast or brunch, but they also make an excellent mid-afternoon snack. You can adjust the recipe to suit your taste – use a higher ratio of feta to ricotta if you want a more savoury pie, or use all ricotta to keep things sweet. Incidentally, if you happen to have any leftover quince, apple and saffron compote (page 198), you can use this to top the tarts instead of making the honeyed quince from scratch.

For the quince
juice of 1 lemon
2 tablespoons runny
 honey
2 quince, peeled, cored
 and cut into 2cm dice
1 tablespoon quince jelly

For the pastry
125ml extra-virgin
 olive oil
100g golden caster sugar
130g half-fat crème
 fraîche
1 egg
500g plain flour
2 teaspoons baking
 powder
finely grated zest of
 ½ orange

For the filling
1 egg, lightly beaten
250g ricotta
200g feta, crumbled
50g icing sugar
¼ teaspoon ground
 cardamom or
 cinnamon
50g flaked almonds
 or roughly chopped
 blanched hazelnuts

First, prepare the quince. Put the lemon juice, honey and 250ml of water in a medium saucepan over a high heat, and bring to the boil. Add the quince pieces, then lower the heat to a gentle simmer. Cover the pan with a lid and cook for 40 minutes, until the quince is just tender to the point of a knife. If the pan starts to dry out, add a little more water to keep the quince moist.

Meanwhile start the pastry. In an electric mixer or with an electric hand whisk, beat the olive oil with the caster sugar for a couple of minutes on high speed, until slightly increased in volume. Whisk in the crème fraîche and egg, then sift in the flour and baking powder. Add the orange zest, then use the mixer or your hands to bring everything together into a soft, but not sticky dough. Knead for a couple of minutes, then set aside in a bowl under a clean tea towel for 30 minutes to rest.

Remove the lid from the quince pan and add the quince jelly to the quince pieces. Simmer gently, uncovered, for another 10 minutes. The quince should have turned golden red and become glazed in the jelly, and very soft to the pressure of a spoon. There should be only a little liquid left, and it should look sticky and jammy. Remove the pan from the heat and set aside.

Make the filling. Reserve 1 teaspoon of the beaten egg. Use a whisk or wooden spoon to beat together the remaining egg with the ricotta, feta, icing sugar and cardamom or cinnamon in a medium bowl. Set aside.

Pre-heat the oven to 210°C/190°C fan/gas mark 6–7. Grease two muffin tins with olive oil.

When the dough has rested for 30 minutes, roll it out on a floured work surface to a circle roughly 3mm thick. Using an upside-down bowl (or pastry cutter) of about 8–10cm in diameter, cut 14–16 circles out of the dough (the amount will depend on the size of your circles), re-rolling the trimmings as necessary until you have used it all up. Place one dough circle in each hole of the muffin tins and press down gently to shape it into a small cup.

2–3 tablespoons runny
honey, for drizzling

Divide the cheese mixture between the dough cups, placing about 1 heaped tablespoon in each. Gently crimp the edges of the dough with your finger and thumb, gathering it together around the cheese filling at the sides. You don't want to cover the cheese, simply gather the dough around it so the filling sits neatly in the middle.

Divide the honeyed quince between the pastries, placing a heaped teaspoon or so on top of the cheese filling in each, until it is all used up.

Brush the pastry around the cheese mixture with the reserved teaspoon of beaten egg.

Bake the pastries for about 20–25 minutes, until the cheese filling has set and the pastry is golden. Remove from the oven and set aside to cool. As the pastries are cooling, put the 50g flaked almonds or hazelnuts on a small baking tray and toast in the oven for 10 minutes. Remove and set aside to cool.

To serve, drizzle the pastries with honey and sprinkle with the toasted nuts.

Aubergine burgers
with feta, walnuts, sour cherries & garlic tahini sauce

Serves 4

Vaguely inspired by falafel, these combine all my favourite flavours from Middle Eastern mezze: smoky, burnt aubergine, earthy chickpeas, bitter walnuts and creamy feta. Jewel-like sour cherries are a surprising but wonderful addition, peppering the mixture with a little sweetness and harmonising all the other flavours. These are a nod to my love of dried fruit in the savoury dishes of Middle Eastern and North African cuisine. You could even use fresh cherries in season, although dried ones will have a slightly richer flavour. Dried cranberries or chopped dried apricots will work in place of dried cherries, if you prefer.

For the burgers

2 aubergines
70g dried sour cherries
50g walnuts
1 tablespoon rapeseed
   or olive oil, plus extra
   for frying
1 red onion, very finely
   chopped
½ teaspoon ground
   cumin
½ teaspoon ground
   coriander
1 teaspoon sumac
¼ teaspoon sweet
   smoked paprika
¼ teaspoon ground
   cinnamon
50g fresh breadcrumbs
400g can of chickpeas,
   drained well
20g flat-leaf parsley
   leaves, roughly
   chopped
120g feta cheese,
   crumbled
1 tablespoon
   pomegranate molasses
1 teaspoon sea
   salt flakes
plain flour, for dusting
pitta, flatbreads or
   burger buns, to serve

Heat the grill to high. Line an oven tray with foil and lay the aubergines on top. Place them under the grill and cook for about 30–45 minutes, turning occasionally, until the skins are blackened and the flesh inside is completely soft to the point of a knife. Remove the aubergines from the grill, pierce the skins to let the steam out, and leave to cool.

While the aubergines are cooking, put the sour cherries in a small bowl and cover with hot (but not boiling) water. Set aside.

Pre-heat the oven to 200°C/180°C fan/gas mark 6.

Place the walnuts on a small baking tray and cook in the oven for 10 minutes, until toasted, then set aside to cool.

Once the aubergines are cool, scoop out the flesh (discard the skin) and place the flesh in a colander over the sink or a bowl to drain while you carry on preparing everything else.

Heat the 1 tablespoon of rapeseed or olive oil in a small frying pan over a medium heat. Add the onion and sauté, stirring occasionally, for about 5–10 minutes, until soft and translucent. Add the spices and breadcrumbs and cook for a final 1 minute, then set aside to cool.

While everything cools, make the sauce. Simply whisk all the sauce ingredients together. Season to taste – add more salt or lemon juice if you think it necessary.

Drain the cherries and pat them dry with kitchen paper.

Put the onion mixture, aubergine flesh, drained cherries, toasted walnuts, chickpeas, parsley, feta, pomegranate molasses and sea salt in a food processor with a good grinding of black pepper. Pulse a couple of times so the ingredients mingle, but do not over-mix – you don't want to turn it into a purée, more of a chunky mixture with individual ingredients still visible.

little gem lettuce leaves,
    to serve
freshly ground black
    pepper

For the sauce
1 garlic clove, crushed
juice of ½ lemon,
    plus extra to taste if
    necessary
90g tahini
180g full-fat plain
    yoghurt
½ teaspoon salt, plus
    extra to taste if
    necessary

Spoon the mixture into a large bowl and refrigerate for 1 hour to make the burgers easier to shape.

Dust a plate with a thin layer of plain flour. Using your hands, shape the aubergine mixture into 8 small patties (each about 7.5cm in diameter) and dust them with flour on each side.

Heat a large frying pan over a medium-high heat and add a couple of tablespoons of rapeseed or olive oil. Once the oil and pan are hot, fry the burgers for about 4–5 minutes on each side, until crispy and fragrant. You may need to do this in batches – if so, keep the cooked burgers warm in a low oven while you cook the rest.

Serve the burgers piled into flatbreads, pitta breads or burger buns, with a couple of crunchy little gem leaves and a good dollop of the garlic and tahini sauce. A tomato and red onion salad is also nice on the side.

Grilled harissa chicken
with griddled peach bulgur wheat & cucumber yoghurt

Serves 3–4

When I asked my friend Patrick to test this recipe, he reported back that grating a cucumber 'is an activity not seemly to perform in sight of any observers'! I promise it's the only unseemly thing you'll be required to do in the preparation of this vibrant dish. I love the contrast in both texture and temperature between spicy, sizzling meat, warm grains and thick, cold yoghurt made extra refreshing with grated cucumber and fresh mint.

Peaches are a particular favourite of mine in summer salads, brightening up whatever you want to throw them in and providing a welcome burst of silky sweetness alongside the charred meat and cooling cucumber. You could also try using apricots or plums. This recipe lends itself well to barbecue season, but just use the grill or a griddle pan if you want to make it all year round. If you have vegetarian or vegan guests, the peach bulgur wheat also works excellently with some slices of grilled halloumi, some crumbled feta or some sliced smoked tofu, and it is surprisingly good with grilled or smoked mackerel, too. If you can't find harissa, you can substitute for a teaspoon of chilli powder or chipotle paste.

For the chicken
1 tablespoon harissa
$\frac{1}{2}$ teaspoon sea
   salt flakes
1 teaspoon sweet
   smoked paprika
finely grated zest of
   $\frac{1}{2}$ lemon and
   1 tablespoon juice
a generous pinch of
   chilli flakes
300ml full-fat plain
   or Greek yoghurt
3 garlic cloves, crushed
2 tablespoons rapeseed
   or olive oil
8 skin-on, boneless or
   bone-in chicken thighs

For the yoghurt
1 cucumber, roughly
   grated

First, marinate the chicken. Mix together all the ingredients except the chicken in a non-reactive mixing bowl. Stab the chicken thighs all over with a metal skewer or cocktail stick, then add them to the marinade and coat thoroughly. Cover with cling film and refrigerate, preferably overnight but for a few hours is fine.

When you're ready to cook, prepare your barbecue (wait for the flames to die down, until you have glowing coals) or heat your grill to medium. Remove the chicken pieces from the marinade and place them on the barbecue or under the grill. Cook for about 15 minutes, until the skin is starting to become golden, then turn them over. Brush them with any remaining marinade and cook for another 15 minutes or so, until the skin is crispy and the juices run clear. (Bear in mind that if you're using thighs on their bone, they will take a bit longer than boneless versions.)

Meanwhile, start the yoghurt. Put the grated cucumber in a colander and toss it with the salt. Suspend the colander in a bowl and leave the cucumber to drip through for about 15 minutes, stirring occasionally, then squeeze out as much remaining water from the cucumber flesh as you can. Set aside.

Put the bulgur wheat in a large bowl and pour over enough boiling water to cover by about 2.5cm. Put a plate over the bowl and leave the wheat for 15 minutes,

…method & ingredients continued on page 36

1 teaspoon salt
300ml thick, full-fat
  plain or Greek yoghurt
2 tablespoons chopped
  mint leaves, plus extra
  to garnish

For the griddled peach bulgur wheat

200g bulgur wheat
juice and finely grated
  zest of 1 lemon
$\frac{1}{2}$ teaspoon salt
$\frac{1}{2}$ teaspoon freshly
  ground black pepper
4 spring onions,
  finely chopped
2 tablespoons chopped
  mint leaves
2 tablespoons chopped
  coriander leaves
1 tablespoon chopped
  parsley leaves
3 tablespoons good-
  quality olive oil, plus
  extra for griddling
  the peaches
3 peaches, stoned
  and cut into roughly
  1cm slices

then transfer the grains to a sieve and drain off any remaining water. Fluff up the bulgur wheat with a fork. Add the lemon juice and zest, along with the salt and pepper, and the spring onions, herbs and olive oil. Toss well.

Get a griddle pan hot, then brush it lightly with a little olive oil. Griddle the peach slices for about 2–3 minutes on each side, until tender and slightly charred, then stir them through the bulgur. You could also do this on the barbecue, but use a clean grill (or wash the one you used for the chicken).

To finish the yoghurt, mix the drained cucumber with the Greek yoghurt, mint and some seasoning.

Serve the chicken with the bulgur and a generous dollop of cucumber yoghurt alongside. A green or avocado salad is also a nice addition.

Basil & goat's cheese stuffed chicken
with pickled cherry & spelt salad

Serves 4

There are a few different components here, but everything is very easy to prepare and the finished dish would make an impressive dinner party main course. I always think cherries are better suited to savoury than sweet dishes: here, they pair beautifully with tart vinegar and lemon juice, the addition of star anise complementing the basil in the chicken stuffing. Spelt is an underused ingredient, so here I've tried to showcase its ability to soak up flavoursome dressings while retaining a delightfully nutty bite. It is the perfect foil to the rich, tender chicken and molten goat's cheese, accentuated by the sharp bite of juicy, tangy cherry.

Orchard Fruits

For the pickled cherries
200g cherries, halved and stoned
1 teaspoon light brown soft sugar
¼ teaspoon sea salt flakes
1 tablespoon balsamic vinegar
1 tablespoon red wine vinegar
1 star anise, broken into pieces
a squeeze of lemon juice

For the chicken & stuffing
1 tablespoon rapeseed or olive oil
50g butter, softened, plus a knob of butter
1 small onion, very finely chopped
2 garlic cloves, finely chopped
30g fresh breadcrumbs
125g soft goat's cheese
25g basil leaves, finely shredded

First, make the pickled cherries. Put the cherries in a bowl and mix with the sugar, salt, vinegars, star anise and lemon juice. Set aside to macerate, stirring regularly.

For the chicken stuffing, in a small frying pan, heat the rapeseed oil and the knob of butter over a medium heat. Add the onion and sauté for about 10 minutes, until golden and soft. Add the garlic and cook for another 2 minutes, then add the breadcrumbs and cook for 2–3 minutes, until everything is golden and toasted. Tip the lot into a small bowl and leave to cool. When cool, mash together with the goat's cheese and basil leaves. Season well with salt and pepper.

Pre-heat the oven to 200°C/180°C fan/gas mark 6. Line a baking tray or roasting tin with baking parchment.

Put the 50g butter in a bowl, season it well with salt and pepper and mash it.

Using a sharp knife, slice a deep cut into the side of each chicken breast, lengthways, so you create a small pocket for stuffing – be careful not to cut all the way through. Arrange the chicken breasts on the baking tray and season well, inside and out. Stuff each breast with a quarter of the goat's cheese stuffing, packing it as tightly as possible and closing the meat around it (as much as you can). Place the breasts in the tray, skin-side up.

Smear the seasoned butter over the skin of each chicken breast. Place the roasting tin in the oven and cook for 30–40 minutes, basting the breasts occasionally with the buttery juices that accumulate in the base. The breasts are cooked when the juices run clear when the thickest part is pierced with a knife, and there are no pink bits (or when a meat thermometer shows 74°C).

...method & ingredients continued on page 39

4 skin-on, boneless
  chicken breasts
salt and freshly ground
  black pepper

For the spelt salad
1.4 litres vegetable stock
300g pearled spelt
140g kale, shredded
1 tablespoon
  cider vinegar
½ teaspoon Dijon
  mustard
1 teaspoon wholegrain
  mustard
1½ tablespoons maple
  syrup
3 tablespoons good-
  quality olive oil
2 tablespoons
  rapeseed oil
2 tablespoons
  lemon juice
40g pumpkin seeds

While the chicken is in the oven, cook the spelt. Place the vegetable stock in a large saucepan and bring it to the boil over a high heat. Add the spelt and cook for 17 minutes at a robust simmer, then add the shredded kale and cook for a further 3 minutes until the kale is tender. Drain everything in a colander and return the mixture to the pan (off the heat).

Whisk together the remaining salad ingredients, except for the pumpkin seeds, to make a dressing and add it to the pan with the spelt while the grains are still warm. Toss well to coat.

Heat a small frying pan over a medium heat. Add the pumpkin seeds and toast, shaking the pan, until they start to pop. Tip the toasted seeds into the spelt salad and toss to mix. Keep the salad warm until the chicken is ready.

Serve the chicken breasts, hot from the oven, with the spelt salad and a spoonful or two of the pickled cherries and their juices.

Blue cheese crusted pork escalopes
with a fennel & apple slaw

Serves 2

This is a lighter riff on the classic roast pork with apple sauce. I have been making variations of this for many years, and the combination of the buttery, crunchy crust with the tender meat and tangy salad makes for the perfect dinner – light yet decadent. It is a great dish for when apple season is in full swing and you need a bit of a break from pies and crumbles.

Inspiration for the slaw comes from Heidi Swanson's wonderful blog *101 Cookbooks*. Try experimenting with different herbs, vinegars and vegetables to keep things interesting. Very thinly shaved celeriac works wonderfully instead of fennel, for example, and a gooseberry, raspberry or elderflower vinegar can take the dressing in interesting new directions. I also encourage you to hunt down some interesting apple varieties in season – they all bring a slightly different characteristic to this timeless pairing. My favourites are Discovery, Egremont Russet and Cox's Orange Pippin. A crisp pear would also be rather lovely. Goat's cheese works well instead of blue cheese, if you're not a fan of the latter, and you could also use chicken breast fillets – bashed with a rolling pin to flatten them – instead of pork escalopes.

For the slaw

1 teaspoon lemon zest
¼ teaspoon sea salt flakes
1 garlic clove, roughly chopped
1 tsp finely chopped rosemary needles
1 teaspoon caster sugar
1 tablespoon cider vinegar
½ teaspoon wholegrain mustard
2 tablespoons plain yoghurt
½ fennel bulb, very finely sliced
1 large eating apple (Granny Smith, Discovery, Cox or

First, prepare the slaw. Put the lemon zest, sea salt, garlic, rosemary and sugar into a mortar and pound with the pestle to a paste. Add the vinegar and mustard and briefly pound until you have a fairly homogeneous liquid. Stir in the yoghurt, season well with black pepper and set aside.

Put the fennel and apple slices, and the kale or cavolo nero in a medium bowl. Pour the yoghurt dressing into the bowl and toss well to combine. Set aside.

Use the oven-assisted grill function on your oven, and pre-heat it to 200°C/180°C fan/gas mark 6 (or pre-heat a grill to high).

Put the hazelnuts on a small baking dish on the middle shelf of the oven and toast for about 5 minutes, until lightly golden and fragrant. Set aside to cool. Once cool, roughly chop and add the chopped pieces to the slaw. Toss gently to mix. Keep the oven/grill on.

Make the pork. If your pork escalopes are quite thick, place them between two sheets of baking parchment or cling film and bash with a rolling pin until they are about 1–1.5cm thick. Place them on an oven tray lined with baking parchment.

...method & ingredients continued on page 42

Russet works well),
quartered, cored and
very finely sliced
a couple of leaves of
kale or cavolo nero,
de-stalked and very
finely shredded
50g blanched hazelnuts
freshly ground black
pepper

For the pork
2 boneless pork
escalopes
30g butter
65g fresh breadcrumbs
30g Gruyère or
Parmesan, coarsely
grated
1 teaspoon thyme or
lemon thyme leaves
60g blue cheese, at room
temperature
salt and freshly ground
black pepper

Melt the butter in a small saucepan over a medium heat. Take the butter off the heat once it is melted, and stir in the breadcrumbs, grated Gruyère or Parmesan, and the thyme. Season well with a little salt and a generous amount of pepper (don't add too much salt, as the cheese will be salty).

Pat dry the surface of each piece of pork with kitchen paper. Divide the blue cheese between the pieces of pork and, using your fingers or a knife, roughly spread the cheese over the surface of each piece. Divide the breadcrumb mixture between the two pieces, and spread it out over the blue cheese, pressing it firmly on top.

Place the pork under the grill (on the highest oven shelf) for 10–15 minutes, until the cheese crust is golden and bubbling, and the pork is cooked all the way through (the exact time will depend on the thickness of your pork pieces, so start checking after 10 minutes). A meat thermometer should show 63°C, and the juices should run clear. Leave the pork to rest for 3 minutes before serving with the apple and fennel slaw.

Chestnut, maple, pear & vanilla cinnamon buns

Makes 15

These are the only thing I want to wake up to on Christmas morning – better than a stocking from Santa (although you can, and should, make them at any time of the year). A festive take on the Scandinavian *kanelsnurre*, these feature all of my favourite winter flavours and are the product of my quest to incorporate the underrated chestnut into as many recipes as possible. The maple pears add a delicious burst of buttery sweetness, but you could use apples instead.

For the dough
180ml whole milk
75g butter
2 eggs
500g strong white flour
60g light brown
  soft sugar
1 teaspoon ground
  cinnamon
1 teaspoon salt
7g fast-action dried yeast

For the filling
70g butter, softened at
  room temperature,
  plus extra for greasing
50g light brown
  soft sugar
200g chestnut purée
1 teaspoon vanilla paste
  or extract
a pinch of salt
2 ripe but firm pears
  (Conference or Comice
  works well)
5 tablespoons
  maple syrup

For the glaze
50g unsalted butter
20g demerara sugar

Put the milk and butter for the dough in a small saucepan over a medium heat and allow the butter to melt (about 5 minutes). Turn off the heat and set aside to cool to body temperature, then beat in the eggs.

In the bowl of an electric stand mixer fitted with a dough hook, or in a large mixing bowl if using your hands, combine the flour, sugar and cinnamon. Add the salt on one side of the flour mixture in the bowl and the yeast on the other. Make a well in the centre and pour in the egg and milk mixture. Using the dough hook or your hands, bring the mixture together to form a sticky dough, then knead for about 10 minutes, until the dough is soft and silky, and no longer sticky. Cover the bowl with a clean tea towel and leave the dough to rise in a warm place for 1–2 hours, until doubled in size.

Lightly grease a large roasting tin or baking dish (one with high sides) and line it with baking parchment.

While the dough rises, prepare the filling. In a medium mixing bowl, combine the butter, sugar, chestnut purée, vanilla and salt, mashing them together with the back of a spoon to form a homogeneous paste. Core the pears (you can peel them too if you like, but I don't think it is necessary) and chop them into small dice (roughly 1cm). Put them in a separate bowl and toss them with the maple syrup. Set aside.

When the dough has doubled in size, roll it out on a floured work surface to a rectangle about 45 x 35cm, with the long side facing you. Spread the chestnut filling evenly over the dough, leaving a border of about 2.5cm at the long edges. Scatter the maple pears evenly over the chestnut filling.

Starting with the long side furthest away from you and rolling towards your body, tightly roll up the dough and filling so that you end up with a long log. Using a sharp, serrated knife, slice the log along its length into 15 even rounds. Place each

...method continued on page 45

round, swirl-side up, on the prepared roasting tin or baking dish with about a 2.5cm gap between each. Cover the tin with a clean tea towel and leave the buns to prove until nearly doubled in size (about 30–60 minutes) – the edges will start to touch one another and the edges of the tin.

While the buns are proving, pre-heat the oven to 200°C/180°C fan/gas mark 6. When they have proved, put the tin in the oven and bake the buns for 23 minutes.

While the buns are baking, make the glaze. Place the butter in a saucepan and melt over a medium heat. After 23 minutes, remove the buns from the oven and, using a pastry brush, glaze them with the melted butter. Sprinkle over the demerara sugar and return the buns to the oven to bake for a final 7 minutes, until golden.

Remove them from the oven and leave the buns to cool in the tin (if you can wait that long) before devouring. They freeze well and are easily reheated in an oven at 180°C/160°C fan/gas mark 4.

Little cherry & almond cakes

Makes 12

The main reason I love these dainty little cakes is that they are the perfect solution for the cook's perennial 'What to do with leftover egg whites?' problem (particularly if, like me, you are not a fan of meringue). They are also an incredibly quick, one-bowl bake that you can whip up in minutes, and are extremely versatile. I've used figs, apricots, peaches, pears and various berries in these with great success, so they are also an excellent way to use up any fruit lingering in your kitchen – simply drop small pieces into the batter in the tin.

90g egg whites (from 2–3 large eggs)
100g caster sugar
70g ground almonds
a pinch of salt
½ teaspoon almond extract
35g plain flour
90g butter, melted and cooled slightly, plus extra for greasing
18 fresh or canned cherries, halved and stoned

Pre-heat the oven to 220°C/200°C fan/gas mark 7. Grease a 12-hole cupcake or bun tin well with butter.

In a large bowl, whisk the egg whites lightly with a hand whisk until a little frothy (but definitely not to soft peaks). Whisk in the caster sugar. Add the almonds, salt, almond extract and flour, then whisk again until just combined. Slowly pour in the melted butter, whisking continuously, until you have a thick batter.

Divide the batter between the holes of the muffin tin, then top each cake with 3 cherry halves. Bake for 7 minutes, then lower the oven temperature to 180°C/160°C fan/gas mark 4 and bake for another 3–6 minutes, until the cakes are golden and a skewer inserted in the centres comes out clean. Leave to cool a little before transferring to a wire rack to cool fully before eating.

Spiced apple & date jam

Makes about 5 x 450g jars

I used to have an apple tree in my garden, so this jam was really born out of necessity. When thousands of cooking apples suddenly descended on my lawn within a two-month period, it forced me to start finding creative ways in which to use them. I am still perplexed as to why we don't see more apple jam in the shops. Apples are high in pectin, which means an almost guaranteed set. They are frequently used in compotes for pies and crumbles, so why do we – a nation so enamoured of apples – not take the logical next step of cooking them that little bit longer, so that we can enjoy their sweet-tart flavour on our morning toast throughout the winter? This is my attempt to do just that. It captures the flavours of autumn in a jar: brown sugar, toffeed dates, soothing cinnamon, and the unmistakeable aroma of warm apples.

1.5kg peeled and
cored cooking apples
(prepared weight), cut
into 1.5cm dice
2 cinnamon sticks
(about 8cm each)
6 cloves
1kg granulated sugar
400g light muscovado
sugar
juice of 2 lemons
250g stoned dates,
roughly chopped

Put the apples in a large, heavy-based saucepan or preserving pan. Add the cinnamon sticks, cloves, both sugars and the lemon juice. Heat gently, stirring regularly with a wooden spoon, until the apples start to release their liquid and the sugar starts to dissolve. Increase the heat and leave to cook until everything is watery. (Stir regularly to prevent the mixture catching on the bottom of the pan and burning.) Put a small plate in the freezer (to test for when the jam is set).

When the mixture is boiling, lower the heat slightly and simmer until the apples have softened and the liquid has started to turn golden and reduce (you will still have some chunks of apple left, though – it shouldn't be totally mushy) – about 15 minutes. Add the dates, then continue to simmer vigorously for about 30 minutes, until the jam begins to thicken. (Again, stir regularly to prevent the mixture catching – be careful and wear oven gloves as the jam will bubble volcanically.)

After 30 minutes, start testing for a set. A sugar thermometer should reach 105°C, or you can test using the plate that you have chilled in the freezer: spoon a small dollop of jam onto it, leave to cool for 1 minute, then run your finger through it – if it wrinkles and parts cleanly, the jam is ready. If not, continue to cook for a few minutes more and test again. As soon as the jam sets, remove it from the heat (don't overcook as the jam can quickly 'turn').

While the jam is cooking, sterilise your jars and lids. I do this by washing them well in soapy water, then putting the jars upside down in an oven at 140°C/120°C fan/gas mark 1 for 25 minutes, adding the lids (also upside down) for the last 10 minutes. Turn off the oven and leave the jars inside until you are ready to bottle the jam. You can alternatively run the jars through a hot dishwasher cycle, then pot the jam while they are still warm.

Decant the jam into the sterilised jars. Cover with wax discs, and seal with the lids. I have kept this jam for five or six years, unopened, in a cool larder with no problems, but once opened, keep it refrigerated and consume within a month.

The ultimate crumble
plum, brown sugar, ginger & marzipan

Serves 4–6

Sometimes, during an idle moment, I mentally rank my all-time top five dessert genres. (Crumble, cheesecake, lemon tart, sticky toffee pudding, *tarte tatin*, since you ask.) I've probably made more crumbles in my life than any other dessert (and the number of them in this book is testament to that fact), but I really wanted to come up with a definitive version that exemplifies the very best of what crumble is all about. This is that version. The plums are just sour enough to contrast with the buttery topping, while ginger, anise and orange bring out the plums' robust flavour and create a deep purple syrup that bubbles up and caramelises invitingly around the edges. Oats, spices and tiny cubes of marzipan add crunch to the topping, and the whole thing is a perfect marriage of layered flavours and textures. This crumble is excellent made with blood oranges, when in season.

12 ripe plums, quartered and stoned

3 globes of stem ginger in syrup, finely chopped

2 tablespoons stem-ginger syrup (from the jar)

1 star anise, halved

finely grated zest of 1 orange and juice of ½

60g dark brown soft sugar

1 heaped tablespoon cornflour

150g plain flour

90g cold butter, cubed

40g jumbo oats

90g marzipan, cut into 5mm cubes

90g golden caster sugar

½ teaspoon ground cinnamon

½ teaspoon ground ginger

¼ teaspoon freshly grated nutmeg

1 tablespoon cold water or milk

Pre-heat the oven to 190°C/170°C fan/gas mark 5.

Put the plum quarters in a medium baking dish. Add the stem ginger and syrup, the star anise halves, the orange zest and juice, the brown sugar and the cornflour. Mix well.

Put the flour and butter in a medium bowl and rub the butter into the flour with your fingertips until the mixture resembles fine breadcrumbs. Stir in the oats, marzipan, caster sugar, cinnamon, ginger and nutmeg and mix well. Add the water or milk and mix gently so the mixture turns 'pebbly'.

Tip the crumble over the plums in the baking dish and spread it out to cover the fruit. Flatten it slightly but don't press down too much.

Bake for 45 minutes, until the fruit is bubbling up around the topping and the crumble is golden brown. Leave the crumble to cool for 10 minutes before serving with vanilla ice cream or custard.

Mediterranean Fruits

> The proper way to eat a fig, in society/Is to split it in four, holding it by the stump/And open it, so that it is a glittering, rosy, moist, honied, heavy-petalled four-petalled flower.
>
> ~ D. H. Lawrence, 'Figs'

Trust D. H. Lawrence to get to the heart of a **fig**. After all, when considering a fruit that for centuries has been closely identified with the female genitalia, who better than the author whose novel *Lady Chatterley's Lover* was actually taken to court for obscenity in 1960? The word sycophant originally comes from the Greek *sykophantes*, which literally means 'one who shows the fig', referring to a vulgar hand gesture. Cato the Elder insulted the Roman Senate by offering them a handful of figs to suggest their weakness and effeminacy. The fruit is commonly associated with voluptuousness, temptation and plenty: in Greek myth, Apollo punished a messenger for getting distracted by waiting for a fig tree to ripen; figs were also associated with Dionysus, god of wine and drunkenness, and Priapus, a satyr who represented sexual desire. In her poignant semi-autobiographical novel *The Bell Jar*, Sylvia Plath describes herself sitting amid the branches of a fig tree, 'starving to death, just because I couldn't make up my mind which of the figs I would choose'. The old-fashioned English saying, 'I don't give a fig', similarly suggests the ripe, overwhelming abundance of these fruits.

Yet, conversely, the fig also features in various Mediterranean and Asian cultures as a symbol of precious rarity. There is a Bengali idiom that translates as 'you have become like the fig flower', meaning 'invisible', while in Hindi, 'flower of fig' refers to something incredibly rare. Figs are sacred in the Qur'an, a symbol of prosperity in the Bible and an important emblem of spiritual growth in Buddhism.

It is actually a miracle that the fig grows at all. One of nature's great survival stories, the fig tree flourishes only in the most inhospitable areas, sending roots deep into the ground in search of running water. Original cultivars could be pollinated only by a particular variety of wasp, which actually enters the fruit and dies inside it (try not to think too much about that next time you take a knife to a ripe fig). If you try to grow figs in the garden, the best way to get them to fruit is to grow them in a confined container filled with poor-quality soil. The Stoic philosopher Epictetus used the fig as a reminder that 'no great thing is created suddenly'. In many ways, the fig embodies the paradoxes at the heart of Mediterranean fruit cultivation. Often associated with rich abundance and sensuality, these are fruits born out of some of the least hospitable environments, and for centuries have been symbols of survival rather than luxury.

The **apricot** can also prove tricky to grow. Although the gardener in Shakespeare's *Richard II* refers to apricots dangling on his trees 'which, like unruly children, make their sire stoop with oppression of their prodigal weight', to achieve this state of perfection – certainly in cooler northern climes – is a near-impossible feat. It is said that, like the apple not falling far from the tree, an apricot tree will not grow far from its parent, so picky is it about the soil quality. This fruit – referred to by the ancient Greeks as 'golden eggs of the sun' – has such a short season that, like the fig, it features in several cultures as a symbol of impossibility. The Arabic expression *filmishmish*, 'in apricot season', is the equivalent of the British 'when hell freezes over': something that is highly unlikely to happen.

Consider, also, the **date**. Mentioned more than fifty times in the Bible and twenty in the Qu'ran, this ancient fruit is often described as 'the bread of the desert'. Correctly stored, dates can last for several years, and contain vital minerals and vitamins. It is said that an adult can live on fifteen dates a day, and dates were often essential to the survival of wandering nomadic desert tribes, particularly when combined with nutritious camel milk. The sight of date palms growing on desert horizons is an indication that there is life-giving water nearby. Dates have been integral to the existence of desert peoples for thousands of years, and this tree flourishes in the most arid environments. They are, traditionally, the first foods eaten to break the fast after sunset during Ramadan, a powerful reminder of their links with simple sustenance. Yet we also associate dates, with their furrowed skins and delectably high sugar content, with hedonistic feasting: they are a common inclusion in Christmas desserts or dried fruit selections, and form the toothsome backbone to that indulgent British classic, the sticky toffee pudding. The Spanish, in a truly marvellous act of gilding the lily, stuff dates with blue cheese and wrap them in bacon before grilling them.

Oranges, which are now so abundant that we rarely think twice about downing a glass of their tangy juice in the morning, were once extremely precious. Rich in vitamin C with a relatively long shelf life, they were planted along major trade routes by Portuguese, Spanish and Dutch sailors during explorations of the New World and the Far East, in order to prevent scurvy. In the Middle Ages, citrus fruits were so precious in Britain that they were often left uneaten; perhaps not a surprise for a fruit whose name originally comes from the Indian *narayam*, meaning 'perfume within'. By the seventeenth century, the orange had become a luxury item: it was the height of fashion for grand houses and palaces to contain an orangery. Something of this magic and luxury lingers on in the coveted blood orange, a cultivar thought to have originated in the southern Mediterranean around the eighteenth century and which appears in the shops for a short season in late winter and early spring. Its flesh – ranging from deep orange to crimson-black – is sharper than that of the sweet orange, with a hint of raspberry, making it excellent for use in savoury and sweet dishes alike. It is sometimes marketed, rather prudishly, as 'blush orange', a denomination that seems to rather miss the point of this fruit's dramatic, vital essence.

Although the image of a bowl piled high with fragrant citrus, glossy leaves still attached and skins glowing 'like golden lamps' – to quote the poet Andrew Marvell – is something we associate with sun-soaked Mediterranean vitality, oranges and **lemons** originally come from the Far East. They have been used medicinally for far longer than they have graced our tables, valued for their antibacterial properties, their vitamin content and, if you follow the example of the Roman Emperor Nero, their capacity as an antidote to poison. Now we zest, juice and slice our way through them with barely a second thought: in fact, the

taste of orange is ranked as the third favourite flavour among Americans (second only to chocolate and vanilla), who drink on average 16.6 litres of orange juice per person per year.

Another somewhat paradoxical Mediterranean fruit is the **bergamot**, which manages to be both tiringly ubiquitous and enticingly rare at the same time. The name is a corruption of the Turkish *bey armudu*, meaning 'prince of pears'. Its tell-tale perfume scents teacups the world over in the form of Earl Grey. The only places I have ever come across fresh bergamots in the UK are Waitrose, farmers' markets and online delivery schemes that often charge handsomely for them (see page 261 for stockist suggestions). Thought to be a hybrid of the bitter orange and the lemon, these underrated fruits are mostly grown in the Calabria region of Italy, where production is strictly controlled to guard against adulteration of expensive bergamot oil with cheaper substitutes. This oil, made from the aromatic peel, is used the world over in everything from Earl Grey and Lady Grey teas to marmalade, liqueurs, perfumes, confectionery and even *snus*, a form of powdered tobacco popular in Norway and Sweden. The Italians also produce a delightful olive oil scented with the peel, wonderful in fish or baking recipes (see page 261 for stockists). Yet despite its global incorporation in such a variety of products, the bergamot is something of a problem child in the kitchen. While the zest is beautifully fragrant, the flesh is exceedingly bitter and packed with knobbly seeds. Even the internet, ever the gastronomic hive mind, comes up short for ideas when bergamot recipes are at stake – there is little beyond sorbet and marmalade. I feel that this fruit is something of a Robinson Crusoe island upon which to lay one's culinary footprints, and have attempted to rise to the challenge with a couple of exciting bergamot recipes in this book. Persevere with these rather bulbous, green-tinged citrus and you will be rewarded with an aromatic and tangy sunshine-yellow curd, the stickiest syrupy cakes and a refreshingly fragrant ceviche.

This chapter embraces the complex heritage of the Mediterranean fruit basket, using these ingredients both as the central focus of a recipe – a plate of honeyed baked figs, for example – but also as supporting acts that bring a small twist to simple dishes: a few slivers of glowing apricot strewn through an earthy couscous salad, or a handful of dates transformed into a piquant salsa to serve alongside crispy, fried mackerel.

'Every fruit has its secret', wrote D. H. Lawrence. Apply a small amount of kitchen know-how, and you might just get closer to a little of that elusive promise.

Tips & tricks

* 'Not to live in a country where figs grow or can readily be bought in the season, seems to me a deprivation,' remarked Jane Grigson. I agree. Luckily it is possible to find good imports, occasionally, but there are also many inferior specimens on the market. When buying figs, choose the ripest ones you can find – they don't ripen any further once plucked from the tree. They should feel heavy in your hand, swollen, faintly warm and soft to the touch. The best ones are imported from Turkey in early autumn. And remember Lawrence's advice: 'ripe figs won't keep, won't keep in any clime'. Enjoy them as soon as possible. If they do start to turn, though, becoming mushy and sticky with the odd furry spot, you can still make them into an excellent jam. Just cut off any really bad bits.

* Disappointing figs can always be remedied with a little heat and honey. The same is true of fresh apricots, which are often unpleasantly woolly because they have been shipped underripe. To quote Grigson again: 'you will perhaps be wise to regard apricots as a fruit for the kitchen, then you will not be disappointed'. Fortunately, there are several suggestions in this book.

* Homemade apricot jam is a revelation, and incomparable to cheap shop-bought versions. Add a little vanilla, lavender or cardamom to make real magic happen.

* Generally speaking, markets and greengrocers are much cheaper places to buy fresh apricots, when in season, than the supermarkets. I have picked them up for as little as £2 a kilo – perfect for cakes and jams.

* If you crack an apricot kernel with a nutcracker or hammer, the small pit inside has a delicious almond flavour that you can use to infuse ice cream or homemade apricot jam. In northern France, apricot kernel is a key ingredient in noyau, a brandy made also with almonds. Be careful though – the kernels contain small quantities of cyanide, so don't be tempted to eat them raw! One cracked kernel in the bottom of a jar of jam is all you need for the flavour to percolate.

* Dates, especially the coveted Medjool variety, can be expensive. Middle Eastern grocers are good places to buy them in bulk, saving you money and giving you access to a host of different varieties. It's also worth looking out for date syrup or date molasses, treacly sweeteners that you can use in baking or drizzled over hummus or grilled meats.

* Keep your eyes peeled (pun intended) for Sicilian blood oranges in late winter; their vibrant colour and sharp flavour make a gorgeous addition to sweet and savoury dishes. You can replace blood oranges in any recipe with normal oranges, but add an extra squeeze of lemon to replicate the sharpness. Amalfi lemons also emerge in early spring, and are well worth the price tag, especially if you use them in dishes that really showcase their flavour, such as a lemon tart or ice cream. They are often sold with the leaves attached, which can be used to imbue recipes with a delightful herbal citrus flavour.

* If you ever come across Persian or Meyer lemons, snap them up. The former are excellent for making Moroccan preserved lemons, and the latter make an utterly sublime lemon curd or lemon tart.

* Similarly, if you are lucky to find fresh kaffir limes (also called makrut limes, as the former name now has problematic discriminatory connotations), grab them while you can. They freeze well and the peel makes an authentic addition to a homemade Thai curry paste. For more information on using lime leaves, see the Leaves chapter.

* Should you get your hands on some fresh bergamots, don't waste anything. The peel, along with slices of the fresh fruit, can be dried on a wire rack in a sunny windowsill and used to flavour homemade iced teas.

* For more advice on oranges, lemons, limes and everything in between, I recommend Catherine Phipps's excellent book *Citrus*.

* Grigson cautions us not to waste the squeezed halves of lemons – she suggests using them to whiten your elbows! If you're already blessed with snow-white joints, however, I'd advise you to use the squeezed halves of any citrus (especially precious varieties like bergamot and blood orange) to make a flavoursome and versatile syrup – see the (very easy) method in the Tunisian citrus cake on page 87.

Giant couscous tabbouleh
with fresh apricots

Serves 6 as a side

This is not an authentic tabbouleh – there is no bulgur wheat and nowhere near the requisite quantity of parsley. Instead, I've used wholewheat giant couscous, which I love for its nutty flavour and big, toothsome grains. The recipe is inspired by the flavours of Middle Eastern salads: the crunch of cucumber, the fragrance of grassy parsley and mint, and a good glug of olive oil to dress the lot. It's brightened with lemon and the intriguing perfume of orange blossom, and finally tossed with slivers of golden apricot. This is one to make when you are lucky enough to find perfectly ripe apricots. Out of season you can use dried, and if you find yourself with woolly, lacklustre fresh apricots, the searing heat of a griddle pan is a good way to pep them up. This salad works very well as a side with barbecued meats and fish, but is also very good with fried halloumi, or crumbled feta or goat's cheese for a simple vegetarian main course.

200g giant couscous (preferably wholewheat)
2 small (Lebanese) cucumbers or 1 regular cucumber, sliced lengthways and deseeded
500g ripe apricots, halved and stoned, or 200g dried apricots, soaked in hot (not boiling) water for 1 hour
25g parsley, finely chopped
30g mint leaves, finely chopped
finely grated zest of 2 lemons and juice of 1
1 teaspoon sumac
3 tablespoons good-quality olive oil
$\frac{1}{2}$ teaspoon orange-blossom water
salt and freshly ground black pepper

Bring a large pan of salted water to the boil and add the couscous. Cook according to the packet instructions until al dente (usually around 10–12 minutes). Drain well and set aside.

Chop the cucumber(s) into 1cm dice and place the dice in a large mixing or salad bowl. If using fresh apricots, chop them into thick slivers. (If they are not very flavoursome, or a bit dry, toss the slivers with a teaspoon of olive oil and cook them on a hot griddle pan for a couple of minutes on each side.) If using dried apricots, drain them, dry them on kitchen paper and roughly chop. Add the apricot pieces to the bowl along with the parsley, mint and lemon zest. Then, add the couscous, lemon juice, sumac, olive oil and orange-blossom water. Season with salt and pepper to taste, toss well to combine, and serve.

Pumpkin, fig & goat's cheese tart
with candied pumpkin seeds

Serves 6

This is what I would like to be served at the Christmas or Thanksgiving dinner table if I were vegetarian. It is a hymn to the flavours of autumn, with a luscious, silky pumpkin custard offset by the grassy tang of goat's cheese and the sumptuous syrupiness of fresh figs. Best of all, you can make the pastry case, pumpkin purée and candied seeds in advance, leaving you with a simple assemble-and-bake job on the day. If you're using a different type of pumpkin (not a Crown Prince), you may want to put the purée in a sieve lined with muslin for a couple of hours to drain, as other types can be watery – and no one wants their tart to have a soggy bottom.

For the filling
600g Crown Prince
   pumpkin wedges
   (deseeded but skin
   on) or 300g pumpkin
   purée from a can
3 eggs
100g soft goat's cheese
100ml whole milk
1 teaspoon thyme or
   lemon thyme leaves
½ teaspoon salt
½ teaspoon sweet
   smoked paprika
¼ teaspoon freshly
   grated nutmeg
¼ teaspoon freshly
   ground black pepper
6 figs

For the pastry
140g spelt flour
40g fine polenta
100g cold butter, cubed
½ teaspoon salt
1 tablespoon rosemary
   needles
2–3 tablespoons ice-
   cold water

Pre-heat the oven to 200°C/180°C fan/gas mark 6.

If you're using fresh pumpkin, place the wedges on a baking tray. Roast them for 30–60 minutes, until completely tender to the point of a knife (the exact time will depend upon your pumpkin). Remove the pumpkin from the oven, turn the oven off and leave the pumpkin to cool. Once the pumpkin is cool, remove the skin and discard it. Blitz the flesh to a rough purée in a food processor and transfer it to a large bowl. (If you're using canned pumpkin, empty the purée into a large bowl.)

While the pumpkin is roasting, make the pastry. Put the flour, polenta, butter, salt and rosemary in a food processor and pulse until the mixture resembles fine breadcrumbs and the rosemary is roughly chopped. Add the iced water, 1 tablespoon at a time, and pulse gently until the mixture just comes together – don't over-mix. Tip out the pastry onto a floured work surface and bring it together into a ball with your hands. Flatten it into a disc and chill it in the fridge for 1 hour. (You can do this in advance, if you like.)

When you're ready to cook the tart, pre-heat the oven to 210°C/190°C/gas mark 6–7.

Roll out the pastry on a floured surface to a circle roughly 5mm thick. Tear off a little bit of the pastry to make a small ball. Use the pastry circle to line a 23cm tart tin, using the small ball of pastry to press it into all the edges. Run a rolling pin over the top of the tin to trim the pastry case, then lightly prick the bottom with a fork.

Line the pastry case with a disc of baking parchment (make sure it's large enough to come up the sides as well as cover the base) and fill with baking beans. Blind

4 tablespoons
    pumpkin seeds
a generous pinch of salt
1 tablespoon maple
    syrup

bake for 20 minutes, then remove the paper and baking beans and bake for a
further 8–10 minutes, until golden.

Meanwhile, make the candied pumpkin seeds. Mix the seeds, salt and maple
syrup in a small bowl, then tip the mixture into a small baking dish. Bake for
15 minutes in the oven while the pastry cooks, stirring halfway through the
cooking time, then remove the seeds from the oven and tip onto some baking
parchment to cool. Once cool, roughly chop.

Add the remaining filling ingredients, except the figs, to the pumpkin purée in
the bowl, and whisk well to combine. Taste and adjust the seasoning as necessary.

When the pastry case is ready, pour the pumpkin filling into it. Halve the figs
and arrange the halves over the top of the tart, cut side up.

Bake the tart for 30–35 minutes, or until the tart is set with just a very slight
wobble. Remove from the oven and allow to cool for at least 15 minutes before
serving warm or at room temperature, scattered with the candied pumpkin seeds.

Cauliflower, date & preserved lemon dumplings
with pomegranate & tahini dipping sauce

Serves 4–5

Combining much of what I love about Middle Eastern and North African cooking in a plethora of moreish little parcels, this recipe actually showcases three different Mediterranean fruits: date, lemon and pomegranate. Dates add a wonderful rich sweetness that balances the slightly sulphuric bitterness of roasted cauliflower, while preserved lemons – a salty staple of North African cooking – lend an intriguing depth of flavour that combines perfectly with warming spices. A ripple of syrupy pomegranate molasses (or you can use date molasses for a double date hit) lifts the tahini dipping sauce both visually and on the tongue. Altogether, this might sound like an odd fusion of east Asian and Middle Eastern, but the result is a delightfully satisfying taste adventure, with a textural depth and richness sometimes lacking in vegetarian dumplings. A true homage to Mediterranean botanicals.

For the filling
1 cauliflower, broken into rough 2.5cm florets, stalks and leaves reserved
1 red onion, thinly sliced
2 tablespoons rapeseed or olive oil, plus extra for frying
½ teaspoon cumin seeds
½ teaspoon sweet smoked paprika
½ teaspoon sea salt flakes
½ teaspoon chilli flakes
a generous pinch of ground cinnamon
40g pine nuts
20g coriander, roughly chopped
70g dates (preferably Medjool), stoned and roughly chopped
120g feta, crumbled

Pre-heat the oven to 220°C/200°C fan/gas mark 7.

Put the cauliflower florets into a baking dish or tray. Tear any tender cauliflower stalks and leaves into small pieces and add these, along with the red onion. Drizzle over the rapeseed or olive oil and scatter over the cumin, sweet smoked paprika, salt, chilli, cinnamon, and a generous grinding of black pepper. Toss everything together with your hands or a spoon.

Put the tray in the oven and roast the vegetables for around 20 minutes, giving everything a stir halfway through, until the cauliflower is slightly charred and just tender. Be careful not to overcook it or it will turn to mush, so check its progress after 15 minutes. Set the tray and its contents aside to cool.

Lower the oven temperature to 180°C/160°C fan/gas mark 4.

Put the pine nuts in a small oven dish or tray and place them in the oven for 8–10 minutes, until lightly toasted and fragrant. Set aside to cool. Turn off the oven.

While everything cools, prepare the sauce. In a small bowl, whisk together the crushed garlic, lemon juice and tahini. Gradually add enough water (you'll need about 50–100ml) to make a fairly thin dipping sauce, whisking as you go – it should be the consistency of double cream. Set aside.

Once the cauliflower is cool, put it in a food processor and add the coriander, dates and feta. Cut the preserved lemon in half, scoop out the flesh and discard.

…method & ingredients continued on page 66

1 preserved lemon,
   or finely grated zest
   of 2 lemons
300g pack gyoza
   or wonton skins,
   defrosted if frozen
2–3 tablespoons plain
   flour, for dusting
freshly ground black
   pepper

For the sauce

1 garlic clove, crushed
juice of ½ lemon
80g tahini
3–4 tablespoons
   pomegranate or date
   molasses

Finely chop the peel and add this to the food processor, too. If using lemon zest, just add that to the processor. Pulse a couple of times, just to bring the mixture together and disperse the ingredients. You definitely do not want it to turn to a homogeneous paste – you should be able to see small pieces of individual ingredients. Use a spatula if necessary to move the mixture around a little so it pulses evenly. Scoop the mixture out into a large bowl and gently fold in the cooled, toasted pine nuts.

Now it is time to fill the dumplings. Have a small bowl of cold water to hand, and a large baking tray lightly dusted with plain flour. Take one gyoza skin from the packet. If you're right-handed, hold it flat on the palm of your left hand; hold it in your right hand if you are left-handed. Dip a finger of the opposite hand in the bowl of water and moisten the edge of the wrapper in your palm to create a border of around 1cm. Place a heaped teaspoon of the filling in the centre of the wrapper, then fold the wrapper in half to enclose the filling. You should end up with a half-moon shape. Moisten one side of the curved edge of the wrapper, then use your fingertips to pinch small pleats into the curved edge of the dumpling. (There are lots of helpful internet tutorials on dumpling shaping, if you want to brush up on the technique.) Place the finished dumpling on the floured baking tray, then repeat with the remaining filling and dumpling skins until everything is used up and you have a tray of beautiful dumplings.

You will need to cook the dumplings in about three or four batches, depending on the size of your pan. Heat a large, non-stick frying pan with a tight-fitting lid, over a medium-high heat. Add 2 tablespoons of rapeseed or olive oil to the pan and swirl it around to coat the bottom. Once the pan is hot, place some of the dumplings in the pan, with the pleated edge facing upwards – you want to cover the base of the pan with dumplings, but don't overcrowd it – they should not be touching one another. Fry them for 3–5 minutes, until the bottoms have become golden and crispy. Then, splash 25ml of water into the pan – it will immediately hiss and start to steam. Quickly put the lid on the pan and leave the dumplings for about 2–3 minutes, until the water has been completely absorbed. Transfer the cooked dumplings to a plate and keep them warm in a low oven while you repeat the process to cook the remaining dumplings.

Divide the tahini sauce between small bowls or dipping dishes, one for each guest. Drizzle a little pomegranate or date molasses into each bowl using a circular motion so you have a pretty swirl of dark syrup. Place the dumplings on a large platter in the centre of the table and let each guest take and dip as they please.

Crispy mackerel
with tahini sauce & toasted pine nuts, date & blood orange salsa

Serves 2

This dish combines many of my favourite ingredients. I was first introduced to the idea of serving mackerel with dates in the wonderful book *Crazy Water, Pickled Lemons* by Diana Henry. I've added blood orange, tahini, toasted pine nuts and caramelised onions for a dish that is as vibrant and luxurious as it is healthy. I like to serve this with wilted spinach and boiled giant couscous, but bulgur wheat or freekeh would also work well. Try doubling the date salsa and serving it with cold meats, smoked fish or – my favourite way – with pan-fried halloumi. I hope it becomes a new kitchen staple.

For the blood orange salsa

15g pine nuts
80g (about 4) Medjool dates, stoned and chopped
1 green chilli, deseeded and very finely chopped
3cm piece of ginger root, peeled and very finely chopped
zest of 1 blood orange and juice of ½
1 tablespoon good-quality olive oil
¼ teaspoon sea salt flakes
15g coriander, finely chopped
freshly ground black pepper

For the mackerel

2 tablespoons rapeseed or olive oil
2 onions, thinly sliced
a pinch of salt, plus extra to season
60g tahini
3 tablespoons lemon juice
1 garlic clove, crushed
4 mackerel fillets

First, make the salsa. Toast the pine nuts in a dry frying pan over a medium heat for a couple of minutes (watch them like a hawk so they don't burn), until golden, then set aside to cool. Place the date pieces in a small bowl. Add the chilli, ginger, blood orange zest and juice, olive oil and salt, and season with a good grinding of pepper. Then, add the chopped coriander and the toasted pine nuts. Stir well and set aside.

Make the mackerel. Heat half the rapeseed or olive oil in a large frying pan over a medium heat, then add the onions and a pinch of salt. Sauté for 10–20 minutes, until the onions are soft and caramelised – do not allow them to burn (you may need to turn the heat down).

While the onions are cooking, put the tahini, lemon juice and garlic in a small jug. Add a little water, whisking well, then continue to add water (you'll need about 30–50ml in total) until you have a sauce a little thicker than double cream. Taste and season with salt and pepper, as necessary.

When the onions are ready, divide them between two plates. Heat the remaining rapeseed or olive oil in the frying pan over a high heat. Season the mackerel fillets well on both sides, then add them to the pan, skin-side down. Cook for 2–3 minutes without moving the fillets (this helps the skin to crisp up) and until you can see that they are nearly opaque on the side facing you. Then, flip them over and cook for a further 1 minute, until the flesh is opaque all the way through (you can check gently with a sharp knife).

Place the mackerel fillets on top of the caramelised onions, then drizzle over the tahini sauce. Garnish with a spoonful of the blood orange salsa and serve immediately, with the remaining salsa on the side and some wilted spinach and couscous or bulgur wheat.

Salmon ceviche

with bergamot, avocado, coriander & toasted pine nuts

Serves 2 as a main or
4 as a starter or snack

I am always trying to find new things to do with bergamots, but their intense bitterness makes them a bit of a problem in the kitchen. However, it occurred to me that their potent juice would work beautifully for curing fresh fish in the style of ceviche. Adding some of the fragrant zest, too, results in a beautifully aromatic ceviche that fuses Latin American and Mediterranean flavours, the latter a nod to the bergamot's culinary roots. You can substitute bergamot juice with lemon and lime, or even yuzu for a more Japanese feel. If you struggle to slice the salmon, place it in the freezer for 20–30 minutes to firm it up beforehand. You can either serve this as a main course with some brown rice, or in crunchy lettuce-leaf 'cups' as a starter or snack.

¼ red onion, very
  thinly sliced
2 generous pinches
  of salt
300g very fresh (sushi-
  grade) salmon fillet
juice of ½ large
  bergamot (to
  give 70ml)
3 teaspoons finely grated
  bergamot zest
1 red chilli, halved
  lengthways and thinly
  sliced (deseeded if you
  want less heat)
2cm piece of ginger
  root, grated
1 garlic clove, very
  thinly sliced
½ teaspoon caster sugar
1 teaspoon very good-
  quality olive oil
1 small fennel bulb, very
  thinly sliced
1½ tablespoons
  pine nuts
1 ripe avocado
10g coriander leaves

Soak the red onion in very cold water, just enough to cover, with a generous pinch of salt, for 30 minutes. After 30 minutes, drain and pat dry with kitchen paper. Set aside.

Meanwhile, slice the salmon very thinly. Sprinkle with another generous pinch of salt and set aside for 10 minutes while you prepare the remaining ingredients.

In a small jug, whisk together the bergamot juice and zest with the chilli, ginger, garlic, sugar and olive oil. Place the salmon in a bowl and pour over the bergamot mixture. Mix well, then refrigerate for 10 minutes, then remove from the fridge, add the fennel and soaked red onion and mix well, then leave for a further 5 minutes at room temperature.

Heat a small frying pan over a medium heat, then add the pine nuts. Toast in the dry pan, shaking it regularly, until they are lightly golden and fragrant (don't take your eye off them, as they burn easily!). Remove from the heat and set aside to cool.

Halve, stone and cut the avocado into roughly 2cm dice. Mix the diced flesh gently with the salmon. Arrange the salmon on a plate, then scatter over the coriander and toasted pine nuts. Serve with brown rice or in lettuce wraps.

Black barley

with beetroot, blood orange, olives & smoked fish

Serves 2–3

This is a good, easy weeknight dinner, but one that is so much more than the sum of its parts. Blood oranges and crunchy fennel are perfect partners for the rich oiliness of smoked fish, and even more so when outlined against a dramatic canvas of black barley (but you can use ordinary pearl barley, if you prefer). If you're making this when blood oranges are out of season, use regular oranges and add an extra squeeze of lemon juice to the dressing.

400g beetroot, trimmed and sliced into 1.5cm wedges
1 tablespoon rapeseed or olive oil
1 teaspoon sea salt flakes
150g black or pearl barley, soaked in cold water for 1–2 hours
3 blood oranges
1 teaspoon wholegrain mustard
2 tablespoons good-quality olive oil
1 teaspoon maple syrup or agave nectar
1 tablespoon red wine vinegar
50g pitted black olives, roughly chopped
4 tablespoons finely chopped flat-leaf parsley
1 small fennel bulb
juice of ½ lemon
250g hot-smoked fish fillet, such as trout, mackerel or salmon
salt and freshly ground black pepper

Pre-heat the oven to 210°C/190°C fan/gas mark 6–7.

Toss the beetroot wedges in a bowl with the rapeseed or olive oil, sea salt, and a good grinding of black pepper to season. Tip the seasoned wedges onto a baking tray and spread them out in a single layer. Place them in the oven to roast for about 30 minutes, or until they are tender to the point of a knife. Set aside.

While the beetroot is roasting, drain the barley from its soaking water and put it in a medium saucepan. Cover with cold water by 5cm or so, place it over a high heat and bring it to the boil. Once boiling, lower the heat to a lively simmer and cook, covered, for 30–40 minutes, until the grains are tender but still have some chewy bite to them. They should not be chalky and crunchy in the centre. Drain the barley well in a colander, then return it to the saucepan to keep warm.

While the beetroot and barley cook, make a dressing. Using a sharp knife, slice the skin and pith off the blood oranges, then, holding the orange over a sieve placed over a bowl, cut out the segments of flesh, dropping them into the sieve. Squeeze the remaining pith and membranes over the sieve to get all the juice.

Pour the blood orange juice into a jug and add the mustard, olive oil, maple syrup or agave and red wine vinegar, and season generously with salt and some black pepper. Taste and adjust if necessary – remember, the olives and fish will be salty, so err on the side of under-salted.

When the barley and beetroot are ready, put the drained barley into a large bowl and add the blood orange segments, roasted beetroot, olives and parsley. Pour the dressing over and mix well – it is important to do this while the barley and beetroot are still warm, so they soak up the dressing.

Pick any fronds off the fennel and add them to the barley mixture. Slice the fennel bulb as thinly as possible, ideally using a mandoline. Place in a small bowl and toss well with the lemon juice and a sprinkling of salt.

When you're ready to serve, flake the fish into large chunks and fold it gently into the barley mixture. Divide the salad between two or three plates, then top each plate with a little of the lemony fennel to serve.

Chickpea, blood orange, kale & almond salad
with smoky chargrilled chicken

Serves 4

This is one of my go-to dishes as soon as blood oranges start to appear in the shops in late winter. The heartiness of bolstering chickpeas, buttered almonds and smoky chicken makes for a supremely satisfying plateful, not to mention one packed with nourishing ingredients. Vegetarians can swap the chicken for slices of chargrilled halloumi, which are just as good (they don't need marinating, just slice and grill). Try to get very good-quality chickpeas for this – they should be tender and creamy, not hard like bullets. You can also use normal oranges, but add a good squeeze of lemon juice to the chickpeas to compensate.

For the chicken
3 garlic cloves, crushed
zest of 1 lemon and juice
   of ½
2 teaspoons smoked
   paprika
1 teaspoon sea salt flakes
½ teaspoon dried thyme
3 tablespoons good-
   quality olive oil
2 chicken breast fillets,
   cut into 2.5cm strips

For the salad
3 blood oranges
1 or 2 red chillies,
   deseeded and
   finely chopped
30g butter
80g whole blanched
   almonds
4 garlic cloves,
   thinly sliced
a generous pinch of salt
1 red onion,
   thinly sliced
150g curly kale
2 tablespoons olive oil
2 x 400g cans of good-
   quality chickpeas,
   rinsed and drained
20g basil leaves,
   roughly torn

Make a marinade. Combine all the ingredients for the chicken, except the chicken itself, in a small bowl. Add the chicken strips and toss well to coat, then refrigerate for 30–60 minutes.

When you're ready to make the salad, grate the zest from two of the oranges. Place it in a bowl with the chilli. Cut the skin off all the oranges with a sharp, serrated knife, then cut the orange segments away from the pith. Do this over the bowl containing the zest and chilli to catch any juice. Place the orange segments in the bowl, then squeeze in any juice from the remaining pith too, then discard the pith. Set aside.

In a large, non-stick frying pan, melt the butter over a medium heat. Add the almonds and cook for 2–3 minutes, until starting to turn golden, then add the garlic and cook until that also starts to turn golden (a further 2–3 minutes). Season with the salt. Use a slotted spoon to remove the almonds and garlic from the pan and set them aside on a piece of kitchen paper.

Add the onion and kale to the butter in the pan with 1 teaspoon of the olive oil. Stir-fry for about 5 minutes, until the vegetables are starting to soften, adding a splash of water if they start to catch or burn. Add the chickpeas and the orange mixture, and cook for another 2–3 minutes, until everything is warmed through. Add the almonds and garlic back to the pan along with half the basil, and stir everything together. Turn off the heat, add the remaining olive oil and mix well, tasting for seasoning.

To cook the marinated chicken, pre-heat a griddle pan over a medium-high heat. Remove the chicken pieces from the marinade and cook for about 5 minutes on each side, or until cooked through – the juices should run clear and the meat should be opaque. (You can do this in a non-stick frying pan if you don't have a griddle pan.)

Divide the salad between four plates and place equal amounts of the chicken strips on top. Garnish with the remaining basil.

Apricot & pistachio clafoutis
with candied sage

Serves 6

Candied leaves are a beautiful way to take your cooking with herbs to the next level. They are very easy to make – simply dip in egg white and then sugar – but look impressive, as if they have been touched by the frosty fingers of the Snow Queen. Sage, with its downy softness, lends itself particularly well to the process, but you could also use the same technique with mint, lemon balm or young lemon verbena leaves. You will need to prepare them a day or two in advance, so bear that in mind.

This classic clafoutis combines succulent roast apricots with verdant pistachio, adding a double hit of aromatic sage to temper the sweetness with its slightly resinous fragrance. It is a perfect pudding for high summer, perhaps with a drizzle of double cream or a scoop of vanilla ice cream to gild the lily. You could also use peaches or plums in place of apricots, and consider adding a few blackberries or raspberries to the batter too, if you happen to have any lying around. The tart fruit paired with the pillowy softness of the custard is really quite something. Unorthodox though it may be, I sometimes eat the leftovers of this for breakfast.

For the candied sage
18 sage leaves
1 egg white
5 tablespoons
  caster sugar

For the clafoutis
150ml whole milk
150ml double cream
15 sage leaves
butter, for greasing
600g apricots, halved
  (or quartered if large)
  and stoned
1 teaspoon finely grated
  lemon zest
3 eggs
2 tablespoons plain flour
100g caster sugar
75g shelled
  pistachio nuts
2 tablespoons
  demerara sugar

Make the candied sage leaves the day before you want to serve the clafoutis. Put the egg white in a small bowl or cup and sprinkle the caster sugar over a plate. Have a sheet of baking parchment nearby. Dip each sage leaf in egg white to coat thoroughly, then dredge it in the sugar, ensuring it is completely covered on both sides. Lay it gently on the sheet of baking parchment and repeat with the remaining leaves. Leave the leaves on a worktop or oven rack to dry out for at least 24 hours. They should become crisp and sparkling.

The next day, about 2 hours before you want to serve the clafoutis, put the milk and cream in a small saucepan. Roughly crush the 15 uncandied sage leaves (not the ones you just covered in sugar!) in your hand then add them to the pan. Bring the mixture to just below the boil, then turn off the heat and leave to infuse for about 1 hour.

Meanwhile, grease a baking dish of about 28–30cm in diameter and at least 4cm deep with butter. Place the apricot halves, cut sides up, in the dish in a single layer.

Once the milk and cream mixture has infused, pre-heat the oven to 200°C/180°C fan/gas mark 6.

Strain the milk mixture through a fine sieve into a jug or bowl to remove the sage (you can discard this sage now). To the mixture in the jug, add the lemon zest, eggs, flour and caster sugar and whisk well using a hand whisk or electric

…method continued on page 78

hand whisk until smooth. (A few small lumps are fine, but aim for it to be as smooth as you can get it.)

If you have a food processor, blitz the pistachios to a fine powder. Otherwise, chop as finely as you can. Whisk them into the milk and egg mixture.

Pour the mixture over and around the apricots in the baking dish – it may cover a few, which is fine. Sprinkle the demerara sugar evenly over the dish.

Put the dish in the oven and bake for about 35–45 minutes, or until the custard is evenly set with a slight wobble. It should be golden and puffed up around the fruit. Leave to cool for about 15 minutes before scattering with the candied sage leaves. Serve immediately.

Steamed apricot dumplings
with poppy seed butter sauce

Makes 10

I no longer live in Oxford, but on my rare visits back to my alma mater, I make it a matter of urgency to return to Moya, an unpretentious Eastern European restaurant whose food remains some of the best I have ever tasted. My main course is of little importance, as long as it leaves room for the apricot dessert dumpling with the poppy seed butter sauce. It's impossible to explain the sensation of startlingly sharp, sweet, collapsing fruit cosseted in a cocoon of fluffy dough, slicked with butter that has been punctuated with the nutty rasp of poppy seeds. Instead, you'd best try it for yourself – this is the closest I could get to a recreation, although I heartily advise you to seek out the original, too. I'd recommend serving one or two dumplings per person as a dessert (depending on what you've eaten beforehand), but they also reheat well in a steamer, should you be unable to consume the entire batch in a single sitting. Out of season, this recipe works quite well with tinned apricot halves in syrup, and you can even try a dollop of apricot jam instead of the whole fruit (omit the sugar cubes in that case).

For the dumplings
125ml whole milk
35g butter
finely grated zest of
 ½ a lemon
1 egg
1 teaspoon vanilla paste
270g plain flour
90g golden caster sugar
¼ teaspoon salt
15g fresh yeast
10 ripe apricots
10 sugar cubes (I prefer
 brown for the flavour,
 but white also works)
icing sugar, for dusting

**For the poppy
 seed sauce**
100g butter
5 tablespoons
 poppy seeds
½ teaspoon ground
 cinnamon
2 teaspoons caster sugar

First make the dumplings. Put the milk, butter and lemon zest in a small saucepan over a medium heat and bring to just below the boil, until the butter has melted. Leave the mixture to cool to body temperature, then beat in the egg and vanilla paste (it is important to leave the mixture to cool as otherwise it will kill the yeast).

Put the flour and caster sugar in the bowl of an electric mixer fitted with a dough hook, or a large bowl if you plan to make the dumplings by hand. Add the salt to one side of the flour mixture in the bowl and crumble the yeast onto the other. Make a well in the centre and add the milk mixture.

Using the dough hook or your hands, bring everything together to form a sticky dough. Knead using the dough hook, or your hands on an oiled work surface, for about 10 minutes, until you have a soft, elastic dough that is slightly sticky, but not wet. Try to avoid adding more flour unless really necessary.

Put the dough back in the bowl if necessary, cover with a clean tea towel and leave it to rise for about 1 hour, or until doubled in size.

Meanwhile, cut the apricots in half and remove the stones. Set aside. Line a baking sheet with baking parchment or non-stick silicone.

Once the dough has risen, divide it into 10 pieces of about 50g each. Take each piece and roll it into a ball in your hands, then flatten it into a circle about 5mm thick. Take two apricot halves and place one half in the centre of the circle, cut

...method continued on page 80

side upwards. Place a sugar cube in the centre of the apricot, where the stone had been. Sandwich the other half of the apricot on top of the sugar cube. Bring the dough circle upwards around the apricot, so that it is fully enclosed in the dough, and pinch the ends together to seal, to give a uniform ball of dough with an apricot inside. Roll the ball gently in your palm to smooth over the sealed end. Set the dumpling aside on the lined baking sheet, and repeat the process with the remaining pieces of dough, apricots and sugar cubes.

Once you have shaped the dumplings, leave them to rest on the baking sheet for 20 minutes. Prepare a metal or bamboo steamer over a pan of simmering water (if using bamboo, you may want to line it with greaseproof paper to avoid bits of dough getting stuck onto it and making it a nightmare to clean). Steam the dumplings for 20 minutes, until the dough is puffed up, fluffy and slightly shiny on the surface.

While the dumplings steam, prepare the sauce. Melt the butter in a medium saucepan over a medium heat, then reduce the heat to low. Grind the poppy seeds in a spice grinder or powerful blender (such as a Nutribullet) until you have a dark, slightly moist mixture that begins to stick together (it shouldn't be a paste, though). You can do this with a mortar and pestle, but it will take more effort and you will probably need to do it in batches to avoid seeds pinging out all over your kitchen. Stir the ground seeds into the butter along with the cinnamon and caster sugar. Keep the sauce warm on a very low heat until you're ready to serve.

Serve the dumplings with the sauce poured over, and dusted with a little icing sugar.

Fig, hazelnut & raspberry pudding cake

Makes one 20cm cake, serving 6–8

Really good, ripe figs are wasted in baking – you should enjoy them as they are, perhaps with a smattering of fresh goat's cheese or ricotta. However, they are also rather hard to find, so I came up with this cake as a way to enjoy their autumnal flavour even when all you can find are bullet-hard supermarket specimens. The sharpness of raspberries (you can use blackberries instead) accentuates the figs' honeyed notes, and they are excellent with buttery hazelnuts and treacly brown sugar. This cake is best served warm on the day it's made, as a pudding with some ice cream or crème fraîche.

130g butter, softened at room temperature, plus extra for greasing
80g golden caster sugar
50g light brown soft sugar
2 large eggs, lightly beaten
1 teaspoon vanilla extract
a pinch of salt
½ teaspoon ground cinnamon
1 tablespoon milk
130g self-raising flour
60g blanched hazelnuts, roughly chopped
4 fresh figs
150g fresh or frozen raspberries
2 heaped tablespoons demerara sugar

Pre-heat the oven to 200°C/180°C fan/gas mark 6. Grease and line a 20cm springform cake tin.

In an electric mixer or with an electric hand whisk, cream the butter and sugars on high speed for 3–4 minutes, until pale and creamy. Gradually add the eggs, whisking well between each addition. Add the vanilla, salt, cinnamon and milk. Sift in the flour, then add two-thirds of the hazelnuts. Fold the mixture together with a spoon until just combined to a thick batter.

Chop two of the figs into small pieces (about 1.5cm) and fold the pieces into the batter along with half the berries. Pour the batter into the tin, level the top with a spatula, then quarter the remaining figs and arrange them on top of the cake, skin side pressed into the batter, along with the remaining berries and hazelnuts. Scatter over the demerara sugar evenly and bake for about 50–60 minutes, until a skewer inserted in the centre comes out clean. Serve warm with vanilla ice cream or crème fraîche.

Bergamot curd

Makes about 2 x 250g jars

Earl Grey tea is named after Charles Grey, Prime Minister of Great Britain in the 1830s, who was gifted a tea flavoured with bergamot oil, probably as a result of a diplomatic connection with China. The exact details of this tale are hazy, but we must be grateful to Grey's mysterious benefactor, for without him (or her!) it is unlikely that the bergamot would be much known outside its Mediterranean homeland. As it stands, you can even buy bergamots in Waitrose during the season, but the number of occasions on which I've seen them reduced to clear suggests that many of us are at a loss for how to use these greenish, sour specimens. This recipe is the answer, and my attempt to rescue those unloved fruit from the supermarket shelves. This exquisite curd is gorgeous spread on a scone or used for sandwiching a Victoria sponge (to be served with a pot of Earl Grey, of course). You can even add a splash of gin to the curd towards the end of cooking. I think the Earl would approve.

juice and finely grated zest of 800g (about 3 large or 4–5 medium) bergamots
100g butter, cubed
200g golden caster sugar
a generous pinch of salt
3 large eggs
2 large egg yolks

First, sterilise your jars. I do this by washing them well in soapy water, then putting the jars upside down in an oven at 140°C/120°C fan/gas mark 1 for 25 minutes, adding the lids (also upside down) for the last 10 minutes. Turn off the oven and leave the jars inside until you are ready to bottle the curd. You can alternatively run the jars through a hot dishwasher cycle, then pot the curd while they are still warm.

Put the bergamot zest in a large, heatproof bowl. Measure out 300ml of the juice (it should be about all of it), and strain it into the bowl with the zest, discarding any pips.

Add the butter, sugar and salt to the bergamot zest and juice. Suspend the bowl over a pan of simmering water (the water shouldn't touch the base of the bowl). Using a wooden spoon, stir the mixture for 5 minutes, until the butter has melted. Remove the bowl from the heat and let the mixture cool for a few minutes before adding the eggs and egg yolks (if it is too hot, they will scramble).

Put the bowl back over the simmering water and whisk the mixture frequently as it heats up for about 30–45 minutes, until the curd thickens and reaches the 'ribbon stage' (when a dollop dropped from the whisk forms a ribbon on the surface of the mixture). You can use a sugar thermometer to check – the temperature should reach 76°C.

When the curd is thick, allow it to cool in the bowl, whisking occasionally, then pour into the warm jars and seal. The curd will keep in the fridge for about 2–3 weeks, and freezes well, too.

Olive oil & candied bergamot syrup cake

Makes one 20cm cake, serving 6–8

This is based on a recipe from Gayle Gonzales's fabulous dessert blog, Pastry Studio. She makes it with oranges, and I would highly recommend trying it with blood oranges if you can't find bergamots – it is one of the most visually stunning cakes I know. Bergamots are usually available for a short period around January to March from certain specialist grocers and suppliers. Resembling squat, yellow-green oranges, they are best known for their fragrant zest, whose oil is used to perfume Earl Grey tea. I will add a small caveat, though: their bitterness isn't for everyone. Despite the candying process, there remains a little residual bitterness in the fruit topping of this cake that tends to divide tasters! However, if you want to keep things sweet, you can just pour the syrup over the cake and simply discard the fruit slices. You can also make it with regular unwaxed lemons, which are a little less bitter. If using lemons or bergamots, make sure you blanch them first as the recipe says, but if you are using oranges you can skip this step and simply put the orange slices straight into the syrup.

This is lovely with a scoop of crème fraîche – or a cup of Earl Grey, for die-hard bergamot fans. It also pairs well, as you might expect, with the London Fog ice cream on page 168. Use your best olive oil and honey here – they make all the difference.

For the candied bergamot & syrup

1 large bergamot, zest grated and reserved, covered, to use in the cake (see below)
130g golden caster sugar
3 tablespoons flavoursome honey
2 sprigs rosemary or thyme, plus extra to decorate

For the cake

150g plain flour
75g semolina
1 teaspoon baking powder
¼ teaspoon bicarbonate of soda

First, make the syrup. Bring a medium saucepan of water to the boil and reduce to a simmer.

Meanwhile, using your sharpest knife, slice the zested bergamot widthways as thinly as possible, discarding the bumpy bit at each end. Remove any seeds with the point of a knife. Put the bergamot slices in the pan of water and simmer for 1 minute. Drain, return the slices to the pan and cover with fresh water. Bring to the boil and allow to simmer gently for 1 minute, then drain again and set aside. This process helps to remove most of the bitterness.

Put 400ml of fresh water in the saucepan and add the sugar. Place over a high heat and bring to the boil, stirring to dissolve the sugar, then reduce the heat to a lively simmer and add the honey and rosemary or thyme sprigs and the blanched bergamot slices. Simmer gently, stirring occasionally, for about 30–40 minutes, or until the fruit is translucent and completely tender to the point of a knife, and the syrup has reduced by half. Set aside.

While the syrup is simmering away, make the cake. Pre-heat the oven to 200°C/180°C fan/gas mark 6. Grease (with olive oil) and line a 20cm springform cake tin.

…method & ingredients continued on page 86

¼ teaspoon sea
   salt flakes
120g golden caster sugar
finely grated zest of
   1 bergamot (see above)
120ml good-quality,
   mildly flavoured
   olive oil, plus extra
   for greasing
3 eggs, separated
200g full-fat plain
   or Greek yoghurt
1 teaspoon vanilla
   extract
icing sugar, for dusting

Mix together the flour, semolina, baking powder, bicarbonate of soda and salt in a bowl. In another bowl, using an electric mixer or electric hand whisk at high speed, whisk together half the sugar, the reserved bergamot zest and all the olive oil for a couple of minutes. Add the egg yolks and beat again for 1 minute. Beat in the yoghurt and vanilla, then use a spatula or wooden spoon to fold in the flour mixture to completely combine.

In a separate, clean bowl and using a clean electric hand whisk (if they aren't clean the egg whites won't whip properly), whisk the egg whites to stiff peaks. Add the remaining caster sugar and whisk again until you have a thick foam. Fold one-quarter of this into the cake mixture, using gentle motions to avoid knocking out the air, then fold in the rest – you want to incorporate the egg-white foam while keeping as much air in the mixture as possible.

Pour the cake batter into the tin, level the top and bake for 30–40 minutes, or until a skewer inserted in the centre comes out clean. Remove the cake from the oven and, leaving it in the tin, prick it all over with a skewer or cocktail stick. Remove the candied bergamot slices from the pan of syrup and set aside. Pour the hot syrup over the warm cake in stages, waiting for each pouring to absorb before adding more. Ensure you distribute the syrup evenly over the whole cake.

Once all the syrup is used up, arrange the candied bergamot slices over the surface of the cake. You can do this neatly or randomly, depending on the kind of cook you are. Finally, scatter over a few sprigs or leaves of rosemary or thyme. Leave to cool before removing from the tin, dusting with icing sugar and serving.

Tunisian citrus cake

Makes one 20cm cake,
serving 6–8

As a teenager, I worked as a waitress at a lovely little organic café in Cambridge. The Tunisian citrus cake was always a favourite among our customers, and is memorable to me for two reasons. First, for its toothsome, slightly crunchy texture – it was made using breadcrumbs from the chef's leftover sourdough – permeated by a heavy slick of sweet, tangy citrus syrup and a whisper of cinnamon perfume. Second, because of an incident with a customer. We used to decorate the cake with whole spices, and the last piece in the counter traditionally ended up with all the spices on top as we removed them from the preceding slices that we served. I served this last piece to the customer, leaving the spices on as I thought it would be a nice touch. When I cleared her table an hour or so later, I noticed that there was not a spice to be seen. The whole cinnamon stick, star anise and handful of spiky cloves had disappeared from the plate. There were only two possible conclusions to be had, both equally unfathomable: said customer had either consumed the whole spices along with her cake, or taken them home, drenched as they were in deeply sticky syrup. I am still mystified to this very day – but I hope she enjoyed them, regardless.

This cake is a beauty because it uses ingredients that we might otherwise waste – leftover citrus peels and breadcrumbs (slightly stale sourdough works best). I must thank Catherine Phipps for introducing me to this way of making citrus syrup. Simply macerate leftover rinds with sugar for a day or so, stirring and squashing occasionally with a wooden spoon before straining, and you'll be rewarded with an intensely flavoursome syrup that can be used in everything from cakes to sorbets and iced teas. If you're buying citrus fruit just to make this recipe, use the zest and juice first for something else, like the bergamot curd on page 83. Thanks also to Diana Henry for the cake inspiration in her wonderful book *Crazy Water, Pickled Lemons*.

For the syrup
the zested, juiced
  halves of 8 bergamots,
  lemons, limes, oranges
  or grapefruit, or
  a mixture
caster sugar, quantity
  depending on the
  weight of your citrus

Make the syrup at least the day before you want to make the cake (but you can make it up to a week beforehand and keep it in the fridge). Roughly chop the citrus halves and weigh them. Put them in a non-reactive bowl (glass is best) and add half their weight in caster sugar. Stir well, cover with a tea towel, then set aside for at least 12 hours, stirring occasionally and pressing the fruit and sugar together with a wooden spoon. After at least 12 hours, strain the mixture through a muslin-lined sieve into a small bowl or jug. Discard the leftover fruit. You should have about 100ml of syrup.

…method & ingredients continued on page 88

For the cake

60g stale, crustless white
    or sourdough bread,
    torn into chunks
100g blanched almonds
1 teaspoon lemon thyme
    leaves, or 2 teaspoons
    finely chopped lemon
    verbena leaves, plus a
    few optional sprigs to
    decorate
150g golden caster sugar
2 teaspoons baking
    powder
150ml good-quality
    olive oil, plus extra
    for greasing
4 eggs, beaten
icing sugar, for dusting
star anise, cloves and
    cinnamon sticks, to
    decorate (optional)

To make the cake, pre-heat the oven to 200°C/180°C fan/gas mark 6. Grease (with olive oil) and line a 20cm springform cake tin.

Put the bread chunks in a food processor or mini chopper with the almonds and lemon thyme or verbena leaves. Blitz the mixture as finely as possible, then put it into a bowl and add the sugar, baking powder, olive oil and eggs. Whisk everything together until well combined.

Pour the mixture into the prepared cake tin and bake for 35–45 minutes, until just set and a skewer inserted in the centre comes out clean.

Remove the cake from the oven and prick it all over with a skewer or cocktail stick, then drizzle 100ml of your syrup all over the cake, letting it sink into the holes (if you have any extra syrup, serve it alongside the cake, or use it in iced tea).

Leave the cake to cool in the tin, then remove it and dust with icing sugar. You can either decorate this with sprigs of thyme or lemon verbena, or with cinnamon sticks, cloves and star anise – just make sure none of your guests eats them or puts them in their pockets! Serve the cake in slices, with fresh berries and a scoop of Greek yoghurt or crème fraîche on the side, if you like.

Tropical Fruits

> Mangoes, a fruit so choice and delectable that, had
> the old rhymers or Poets known of it, no doubt they
> would have given it a place above all the nectars and
> ambrosias of their dream-gods.
>
> ~ *Travels of Fray Sebastien Manrique, 1629–1643*

IF I COULD bottle one smell, it would be that of Mumbai's Crawford Market on a sunny afternoon in May. You may not think that a sweltering Indian city would be top of anybody's list of desirable aromas, but something special happens at that sticky transitional period between spring and summer. For it is then that the Alphonso **mango** comes into season. These, the food world's gold ingots, are widely cited as the best mangoes in the world. They feel warm, almost alive, in your hand, and the marigold skin hints boldly at the promise of treasure within. The flesh is silky, oozing honeyed syrup. Your fingernails will look like a smoker's for days after eating one of these, for they demand to be sucked greedily from the skin; the ceremony of a knife or spoon would be absurd.

For a fleeting period of a few weeks in early summer, Mumbai's giant fruit and vegetable market becomes a cavern of marigold, a hallowed treasure trove for these coveted fruits. They line shelves from floor to ceiling, nestle in baskets on the ground, and vendors sliver and proffer them, eager to prove that their mangoes are the best. The sight alone is splendid enough – radiant yellow orbs as far as the eye can see – but the heavy perfume that hangs in the air is something else altogether. The whole country goes somewhat mad for these mangoes during May: take a trip on any form of public transport in India during that time, and you will more than likely be sharing your space with several crates of these fruit, as families transport them to loved ones across the country.

Like the traveller Fray Sebastien Manrique, who found himself captivated by Indian mangoes nearly four centuries ago, I will never cease to be compelled and fascinated by the sheer abundance and variety of fruit in the tropics. Beyond Mumbai's mango markets I have been wide-eyed over street carts in Bangkok piled high with alien-esque hairy rambutans (whose name is derived from the Malay for 'beard'), gigantic, razor-sharp jackfruit dangling precariously from trees in Kerala, two-foot-long papayas piled by the roadside in Nicaragua and armfuls of fragrant lychees sold in the market in Myanmar. I have torn the spongy skin off a face-sized pomelo while perched on a kerb in Vietnam, and attempted to consume a foot-long papaya on a juddering overnight train in Rajasthan using nothing more than a pocket penknife. I have eaten strange, custardy durian fruit fresh from the tree and carried a gift of five home-grown pineapples from a plantation in south India all the way to the plains of Bagan in Myanmar, loath to leave these unbelievably fragrant fruit behind despite the demands of my itinerary.

Something of an expensive luxury in Europe, tropical fruit near the equator is an everyday staple. Cooks make use of these fruits in all their forms, from the green papaya salads of Thailand to the pineapple curries of Kerala and Malaysia, from mango kulfi to mango chutney, durian ice cream to iced lychee tea. Tropical fruit is incorporated in both sweet and savoury recipes, providing a sweet end to a meal or a juicy foil to rich meat or fish. The recipes in this chapter aim to add a little of that abundance to your everyday cooking, proving the versatility of the tropical fruit basket in a variety of radiant, colourful dishes.

Pineapple works particularly well simmered in curries or seared in stir-fries, contributing bursts of tart sweetness without losing its shape or texture. It functions well as a meat tenderiser because of its high levels of the enzyme bromelain, which breaks down protein chains – hence the Mexican dish *tacos al pastor*, in which pork or chicken is marinated in spices and pineapple before being grilled on a spit. This power can actually be problematic: pineapple processors have to wear gloves and face masks so as to avoid the fruit corroding their skin, and it is not uncommon to find your mouth bleeding after eating large quantities of fresh pineapple (equally, this also makes it excellent for your digestion).

Given the prevalence of pineapple nowadays, it is hard to believe that this formidable-looking fruit was once so sought-after that it gave rise to a thriving rental business. Brought back to Europe by Columbus in the fifteenth century, the pineapple soon won over audiences with its flavour, described delightfully by Edward Terry in 1655 as 'a most pleasing compound made of Strawberries, Claret-wine, Rose-water and sugar well tempered together'. It sparked a frenzy among the gardeners of the wealthy, who grew pineapples on wooden trays placed over pits filled with steaming manure. This was not a quick or easy process, and the pineapple soon became associated with those who could afford such extravagance. Throughout the eighteenth and nineteenth centuries, well-to-do families would often rent a juicy pineapple for use as a dinner-party centrepiece, symbolising wealth and hospitality. No one ate it, but instead they returned it to the rental business intact for the next family to use (sometimes they would whisk it away to the kitchen, making as if to treat their guests to a sliver or two, and bring back a completely different fruit – as the guests would never have tasted real pineapple, they could be relied on not to know the difference!). Pineapples still retain something of this precious status in Hawaii, where they are such an important crop that there is a ban on bringing hummingbirds into the country, in order to reduce pollination and the amount of pesky seeds in the fruit. Take note, would-be hummingbird smugglers.

The vibrant, glowing colour of the **papaya** belies a flesh that is actually rather light in flavour. One of the quickest fruit trees to grow, fruiting within the first year (I have spotted them growing like weeds all over southeast Asia), papaya is valued the world over in both its ripe and unripe state. The latter is vital for the famous Thai salad *som tam*, one of the country's fieriest dishes, while the former makes an excellent breakfast with a squeeze of lime and perhaps some fresh passionfruit or berries. The texture of ripe papaya is addictively fudgy, almost buttery, and functions well in savoury summer salads in the same way that you might use watermelon. Like pineapple, it also works as a meat tenderiser owing to the enzyme *papain* – in tropical countries, freshly butchered meat is sometimes wrapped in green papaya skins. It is said that you cannot make jam out of either papaya or pineapple because of their high enzyme content, but I once made a pineapple, vanilla and papaya jam with great success and would encourage you to do the same for a morning taste of the tropics on your toast.

Similar to the papaya in its egg-yolk hue, the **persimmon** is native to East Asia. There are two main varieties: Fuyu and Hachiya. The former has been developed by Israeli growers in the Sharon valley, hence we often find it sold under the name 'Sharon fruit'. It resembles a squat, sunshine-coloured tomato and, like papaya, is delightful enjoyed simply with a squeeze of lime, or tossed into zesty salads. Its flavour lies somewhere between papaya, peach and mango, making it an excellent substitute for recipes using any of those fruits. The Hachiya persimmon, often sold as the 'kaki fruit', is larger and more bulbous, and must be left to ripen until it is almost as fragile as a water balloon, with a jellied interior that can be scooped out and eaten with a spoon. The name 'persimmon' derives from an indigenous language of the United States, and means 'dry fruit'. You can understand why if you ever try to eat a Hachiya persimmon before it reaches that ripe, water-balloon stage: high tannin levels render it astringent and unpleasant, like licking the inside of a banana skin. The Japanese make *hoshigaki* (dried persimmon) by hanging these fruit, peeled, from strings until they form a dry outer skin, and then massaging them daily for at least a month to bring the natural sugars to the surface and cause a highly prized white bloom to appear on each fruit. They are eaten as a nutritious snack or used to make the famous Japanese sweets, *wagashi*. Persimmon leaves are also brewed to make a tea or to wrap sushi – try this if you're ever lucky enough to get your hands on some. The soft flesh of the Hachiya persimmon is excellent in recipes that normally use ripe banana: think persimmon bread or persimmon pancakes.

Like the pineapple, the **banana** is so ubiquitous in our modern culinary landscape that it is hard to believe it was once an exotic discovery or a sought-after rarity. Early explorers likened the taste of the banana to a combination of parsnips and butter, and food shortages during the Second World War saw this likeness exploited, when resourceful bakers would replace scarce bananas with plentiful home-grown parsnips, often boosted with a splash of banana essence. It is said that (real) bananas and chocolate were the foods most missed by the British during rationing.

Unfortunately, sliced parsnip sandwiches or parsnip cakes may soon become a necessity. Panama disease, an infection that wipes out banana plants, is spreading rapidly across the tropics. The trees on which we grow modern banana crops are genetically identical and so at great risk of extinction, should the infection continue to spread. While modern scientists work tirelessly to fight this threat, let us appreciate the versatility of the humble banana and its eminent usefulness. The leaves are excellent for wrapping rice, meat and fish for cooking (see page 148) or for use as eco-friendly plates, as they do in South India. The flowers (which resemble some kind of space-age alien hanging from the tree) are a common ingredient in fresh southeast Asian salads, adding a delightful crunch reminiscent of artichoke. Even the core of the trunk is used in the Burmese dish *mohinga*. Yet in the UK we apparently throw away 1.4 million perfectly edible bananas *every day*, despite the fact that the blacker they are, the better they perform in baking. I therefore make no apology for the number of banana recipes in this book, many of which are expressly designed to give you something delicious to do with those overripe fruit beyond the classic banana bread. You're welcome – now please stop throwing them away.

The **grapefruit**, and its associated tropical cultivars, remains a somewhat underutilised fruit in the kitchen. Beyond breakfast, where it is often served simply and unimaginatively bisected across its middle (bonus points if you are in possession of a serrated knife or spoon with which to tackle it), the grapefruit has not captured our hearts in the same ways as many other members of the citrus family. This is in spite of decades of selective breeding and cultivation. Originally an accidental cross of two citrus species – pomelo and sweet orange – the grapefruit comes from Barbados, where it grows in clusters on the tree like grapes, hence the name. It has a reputation for being bitter, despite most of its bitterness having been progressively bred out of the fruit, which perhaps explains its somewhat languishing status as a fruit for cooking with – or perhaps it is a result of its less-than-glamorous association with the depressing 'Grapefruit Diet', which claims to harness the fat-burning potential of the fruit's enzymes. Yet few ingredients can match grapefruit for unparalleled freshness and an explosion of sweet-tart flavour, and its potential deserves to be exploited more, particularly in salads where it contrasts perfectly with earthy grains, salty cheeses or buttery avocado. It has a wonderful affinity with basil, a combination exquisitely refined by Yotam Ottolenghi in his recipe for grapefruit, basil and sumac salad in his book *Plenty More*.

Pomelo, so much more than just 'a large grapefruit', as it is often infuriatingly described, gives toothsome texture and a pop of refreshing citrus to southeast Asian noodle dishes and salads. The name comes from the Dutch, combining the words for pumpkin and lemon, and as this substantial citrus starts to become more prevalent on our supermarket shelves, I urge you to experiment. The appearance can put people off, but pomelos are in fact incredibly easy to prepare (see tips on page 96).

Similarly, **lychees** tend to have little role in our repertoires beyond being eaten as a snack or dessert around Christmas, when they are in season. Perhaps this is because of their fiddly nature (an eighteenth-century explorer described them having a thin rind 'like the Scale of a Fish'), but I increasingly come across shelves of tinned lychees in our shops – let them tempt you to get a bit of that delightful lychee flavour (an addictive, refreshing combination of rose and passionfruit) into your cooking. They work particularly well in rich, coconut-scented curries, like the one on page 111.

While some of these fruits might initially appear alien or challenging, with a little preparation know-how and a good staple recipe, tropical fruits can become part of any repertoire. This chapter has perhaps the boldest flavours in the book. It is a celebration of riotous colour, sun-soaked fruits and the hedonistic messiness that often accompanies the consumption of tropical bounty – as anyone who has ever eaten an Alphonso mango will know.

Tips & tricks

* The large, foot-long papayas you sometimes see (particularly in Asian grocery shops) are much better value and much more flavoursome than the mini, mango-sized versions popular in supermarkets (developed by growers in Hawaii in 1919 and aptly named 'Solo', as they are just the right size for one person!). The large versions are more expensive, but you get much more flesh for your money, they have a far superior texture, and they are easier to peel and prepare, too (simply cut into long slivers, slice off the peel in one strip and scoop out the seeds with a knife).

* Papaya seeds (likened by cookery writer Tom Stobart to 'a heap of caviar') apparently have a laxative effect. A friend once proudly brought a papaya salsa to a dinner party of mine, claiming that the seeds added an irresistible nutty flavour so she had left them in. I was apprehensive but suffered no noticeable effects. Still, perhaps something to bear in mind before you go gorging yourself.

* Have a look for Alphonso or Pakistani mangoes in season (May to June). Asian grocers will usually sell them by the box, although sometimes the major supermarkets get in on the act, too. Expect to pay anything from £8 to £14 per box, but they are absolutely worth it. Judge their quality by sticking your face into the box and inhaling.

* Blitz disappointing, stringy mangoes into smoothies to salvage them. (I often freeze the flesh in cubes, then add it straight to the blender, where it has the added benefit of making the smoothie nice and cold.)

* Pomelos look daunting to prepare, but they are no trickier than oranges. Slice in half vertically (with the stalk end on the top), then cut lengthways into quarters. Prise off the spongy peel with your fingers, then simply tear the pomelo flesh into chunks, peeling off the thin pith. I often do this in a 'one-piece-for-the-bowl-one-piece-for-my-mouth' manner.

* Some southeast Asian recipes call for green papaya or mangoes. Rock-hard, underripe supermarket mangoes make a good substitute (grate them using a box grater or julienne peeler), but you can also use tart apples such as Granny Smith, cut into matchsticks.

* The best way to gauge the ripeness of a pineapple is with your nose. Smell the base of it – the oldest and sweetest part of the fruit. If you get a waft of that irresistible candyfloss aroma, buy it. Any sign of grey-blue mould in the furrows on the skin is a bad sign, so watch out for this, too. If you do find yourself with an underripe pineapple, try dipping it in chilli and salt for a snack or refreshing starter, as they do in southeast Asia, or use it for cooking in the recipes in this book.

* Persimmons apparently make a good hangover cure. A good reason to try the recipe on page 113.

* Tinned lychees make a good substitute for fresh in salads or curries, and are one of the few fruits that survive the canning process relatively intact. Major

supermarkets sell these, or you can find them in Asian grocers. Just be sure to drain off all the syrup.

*   If you are lucky enough to find fresh longans or rambutans, use them in much the same way as fresh lychees. They are less sharp and more fragrant, with slightly more chewy flesh. I've never got as far as using them in a recipe, though – I tend to just sit there with a bagful and meditatively peel and chomp until, before I know it, they have all disappeared.

Mango, lime & cardamom frozen yoghurt

Makes 1.5 litres

Although the season for Alphonso mangoes is cruelly fleeting, there is hope for those of us who believe true happiness is a turmeric-yellow mouth and a trickle of mango juice down the forearm. The canned purée – available in most Asian grocers and the World Food aisle of some supermarkets – captures the sunny sweetness of the fresh mango, and is conveniently suited to swirling through thick Greek yoghurt for a luscious ice that tastes of tropical summers. A hint of cardamom and a spritz of lime enhance the musky Alphonso aroma, but you can omit the cardamom if you're not a fan.

This recipe makes 1.5 litres of sorbet, but it's easily halved if you don't have space in your freezer. You can also buy 400g cans of Alphonso mango pulp, so use this if halving the recipe.

145g caster sugar
seeds from 6 cardamom pods, finely ground
juice and finely grated zest of 1 lime, plus extra juice to taste
850g can of Alphonso mango pulp
500ml thick, full-fat plain or Greek yoghurt
¼ teaspoon salt

Put the sugar, cardamom and lime zest in a large bowl and rub together with your fingertips until the sugar is fragrant and starting to moisten and turn light green.

Add the mango pulp, yoghurt, lime juice and salt. Whisk everything together and taste – remember, it will taste slightly too sweet, but freezing dulls flavour, so err on the side of slightly over-sweetened. However, add a little more lime juice if you want it more tangy.

Place the mixture in the fridge for at least 4 hours, before churning in an ice-cream machine until thick and set. You may need to do this in two batches, depending on the size of your ice-cream maker. Freeze for at least 2 hours before serving. Eat within 1 month.

Chickpea, spinach & mango curry

Serves 4

This curry delivers a double whammy of mango – good news for those who are as mad about this luscious botanical as I am. As well as using the fresh fruit, it also contains *amchoor*, a powder made from sun-dried, unripe mangoes that is used predominantly in Indian cooking to deliver a hit of acidity. The earthy chickpeas and iron-rich spinach are balanced perfectly by a thick, fragrant sauce, and chunks of fresh mango deliver a welcome burst of sweetness. It's also a very good, simple curry for a weeknight or for vegetarian or vegan guests. If you can, make this with Alphonso or Pakistani honey mangoes in late spring or early summer.

1 tablespoon rapeseed
  or coconut oil
2 onions, thinly sliced
1 teaspoon
  ground cumin
4 cardamom pods,
  bruised using a heavy
  knife or pestle
2 cinnamon sticks (each
  about 8cm)

4 plum tomatoes,
  roughly diced,
  or 16 cherry
  tomatoes, halved
½ teaspoon salt, plus
  extra to taste if
  necessary
3 tablespoons amchoor
  (dried mango powder)
3 teaspoons ground
  coriander

1 teaspoon garam
  masala
½ teaspoon Kashmiri
  chilli powder
½ teaspoon turmeric
1 teaspoon light brown
  soft sugar
2 x 400g cans of
  chickpeas, drained
500ml hot vegetable
  stock or water

2 large handfuls
  of coriander,
  finely chopped
100g baby
  spinach leaves
2 ripe mangoes,
  peeled, stoned and
  cut into 1.5cm dice

Heat the oil in a large casserole dish over a medium heat and sauté the onion for about 10–15 minutes, until softened and golden. Add the cumin, cardamom pods and cinnamon sticks and cook for 1 minute or so, until fragrant. Add the tomatoes, salt, amchoor, ground coriander, garam masala, chilli powder, turmeric and sugar. Part-cover the pan with a lid and cook for 10–15 minutes on a medium–low heat, until the tomatoes have softened and thickened.

Add the chickpeas, stock or water, and half the coriander. Cook over a medium heat, covered, for 25 minutes, until the sauce has thickened. If too runny, cook uncovered for a few minutes more. Add the spinach and cook for 1 minute or so, until it wilts into the sauce. Season the sauce to taste – you may need more salt if you used water as opposed to vegetable stock. Stir in the mango, and serve immediately, sprinkled with the remaining coriander and with steamed basmati rice.

Stir-fried pineapple
with tofu, greens & toasted cashews

Serves 2

During a hair-raising trip through the stunning scenery of Vietnam on the back of a motorbike several years ago, we stopped for lunch at an unassuming little hut by the sea. It was there that I began a love affair with stir-fried pineapple. The Vietnamese often incorporate it in light seafood dishes, but it also works beautifully with an assertive blend of ginger, chilli and brown sugar. Substitute the fish sauce with soy sauce for a wonderful vegetarian or vegan main course.

70g cashew nuts
2 tablespoons rapeseed or olive oil
250g firm tofu, cut into 2cm cubes
½ pineapple, peeled, cored and flesh cut into 2cm chunks
a couple of large handfuls of baby spinach leaves or shredded kale
1 garlic clove, finely chopped
1 red chilli, finely chopped (deseeded if you prefer less heat)
3cm piece of ginger root, very finely chopped
1 tablespoon fish sauce (or 1 tablespoon soy sauce if you're vegetarian)
2 tablespoons dark soy sauce
1 tablespoon light muscovado, palm or coconut sugar
juice of ½ lime, plus lime wedges to serve
a small bunch of Thai basil or basil, leaves picked, or 20g roughly chopped coriander leaves

Heat a large wok or frying pan over a medium-high heat and toast the cashews in the dry pan until golden – about 5 minutes. Toss them regularly and watch them like a hawk so they don't burn. Set aside.

Add half the oil to the pan and sauté the tofu cubes over a medium-high heat for about 5–10 minutes, until golden brown on all sides. Remove with a slotted spoon and set aside.

Add the remaining oil to the pan. Sauté the pineapple over a medium-high heat, stirring frequently, for about 5–10 minutes, until golden and sticky. You may need to turn up the heat a little if the pineapple looks like it is steaming rather than browning. Add the greens and cook for a further 1 minute, until they are softened. Lower the heat slightly and add the garlic, chilli and ginger. Cook everything, stirring frequently to prevent it from burning, for 2–3 minutes, until fragrant. Return the tofu to the pan.

Mix together the fish sauce (or extra soy sauce if making a vegetarian or vegan version), soy sauce and sugar in a small bowl or jug. Add the mixture to the pan and let it bubble and coat everything, stirring for a couple of minutes. Stir in the lime juice and cook for another 30 seconds. Tip in the cashews and stir well. Remove from the heat.

Serve the stir-fry with the basil or coriander scattered over, and extra lime wedges alongside. Serve with some steamed jasmine rice or boiled rice noodles.

Very green quinoa
with grapefruit, maple pistachios & pan-fried halloumi

Serves 4

I asked my best friend and her husband to test this recipe for me. She told me a few days later that they had made it, enjoyed it for dinner, and put the remaining portions in the fridge for lunch the next day ... only to devour them half an hour later. I couldn't ask for a greater compliment.

You can use almost any herbs for the dressing, as long as the total quantity is around 35g – mix and match according to what you have. Coriander, parsley, dill and chives all work well, and grapefruit mint, if you can find it, works fabulously, echoing the citrus notes of the juice. This is one of my favourite meals in January, when I need a little green and some sharpness to counteract the excess of Christmas – it is packed full of zingy flavours, balanced out by the salty depth of the halloumi, and proves that grapefruit should not be confined to the breakfast table.

For the very green quinoa
200g quinoa
200g frozen peas or broad beans
1 teaspoon salt, plus a generous pinch for the nuts
1 grapefruit
2 avocados, stoned and flesh sliced
3 big handfuls of rocket or baby spinach leaves
60g shelled pistachio nuts
2 teaspoons maple syrup
250g halloumi, cut into 1cm slices

For the dressing
1 teaspoon finely grated grapefruit zest, plus 2 tablespoons juice (from the grapefruit for the quinoa, above)
2 spring onions, roughly chopped
15g mint leaves
20g basil leaves
1 teaspoon Dijon mustard

Place the quinoa in a large saucepan over a medium heat. Shake the pan occasionally as the quinoa toasts. Once it begins to pop vigorously, add the peas or broad beans, 480ml of water and the salt. Bring to the boil, cover, lower the heat and simmer gently for 12 minutes.

Turn off the heat and leave the quinoa covered in the pan for 5 minutes before fluffing it up with a fork. It should be quite dry – if it is wet, drain off any excess water and leave the grains to sit in a sieve or colander to dry out a little.

Meanwhile, zest the grapefruit and set the zest aside. Cut off the top and bottom to expose the grapefruit flesh. Stand the grapefruit on one of its cut ends on a chopping board and use a sharp, serrated knife to slice off the remaining skin and pith. Holding the fruit over a sieve placed over a bowl, use the knife to slice between the membranes of the fruit and cut out the segments of flesh, dropping them into the sieve. Squeeze the remaining membrane into the sieve at the end. Discard the skin (squeeze it, too, to catch any juice).

Make the dressing. Put 2 tablespoons of the grapefruit juice in a mini chopper or food processor along with a teaspoon of the grapefruit zest (keep the rest for later) and the other dressing ingredients. Blitz well to make a creamy, green paste. Check the flavours – you may want a little more grapefruit or lime juice, or honey or maple syrup. The dressing should be quite sharp. Set aside.

When the quinoa is ready, transfer it to a large bowl. Stir in the remaining grapefruit zest, the avocado and the rocket or spinach leaves. Stir in half the dressing. Roughly chop the grapefruit segments into 2cm pieces or so, then gently stir them into the quinoa mixture.

Heat a medium saucepan over a medium-high heat. Add the pistachios and toast, shaking the pan regularly, until they start to smell nutty and turn slightly golden (1–2 minutes). Throw in a generous pinch of salt and trickle in the maple syrup,

½ teaspoon salt

4 tablespoons full-fat plain or Greek yoghurt

2 tablespoons lime juice

½ teaspoon runny honey or maple syrup

1 teaspoon good-quality olive oil

swirling the pan so it bubbles and coats the nuts. Stir everything well to coat, then pour the sticky pistachios onto some baking parchment and leave to cool.

Put the pan back on the heat and add the halloumi slices. Fry them over a medium-high heat for 1–2 minutes on each side, until golden.

Divide the quinoa equally between four bowls, then top with the halloumi. Drizzle the remaining dressing over the halloumi. Roughly chop the candied pistachios and scatter them over. Serve immediately.

Malaysian pineapple, aubergine & coconut curry

Serves 2

Sometimes, you read a menu description that sends you into paroxysms of longing and desire, and has you practically gaping at the waiter as you urge him, wide-eyed, to come over and take your order instantly so that the kitchen can quicken the transition of your food from plate to mouth. There was once a wonderful Malaysian restaurant in York that offered, as a vegetarian option, 'Classic Malay pineapple and aubergine with palm sugar curry', described as a 'sweet coconut milk thick curry'. The rest of the menu became irrelevant to me upon reading those words. I ordered this every single time. Now that the restaurant sadly no longer exists, I have been forced to create my own version, which is – to my delight – just as appealing and delicious as the original. It is a perfect main course for vegans and vegetarians (use the soy-sauce option), but I defy even the most ardent carnivore not to love it.

For the spice paste

2 shallots or ½ a
white onion,
roughly chopped
2 garlic cloves,
roughly chopped
5cm piece of ginger
root, peeled and
roughly chopped
1 tablespoon dried
shrimp, soaked in
200ml water for 1 hour
(reserve the water)
or 2 tablespoons light
soy sauce
2–3 red chillies
(deseeded if you
want less heat)

For the curry

3 tablespoons
coconut oil
1 cinnamon stick
(about 8cm)
5 cloves
5 cardamom pods,
bruised with a heavy
knife or pestle
2 star anise

First, make the spice paste by blitzing everything together in a mini chopper or food processor. Add a little of the shrimp soaking water (or plain water, if using soy sauce) to help everything blend evenly to a paste. Set aside.

Make the curry. Heat the coconut oil over a medium-high heat in a large frying pan or wok. Fry the cinnamon, cloves, cardamom and star anise for 1 minute until fragrant, then add the spice paste, curry powder and salt and cook for 5 minutes, stirring regularly, until fragrant and starting to dry out. Add the pineapple and aubergine and cook for 5–10 minutes, until starting to soften, stirring well to coat everything in the spices.

Pour in the coconut milk and add the lime leaves. Simmer for 10 minutes, then add the green beans and simmer for another 5 minutes, until the sauce has reduced and thickened (add a little water if it looks too thick). Grind the coconut in a mortar and pestle or spice grinder, then add it to the curry. Simmer for another 1 minute or so. Add the tamarind and sugar to taste – the sauce should be tangy and hot, but quite sweet. Simmer for a final 1 minute, then serve with lime wedges and sprinkled with chopped coriander or Thai basil leaves. Serve with steamed jasmine rice.

2 teaspoons medium
  curry powder
1 teaspoon salt
½ pineapple, peeled,
  cored and flesh cut
  into 2.5cm chunks
1 aubergine, cut into
  2.5cm dice
400ml full-fat
  coconut milk
3 kaffir lime leaves
  (fresh, or frozen and
  thawed; avoid dried),
  shredded (tough centre
  stems discarded)
80g green beans, cut
  into 2.5cm lengths
3 tablespoons desiccated
  coconut, toasted in a
  hot, dry pan or oven
1–2 teaspoons
  tamarind paste
2–3 teaspoons palm
  or brown sugar
chopped coriander
  or Thai basil, for
  sprinkling
lime wedges, to serve

Papaya, avocado & feta salad
with blackened corn & crispy tortilla chips

Serves 4 as a starter
or 2–3 as a main

The juicy, mild sweetness of papaya works fabulously in this salad of bright, Mexican-inspired flavours, and adds a pop of vivid orange colour. I could eat this every single day – it is an irresistible blend of sharp, creamy and crunchy, and the blackened corn and tortilla chips elevate it to something rather special. I recommend using the large papaya (about 30cm long) that you can find in some supermarkets and Asian grocers, as they have a better flavour and texture than the smaller, pear-shaped ones. If you can't find good papaya, watermelon makes a decent substitute (remove the seeds where possible). Vegans can simply omit the feta, perhaps substituting for some smoked tofu.

For the salad
½ red onion, thinly sliced
¼ teaspoon sea salt flakes
½ teaspoon caster sugar
juice of ½ a lime
1 tablespoon rapeseed
  or olive oil
250g fresh, frozen or
  canned corn kernels
½ teaspoon sweet
  smoked paprika
400g peeled and
  deseeded papaya
  (prepared weight),
  cut into 2.5cm dice
20g coriander leaves,
  roughly chopped
1 jalapeño chilli,
  deseeded and
  thinly sliced
100g feta, crumbled
125g baby plum or cherry
  tomatoes, halved
1 avocado
2 corn or corn-wheat
  tortillas (about 20cm
  diameter)
salt or freshly ground
  black pepper

For the dressing
juice and finely grated
  zest of ½ a lime

Pre-heat the oven to 200°C/180°C fan/gas mark 6.

Place the red onion in a small bowl with the salt, sugar and lime juice, stir well and set aside while you prepare everything else, stirring occasionally.

Heat a medium frying pan over a high heat, then add 1 teaspoon of the rapeseed or olive oil. If you're using canned corn kernels, drain well and pat dry on kitchen paper. If you're using frozen, simply pat dry. Tip the corn kernels into the hot pan, then add the paprika, a good sprinkling of salt and a generous grinding of black pepper. Cook over a high heat, stirring occasionally, until the corn starts to blacken slightly and smell smoky. Don't stir too much – allow it time to char a bit. It may also start to pop, so watch out for flying corn missiles around your kitchen! You may have to do this in batches, depending on the size of your pan – you want an even layer on the base of the pan but no more, otherwise the corn will steam rather than blacken.

Once the corn is done, tip it into a large mixing bowl and set it aside to cool. Once cool, add the papaya along with the coriander, jalapeño, feta and tomatoes. Slice the avocado in half, remove the stone and cut the flesh into 1.5cm dice. Add those to the bowl, too.

Slice the tortillas into small triangles (roughly the same size as nachos) and spread them out on a large baking sheet in a single layer. Drizzle with the remaining rapeseed or olive oil and sprinkle generously with salt to season. Put the baking sheet in the oven and cook the tortillas for 5 minutes, or until they are golden, but not brown. Remove from the oven and leave to cool.

Meanwhile, whisk together all the ingredients for the dressing in a small jug.

Tip the red onion slices into the bowl with the rest of the salad. Add the dressing and toss everything gently. Just before serving, add the tortilla chips and give it one final stir.

1 small garlic clove,
  crushed
1 teaspoon agave nectar
  or maple syrup
½ teaspoon red wine
  vinegar
2 tablespoons olive oil

Roast duck Thai red curry
with lychees

Serves 4

Yes, it may be called 'roast duck Thai red curry with lychees' in this book, but in my house this is referred to simply as 'delicious duck curry', which hopefully tells you everything you need to know about it. Pairing the dense, rich flesh of duck with the delicate perfume and soft spring of lychees is a luscious marriage (and one that I have experienced several times in Thailand), but even more so when the whole is draped in a sweet, spicy and deeply fragrant coconut cream. You can use fresh lychees, but I don't think it's worth the faff of peeling and stoning them (and I inevitably spray lychee juice in my eye whenever I try). The canned variety work excellently, and can be found at most Asian grocers and even big supermarkets. You could substitute with fresh or canned pineapple, if you prefer.

4 duck legs
2 tablespoons sea
  salt flakes
2 tablespoons
  coconut oil
6 banana shallots,
  thinly sliced
4 garlic cloves,
  thinly sliced
1 lemongrass stalk,
  tough outer layers
  removed, very
  finely sliced
4 kaffir lime leaves
  (fresh, or frozen and
  thawed; avoid dried),
  finely shredded (tough
  centre stems discarded)
400ml full-fat
  coconut milk
2 tablespoons Thai red
  curry paste
4 teaspoons light
  muscovado, palm or
  coconut sugar, plus
  extra to taste
  if necessary

Rub the duck legs well with the salt and place them in a single layer in a shallow dish. If you have time, chill them in the fridge overnight, or for a few hours, uncovered. This will help you to get really crispy skin. If you don't have time to refrigerate the duck legs, simply rub the salt into the duck legs when you are ready to cook.

Pre-heat the oven to 210°C/190°C fan/gas mark 6–7.

Place the duck legs on a wire rack above an oven tray lined with foil, then place them in the oven and roast for 10 minutes to crisp the skin. Lower the oven temperature to 190°C/170°C fan/gas mark 5, add a cupful of water or stock to the oven tray, then roast for 90 minutes, until the duck is tender and cooked through.

Meanwhile, make the curry. Heat the coconut oil over a medium-high heat in a large frying pan or wok, then add the shallots and sauté them for 5–10 minutes, until golden and starting to soften. Add the garlic, lemongrass and lime leaves and cook for another couple of minutes until softened and aromatic.

Lower the heat to medium. Add a couple of tablespoons of the coconut milk and the curry paste, sugar and turmeric, and sauté for a couple of minutes until fragrant – add a little more coconut milk if it starts to stick. This will help to release the aromatics in the paste and prevent the paste from burning.

Add the stock and remaining coconut milk, then simmer for 15 minutes, until the sauce is thick, creamy and aromatic. Stir in the cherry tomatoes and spinach and cook for another 10–15 minutes, until the tomatoes start to break down. Lower

...method & ingredients continued on page 112

1 teaspoon ground
turmeric
200ml hot chicken or
vegetable stock
200g cherry tomatoes
a couple of large
handfuls of spinach
leaves
juice of ½ a lime,
plus extra to taste if
necessary, and wedges
to serve
fish sauce or dark soy
sauce, to taste
400g can of lychees,
drained
a small bunch of Thai
basil, leaves picked, or
30g roughly chopped
coriander leaves, for
sprinkling

the heat, then add the lime juice. Taste and check the seasoning – you may
want to add some fish or soy sauce to make it more salty, depending on the
brands of curry paste and stock you use, and you may want to adjust the lime
juice and sugar.

Stir in the lychees to briefly heat through. Keep the sauce warm until the duck
is ready.

When the duck legs are ready, place one leg on each of four plates. Divide
the sauce equally between the four plates, pouring it over the duck legs. Sprinkle
with the Thai basil or coriander leaves. Serve with steamed jasmine rice and
lime wedges.

Sesame-crusted tuna rice bowl
with gingered persimmon, avocado salsa & sesame cream

Serves 4

This is neither sushi nor poke, but is inspired by both of those wonderful things, as well as the addictive interplay of textures that I so love about Japanese food. I have used persimmon for the salsa, both because it is a sadly underrated fruit and because its mellow crunch works perfectly with other Japanese flavours. Indeed, the persimmon holds a rather special place in Japanese culture so although its pairing with tuna may seem unorthodox, I think this works well. You want the Fuyu persimmon or 'Sharon fruit' here – the one that resembles a squat, bright orange tomato – rather than the more bulbous Hachiya persimmon. Luckily, the former are far more common in our shops anyway. You can also use mango or papaya, depending on the season.

Please don't hate me or be put off by the long list of ingredients: every step is very simple and mostly involves mixing things together in bowls, and you can make the sesame cream and salsa in advance (just be sure to bring them to room temperature before serving). Feel free to omit some of the elements, though – the tuna, rice and salsa on their own will be just lovely. Vegetarians can substitute the tuna for some pan-fried tofu.

For the persimmon salsa
2 ripe Fuyu persimmons (often called Sharon fruit), stalks removed, flesh cut into 1cm dice
1 red chilli or jalapeño chilli, deseeded and finely chopped
3cm piece of ginger root, grated
¼ teaspoon salt
1 teaspoon golden caster sugar
juice and finely grated zest of 1 lime
1 spring onion, very finely chopped
1 ripe avocado, stoned and flesh cut into 1cm dice
2 tablespoons finely chopped coriander leaves

For the salsa, mix all the ingredients except the avocado and coriander in a medium bowl, and set aside for 30 minutes while you prepare everything else, stirring occasionally.

Place the rice in a medium saucepan with a lid. Rinse it a couple of times with cold water, then drain, return it to the pan and add 400ml of water. Bring the water to the boil over a high heat, then immediately turn the heat down to its lowest setting, cover the pan with the lid, and cook the rice for 25 minutes. Then, turn off the heat and leave the rice, without lifting the lid off the pan, for another 10 minutes, until the rice has absorbed all the water. (If there is any left in the pan, drain it off.) Fluff up the rice with a fork and stir in the vinegar, salt and sugar. Taste and check the seasoning – you may want a little more vinegar, salt or sugar.

While the rice cooks, whisk together all the ingredients for the sesame cream in a small jug with 2 tablespoons of water. Taste and adjust – you may want a little more vinegar, soy or sugar. Set aside.

Meanwhile, prepare the dressed carrots. Put the carrot matchsticks into a small bowl and toss with the lime juice, rice vinegar and sugar. Set aside to macerate, stirring occasionally, while you prepare the remaining elements.

...method & ingredients continued on page 114

For the rice

250g brown sushi rice
3 tablespoons rice
  vinegar, plus extra to
  taste if necessary
1 teaspoon salt, plus
  extra to taste if
  necessary
2 teaspoons sugar,
  plus extra to taste
  if necessary

For the sesame cream

3 tablespoons tahini
2 tablespoons rice
  vinegar, plus extra
  to taste if necessary
½ tablespoon dark soy
  sauce, plus extra to
  taste if necessary
2 teaspoons golden
  caster sugar, plus extra
  to taste if necessary
1 teaspoon sesame oil
1 teaspoon mirin
1 teaspoon sake
1 tablespoon yuzu juice
  or lime juice

For the dressed carrots

1 carrot, cut into
  matchsticks
1 tablespoon lime juice
1 teaspoon rice vinegar
a pinch of caster sugar

For the tuna

2 tablespoons white
  sesame seeds
1 tablespoon black
  sesame seeds
2 tuna steaks
1 tablespoon rapeseed
  or olive oil

To serve

150g cooked edamame
  beans
dried yuzu powder
  (optional)
lime wedges

Add the avocado and coriander to the persimmon salsa and stir well.

Prepare the tuna. Put both types of sesame seeds on a small plate and shake to spread them out evenly. Press the tuna steaks onto the seeds, first one side then the other, to coat them in the sesame. Heat the rapeseed or olive oil in a frying pan over a high heat, then sear the tuna for about 3 minutes on each side (timings will depend on the thickness of your steaks, but you should be able to see them cooking from the side, which will help you to judge when they are cooked through). I like my tuna slightly rare, but cook for longer if you prefer it well done. Alternatively, you can use a meat thermometer, which should show 60°C. Remove the tuna from the pan and place it on a chopping board to rest while you assemble everything else.

Divide the rice between two bowls, then top with a couple of spoonfuls of persimmon salsa, the dressed carrots and the edamame beans. Slice the tuna steaks into thick strips and lay the strips across the top, then drizzle everything with a generous amount of sesame cream. Serve immediately, with a sprinkling of yuzu powder (if using) and lime wedges to squeeze over.

Seared salmon salad
with pomelo, avocado & toasted cashews

Serves 2

This is inspired by a Bill Granger recipe, one that has the rare accolade of being something that both my mum and I make on a regular basis (she doesn't have time to ferment her own water kefir and prove her own sourdough, so our repertoires tend to differ substantially). His way of cooking salmon is revelatory: briefly marinate in fish sauce and sugar, then simply sear on each side for 1 minute over a very high heat. The result is a crispy, caramelised exterior while the inside remains deliciously tender and succulent. It combines beautifully with the crunch of fresh greens, the aniseed notes of basil and the sweet freshness of pomelo. Use a pink grapefruit, segmented, if you can't find pomelo.

For the salmon
1 tablespoon fish sauce
1 teaspoon caster sugar
2cm piece of ginger
 root, grated
2 skin-on salmon fillets

For the salad
2 tablespoons lime juice
1 tablespoon fish sauce
1½ teaspoons
 caster sugar
½ red onion, very
 thinly sliced
150g sugar snap peas
½ cucumber, halved
 lengthways, deseeded
 and thinly sliced into
 half moons
1 avocado, stoned
 and flesh cut into
 2.5cm dice
1 red chilli, deseeded
 and thinly sliced (or
 seeds in if you want
 it hotter)
15g Thai basil leaves
 (or normal basil)
15g mint leaves,
 roughly torn
a few drops of sesame oil
a quarter of a pomelo
65g cashew nuts

For the salmon, mix together the fish sauce, caster sugar and ginger in a shallow dish. Add the salmon and set aside in the fridge to marinate while you make the salad – turn the fish occasionally to coat it in the marinade.

Make the salad. In a large bowl, mix together the lime juice, fish sauce and caster sugar, then add the onion and stir well. This will soften the onion and remove some of its raw harshness.

Fill a small saucepan with water and bring it to the boil over a high heat. Add the sugar snap peas. Cook for 1 minute, then drain and refresh under cold, running water. Pat dry with kitchen paper and add the sugar snaps to the bowl with the onion.

Add the cucumber slices to the bowl with the onion and sugar snaps. Add the avocado, chilli, basil, mint and sesame oil.

Peel the thick rind off the pomelo. Peel off the thin, white membrane, breaking the juicy segments into 2cm pieces and adding them to the rest of the salad. Discard the pith and membranes. Toss the salad together.

Heat a large, non-stick frying pan over a high heat. Add the cashews and cook for about 5 minutes, shaking the pan regularly, until they start to toast and become golden. Tip the nuts onto a plate to cool, roughly chop, then add them to the salad. Keep the pan hot.

Remove the salmon from its marinade using a slotted spoon and fry the pieces for 1 minute on each of their four sides (so 4 minutes in total, turning after each minute). The salmon should become slightly black and crispy on all sides. Allow the fillets to rest on a plate for 1 minute, then break them into chunks using a spatula (or your fingers, if you can handle the heat!) and add the chunks to the salad. Toss everything together gently, then divide between two plates. Serve with extra lime to squeeze over, if you like.

Soba noodles
with crab, pomelo, yuzu & avocado

Serves 2

I could eat this dish for every meal: a soft tangle of earthy noodles, the creamy sweetness of crab and the assertive rasp of citrus and galangal. I recommend the pink-fleshed, grapefruit-sized pomelos here, but the big yellow ones will do, too (if so, you may want slightly less – a quarter instead of half). Bottled yuzu juice is available in many major supermarkets now – use lime juice if you can't find it, but it is definitely worth seeking out for this dish. You can vary the herbs according to your taste, and use cooked prawns instead of the crab, or tofu if you are vegetarian. If you can find grapefruit mint (often sold at garden centres), I highly recommend using its fragrant leaves.

For the dressing
1 tablespoon yuzu juice
2 teaspoons
  tamarind paste
2 teaspoons dark
  soy sauce
1 tablespoon neutral-
  flavoured oil, such
  as groundnut or
  sunflower
juice and finely grated
  zest of ½ a lime
2cm piece of galangal or
  ginger root, grated
1 tablespoon light brown
  soft sugar

For the noodles
150g soba noodles
1 tablespoon rapeseed
  or olive oil
3 garlic cloves, finely
  chopped
1 green chilli, deseeded
  and finely chopped
2 spring onions, finely
  chopped
1 tablespoon
  sesame seeds
1 dressed crab, white
  and brown meat
½ fennel bulb, very
  finely sliced

First, whisk all the dressing ingredients together in a small jug. Taste and adjust – you may want it a little sweeter, or more sour, so add sugar or lime juice accordingly. Set aside.

Bring a pan of water to the boil. Cook the soba noodles according to packet instructions (usually 4–5 minutes), then drain well in a colander and rinse under cold running water. Set aside in the colander to drain and dry a little.

Heat the rapeseed or olive oil in a small frying pan over a medium–low heat. Add the garlic, chilli, spring onions and sesame seeds and cook for 3–4 minutes, stirring regularly, until the garlic, spring onions and chilli are fragrant and starting to soften. Do not let the garlic brown or burn. Add the crab meat and cook for another 1 minute, stirring to combine everything, then remove from the heat and set aside.

Put the drained noodles in a large bowl. Pour the dressing over and toss well to coat the noodles. Add the fennel to the noodles in the bowl. Remove the tough outer skin and pith from the pomelo segments, breaking the flesh into small, roughly 1cm pieces. Add the pieces to the bowl with the fennel and noodles.

Gently toss the noodles with the fennel and pomelo, then add the crab mixture, avocado and herbs and toss again gently to combine. Divide between two bowls and serve immediately.

½ pomelo (ideally one
  of the pink, grapefruit-
  sized ones)
1 avocado, stoned and
  flesh cut into 2cm dice
4 tablespoons roughly
  chopped mint, basil
  or coriander

Bali banana pancakes

Serves 4

For some unknown reason, this is one of the most popular recipes on my blog. Perhaps all hotels in Bali serve these pancakes to their guests, so there are always swathes of British holiday returnees frantically googling ways to keep that holiday spirit alive. I certainly enjoyed them for breakfast a few times during a trip to Bali several years ago. So, in the spirit of bringing a little feelgood Indonesian magic to your kitchen, here is my recreation of those lovely, thick pancakes, studded with chunks of ripe banana and golden with brûléed sugar. Incidentally, thin slices of pineapple also work beautifully instead of (or as well as) banana, for a slightly sharper sweetness.

You do need a good non-stick pan of the correct size for this recipe, otherwise it will be difficult to set the bananas in the pancake. Don't use bananas that are too ripe, or they will be difficult to slice thinly.

150g plain flour
1 egg
300ml milk (whole or semi-skimmed works best)
a pinch of salt
¼ teaspoon ground cinnamon
1 tablespoon melted butter, plus extra for cooking
4 teaspoons light muscovado sugar
2 large bananas (not too ripe), sliced on the diagonally as thinly as possible (about 3mm)
4 tablespoons desiccated coconut
maple or coconut syrup, to serve

Sift the flour into a large bowl. Make a well in the centre and crack in the egg. Pour in a little of the milk, then whisk the egg and remaining milk, incorporating a little more of the flour with each whisk, adding more milk gradually until you have a batter. Whisk in the salt, cinnamon and melted butter.

Heat a medium non-stick frying pan (about 20cm diameter) over a medium-high heat. Add a knob of butter and swirl it around the pan. Sprinkle 1 teaspoon of the sugar over the base of the pan, then arrange a quarter of the banana slices over the base of the pan (you can do this in concentric circles if you're feeling stylish, or just scatter it over). Cook for 2–3 minutes, until the bananas start to caramelise (check by lifting up one of the slices with the tip of a knife), then scatter over a quarter of the coconut and cook for another 1 minute.

Pour over a quarter of the pancake batter and tip the pan gently to cover the banana pieces and coconut evenly. Cook for 2–3 minutes, until the batter is almost set, then flip over the pancake carefully using a palette knife or spatula, and cook for another 1–2 minutes, until golden.

Keep the pancake warm in a low oven while you repeat to make the remaining three pancakes. Serve warm with maple or coconut syrup.

Banana & coconut drømmekage

Serves 8

This cake is based on a classic Danish recipe (pronounced 'drummer-kay'), which literally translates as 'dream cake'. It normally features a plain sponge topped with ludicrous quantities of butter, brown sugar and coconut (dreamy indeed), but I've paired this decadent topping with a light banana sponge, livened up with a spritz of fresh lime. The combination of lime, banana, coconut and brown sugar conjures up a tropical beach, and also gives you something excellent to do with those bananas starting to turn brown in the fruit bowl.

For the cake
400g (about 4 medium)
  very ripe bananas
  (peeled weight)
finely grated zest of 1
  lime and 1 tablespoon
  juice
140g golden caster sugar
2 eggs
60g coconut oil, melted
  and cooled slightly
220g plain flour
2 teaspoons baking
  powder
a pinch of salt
1 tablespoon milk

For the topping
80g butter
80g dark brown
  soft sugar
60g coconut sugar (or
  use all brown sugar)
40ml milk
80g desiccated coconut
seeds from 6 cardamom
  pods (optional),
  finely ground

Pre-heat the oven to 190°C/170°C fan/gas mark 5. Grease and line a 20x20cm square cake tin with baking parchment, leaving an overhang on at least two opposite sides that you can later pull up to help get the cake out of the tin.

Lightly mash the bananas with the lime zest and juice – don't mash too much, there should still be some chunks of banana.

Beat the sugar and eggs in an electric mixer until thick and creamy. Pour in the melted coconut oil and whisk briefly. Fold in the flour, baking powder and salt, then the mashed banana and the milk and mix until just combined – do not over-mix. Pour the batter into the cake tin and bake for 35 minutes, until the cake has risen and started to turn golden and firm up.

While the cake is in the oven, make the topping. Place the butter, brown sugar, coconut sugar (if using) and milk in a saucepan over a low heat and heat gently until the butter melts. Increase the heat and bring the butter mixture to the boil, then add the coconut and the cardamom (if using), lower the heat slightly and simmer for 1 minute, to infuse, then remove the pan from the heat.

Once the cake has been baking for 35 minutes, remove from the oven and turn the oven up to 220°C/200°C fan/gas mark 7.

Little by little, add the butter topping to the surface of the cake, spreading it out with the back of a spoon with each addition, to cover the cake evenly. When the oven is up to its new temperature, return the cake and bake for a further 5–10 minutes, until the topping is bubbling and caramelised. Remove the cake from the oven, pull it out of the tin by lifting the baking parchment, and leave to cool on a wire rack before serving.

Banana, coffee & caramel upside-down cake

Serves 8

On a recent trip to Vientiane in Laos I ordered 'fried bananas and coffee' in a delightfully cosy little backstreet café festooned with dangling pot plants (and a healthy population of mosquitoes, but let's not dwell on that). If dipping sweet, crispy bananas fresh from the fryer into a cupful of espresso sounds strange to you, consider the fact that both coffee and bananas contain similar flavour compounds (clove and floral notes). Also consider their very similar growing territories across the world, and suddenly the combination might not seem so strange. The two of them pair beautifully in this cake, the coffee cutting through the richness of ripe banana, butter and brown sugar. This is best as a pudding cake, eaten on the day it is made with some vanilla ice cream.

For the cake

2½ tablespoons instant coffee granules

3–4 teaspoons boiling water

130g soft butter, plus extra for greasing

110g light brown soft sugar or golden caster sugar

2 large eggs, lightly beaten

a pinch of salt

130g self-raising flour

½ teaspoon baking powder

For the topping

3 small, ripe bananas (or 2 large), sliced into 5mm rounds

40g butter

80g dark brown soft sugar

1 teaspoon ground cinnamon

2 teaspoons of the coffee mixture (above)

Grease and line a 20 x 20cm square cake tin (not springform).

Put the coffee granules in a small cup and add the boiling water. Stir to make a thick, dark liquid, almost a paste, ensuring there are no lumps (add a tiny splash more water if there are still lumps). Set aside to cool a little.

Pre-heat the oven to 190°C/170°C fan/gas mark 5.

For the topping, first place the banana slices over the bottom of the prepared cake tin in a single layer. Then put the butter, sugar and cinnamon in a small saucepan over a medium heat, and heat until melted together. Add the 2 teaspoons of coffee mixture, leaving the remainder to use in the cake batter. Stir vigorously with a wooden spoon until it is thick and dark. Pour this evenly over the bananas (you can spread it out using a spoon, but be careful not to dislodge the bananas).

Make the cake. Using an electric mixer or electric hand whisk, cream the butter and sugar on high speed for about 3–4 minutes, until pale and creamy. Gradually add the eggs, whisking well between each addition. Add the remaining coffee mixture and salt, mix briefly, then sift in the flour and baking powder and fold the mixture together with a spoon until just combined and you have a smooth, thick batter.

Pour the cake mixture over the bananas in the tin and level the top with a spatula, then bake for 30 minutes, until a skewer inserted into the centre comes out clean. Leave the cake to cool in the tin for 5 minutes, then invert it onto a cooling rack or plate and leave it to cool a little more before serving warm in slices, preferably with scoops of vanilla ice cream.

Honey mango, coconut & cardamom cheesecake

Serves 8

Honey mangoes start to arrive just as the Alphonso season ends. They come from Pakistan and, like Alphonso mangoes, will rarely be found in the supermarket. You're most likely to obtain these treasures from an Indian grocery shop, where they are sold by the box. The tell-tale sign that these are something special – a far cry from the tough, green supermarket specimens – is the aroma that greets you as you stand within a 3-metre radius of them. 'Honey' suddenly seems a very accurate name for these fruit: the scent of them hangs thick and heavy in the air, sweet and musky, almost sickly, but in a beautiful way, with notes not only of honey but also of toffee and butterscotch. The juice is likely to dribble down your wrist as you eat one. Should you want to elevate their deliciousness to extreme and sublime heights, try making this cheesecake: a smooth, cream cheese and coconut batter, a buttery biscuit base enriched with the heady perfume of crushed cardamom pods, and the sweet flesh of those honey-sweet mangoes (you can alternatively use Alphonsos). If good, flavoursome mangoes elude you, you can use 100g dried mango (preferably a Thai or southeast Asian brand) instead. Place it in a bowl, pour over enough boiling water to cover, then leave for 1 hour. Drain, pat dry and chop it into 1.5cm dice. Use as the recipe directs for fresh mango.

60g butter, plus extra for greasing
200g digestive biscuits, blitzed to crumbs in a food processor
seeds from 15 cardamom pods, finely ground; or 1 teaspoon ground cardamom
300g Quark or ricotta
200g full-fat cream cheese
150g icing sugar
finely grated zest of 1 lime and juice of ½
1 teaspoon coconut essence or 1 teaspoon vanilla extract
4 gelatine leaves
1 large, ripe mango or 2 small, ripe Indian/ Pakistani mangoes (in season), peeled, stoned

Pre-heat the oven to 200°C/180°C fan/gas mark 6. Grease and line a 20cm springform cake tin.

Melt the butter in a small saucepan over a medium heat, then stir in the blitzed biscuits and cardamom. Press the biscuit mixture into the bottom of the cake tin, using the back of a spoon to flatten gently to form a crust. Bake the crust for 10 minutes, until golden and aromatic. Remove from the oven and set aside to cool while you make the filling.

Mix the Quark or ricotta, cream cheese, icing sugar, lime zest and coconut essence or vanilla extract together in a large bowl using an electric mixer or electric hand whisk. Set aside.

Soak the gelatine leaves in a bowl of cold water until softened (about 5 minutes).

While the gelatine soaks, put the lime juice in a small saucepan along with 2 tablespoons of water. Place the pan over a medium heat until the liquid starts to steam, then turn off the heat. Squeeze the softened gelatine sheets in your hand over the sink to remove any excess water, then add to the lime juice and water mixture in the pan. Stir to melt the gelatine completely in the liquid.

Have the electric mixer or whisk ready, and pour the gelatine mixture slowly into the cheese mixture, whisking continuously to incorporate, then, using a spatula,

and flesh cut into
 1cm dice
2 tablespoons desiccated
 coconut, lightly toasted
 in a hot, dry pan
 or oven
mint leaves, to decorate

quickly fold in the diced mango. Pour the filling over the biscuit base and place the cheesecake in the fridge for at least 6 hours to set.

When you're ready to serve, sprinkle the cheesecake with the desiccated coconut and finish off with the mint leaves to decorate.

Pineapple, vanilla, pepper & coconut crumble

Serves 6

The wonderful Dishoom restaurant in London used to have a pineapple and black pepper crumble on its dessert menu, which inspired my version many years ago. I was recently devastated to discover that it is no longer on the menu, which makes this recipe even more important: if you haven't yet tried the heady combination of tangy, buttery pineapple buried beneath a lightly spiced, crunchy crumble, you now can address this significant gap in your gastronomic life. Enjoy with cold, cold ice cream and perhaps a cup of chai.

For the crumble
200g plain flour
120g cold butter, cubed
90g demerara sugar
seeds of 8 cardamom
  pods, finely ground
70g desiccated coconut
40g sunflower seeds
40g pistachio nuts,
  roughly chopped
2 tablespoons cold
  water or milk

For the filling
30g butter
2 pineapples, peeled,
  cored and flesh cut into
  2.5cm chunks
3 tablespoons dark
  brown soft sugar
1 teaspoon ground
  cinnamon
1/2 teaspoon ground
  ginger
1/4 teaspoon freshly
  ground black pepper
1/2 teaspoon vanilla
  extract or vanilla
  powder
finely grated zest
  of 1 lime

First, prepare the crumble. Using your fingertips, rub the flour and butter together until the mixture resembles fine breadcrumbs. Stir in the sugar, cardamom, coconut, sunflower seeds and pistachio nuts, and mix well. Add the water or milk and mix gently so the mixture turns 'pebbly'. Refrigerate while you prepare the fruit.

Pre-heat the oven to 190°C/170°C fan/gas mark 5.

For the filling, heat the butter in a large frying pan over a high heat. Add the pineapple and cook, stirring frequently, for 5–10 minutes, until the fruit starts to turn golden and loses some of its juice. Then, lower the heat slightly, add the sugar and cook for a further 5 minutes, until the pineapple is caramelised. You may need to do this in batches depending on the size of your pan – if the pineapple is too crowded, it will steam rather than caramelise. Remove the pan from the heat and stir in the cinnamon, ginger, pepper, vanilla and lime zest.

Tip the fruit into a medium baking dish and top it evenly with the crumble mixture. Bake the crumble for 35 minutes, until the fruit is bubbling and the crumble is crunchy and golden. Serve with vanilla ice cream.

Leaves

And the eyes of them both were opened, and they knew that they were naked; so they sewed fig leaves together, and made themselves aprons.

~ *The Holy Bible*

S O READS the story of Adam and Eve's fall from grace, the bitter knowledge imparted by the forbidden apple bringing forth shame and humiliation, and leading to the expert crafting of loincloths out of a piece of foliage so perfectly suited to cloaking the human genitalia that you'd almost think God had all this planned out. Whether the forbidden fruit of Genesis was, as many have speculated, actually a fig rather than an apple (other contenders are pomegranates and quinces) or not, there's no denying that fig leaves are associated with a certain *frisson* of eroticism and desire in Western culture. Depictions of Adam and Eve from the medieval period onwards feature modesty-preserving fig leaves, strategically and titillatingly placed, and the Renaissance period witnessed the fabulous 'fig leaf campaign', during which lascivious artworks were hurriedly covered with branches from nearby bushes to avoid offending delicate religious sensibilities.

Despite the cultural capital of the fig leaf, which is also useful for making an excellent ice cream, there are some underrated edible leaves out there that deserve a chance in the limelight. **Blackcurrant leaves**, for example. Where the vibrant, swollen blackcurrants are the beating heart of the plant, the leaves are its limbs; they are delicately imbued with that same fragrance, branched with aromatic capillaries that carry an intriguing herbal tang and mellow beautifully into ice cream or tea. Despite this potential, there are perhaps several reasons why blackcurrant leaves have never acquired the same resonance as those of the fig. For one thing, Adam and Eve would have had to work pretty hard to stitch loincloths out of these, and a single blackcurrant leaf would probably have been insufficient to cover Adam's modesty (and if it did manage to do so, then I feel a little sorry for Eve). Blackcurrants are less exotic than figs, growing in colder climes and lacking those heady associations with the perfumes of Arabia and the whitewashed, sun-drenched terraces of the Mediterranean. Blackcurrants are also rather less sexy than figs; where a fig presents you coquettishly with downy skin, voluptuous curves and a sweet, dripping interior, a blackcurrant is small, hard, and essentially mounts an assault on your taste buds with its astringent juice. It's the chastity belt of fruits.

Where flowers and fruits are the ostentatious – even flirtatious – parts of the plant, leaves have a stalwart usefulness that often means we overlook them. It's hard to care much for the mundane foliage of the blackcurrant plant when one is reaching to snare a particularly perfect tangle of inky berries, or to notice the swaying, umbrageous leaves of the banana tree when observing the way its fruit hangs coiled like some alien contraption. Peach leaves have a faint taste of almonds, but given a choice between a glowing, curvaceous peach and a piece of foliage, few would bother to gain better acquaintance with the latter. No wonder **tea** was apparently invented by accident, when the leaves of the *Camellia sinensis* plant fell into a monk's boiling water in ancient China. The tea plant is a fairly nondescript bush, the kind an unsuspecting gardener might turn into a hedge. Seeing hundreds of thousands of these plants sweeping the mountainous landscapes of India, you'd never guess at the infinite manifestations such a humble bush will eventually yield, from exclusive matcha to a mug of builder's brew. Perhaps the world's most culturally significant leaf – consider its association with fortune telling, the tea ceremonies of China and Japan, and our own British traditions – the infinite versatility of tea makes it a wonderful partner in the kitchen. In Myanmar, fermented tea leaves are tossed into an unusual salad with crunchy fried beans, roasted sesame seeds, peanuts and crispy, fried garlic. The Japanese pour tea over rice to finish a meal. In Britain, putting the kettle on serves as a sublimated way for us stiff-upper-lippers to express a whole host of otherwise awkward emotions, particularly when helped along by the presence of scones. Infusing tea into a dish is a way of bringing the centuries-old magic of this ingredient to your everyday cooking: as in life, tea provides a supporting role for the rest of the drama. It can add depth and aroma to a smooth scoop of ice cream, a whisper of perfume to a bowl of steaming, fragrant rice, or a malty back note to a fruity loaf cake. This versatility is a boon in both the teacup and the kitchen, with different varieties of tea all contributing their own unique qualities to a dish: romantic jasmine, feisty rooibos, aristocratic Earl Grey and tarry lapsang souchong, to name but a fraction of the available possibilities. On a recent trip to Laos, I found myself enjoying a pot of silkworm poo tea, although the delicate flavour of this one (yes, really!) is best enjoyed unadulterated, rather than used to enhance cooking.

We can deploy leaves in the kitchen in myriad ways. First, we can exploit them for practical purposes. **Banana leaves** (which Jane Grigson suggests would have made a better covering for genitalia than those of the fig, owing to their size) make fabulous, eco-friendly wrappings for food intended for grilling, baking, steaming or barbecuing. Not only are they practical and biodegradable, but they also contribute a smoky, slightly bamboo-like taste to whatever they are being used as a vessel for. Unwrapping a verdant parcel of fish steamed in coconut curry is always going to be much more appealing when the parcel in question is a neatly folded banana leaf, as opposed to an anaemic piece of kitchen foil. If you are lucky enough to have access to a lemon tree, the leaves make wonderful wrappings for grilled halloumi, chicken or fish, lending a subtle citrus perfume to what lies within.

Perhaps one of the reasons we enjoy cooking with **herbs** so much is that they are rarely necessary in a dish – instead, they are the proverbial cherry on top, a way to personalise a meal or elevate it to another level. Herbs can add surprising or unusual touches, especially if you can get your hands on some of the more unusual variants. I love grapefruit mint, which smells as glorious as it sounds and is fabulous in zesty salads with citrus and fish, or crushed in a mojito. Pineapple sage works beautifully in pork and cheese recipes, while lemon basil makes an excellent pesto and couples well with chicken in Italian dishes. Cinnamon basil partners intriguingly with strawberries and peaches in desserts, and purple basil

tastes similar to the normal green variety, but adds dramatic colour and interest. Thai basil is essential in many Thai and Vietnamese dishes; its aniseed flavour is difficult to substitute. Lemon thyme is fairly common now in supermarkets, thankfully, and wonderful with fish, chicken and dairy, as well as stirred into a simple omelette or pan of scrambled eggs. Experiment with adding herbs to sweet dishes: a few delicate lemon verbena leaves work beautifully scattered over a blackcurrant cheesecake, while finely chopped rosemary needles add a delicious herbal note to an apple tart. Basil has a curious affinity with strawberries, and you can cast your culinary net even wider if you start to branch out into the numerous varieties available.

Herbs often provide useful substitutes for one another, too – lemongrass, lemon verbena, lemon myrtle and lemon balm all contain high levels of citronella and citral, as do the leaves of the **kaffir or makrut lime** plant. Aside from their curious habit of sprouting one leaf from another like a parent and child, these leaves are visually unremarkable; it is only when shredded and infused in the enveloping richness of coconut milk that their potent citrus qualities come to the fore, and they are essential in many southeast Asian dishes. Only the fresh or frozen leaves – the latter of which defrost in minutes and are every bit as aromatic as their just-off-the-plant counterparts – will offer you the strong, citrus snap of the kaffir lime plant, particularly when shredded finely and stirred into simmering sweet coconut milk or pounded with chilli, ginger and coriander in a pestle and mortar.

One of the best ways to bring out the qualities of many leaves is to cosset them in milk or cream. Dairy coaxes out the flavour of these aromatic botanicals, allowing it to permeate your cooking: think lemon thyme or lemon verbena added to a creamy white sauce for baked salmon, or the grassy tang of blackcurrant leaves rippled through an ice-cream custard. Hot water is also a good way to extract the freshness of herbs: both lemon verbena leaves and lemongrass (pounded briefly in a pestle and mortar) make a wonderfully palate-cleansing tea. As should be obvious from the very concept of pesto, whose name derives from the Italian verb *pestare* (to pound or crush), applying pressure to fragile herbs releases much of their fragrance. It is a surefire way to unleash their full potential in a dish, whether it be crushed lemon thyme leaves stirred through crumbly ricotta to serve with honeyed figs, or a spice paste, pounded and scented with lime leaves, for baking tender pieces of white fish.

Reading leaves, whether those of tea or books, has long been a magical, transporting experience. Edible leaves are no exception. Learn to 'read' these delicate botanicals and harness their potential in the kitchen: it will open up a world of culinary discovery.

Tips & tricks

* In my opinion, dried kaffir lime leaves are not worth bothering with. Vacuum drying these thick, intensely zesty leaves sucks the life out of them like a well-positioned aphid. Buy boxes of frozen leaves from Asian grocers – they are cheap, will last for years and the flavour is incomparable. You can now buy the fresh leaves in some supermarkets, or you could try growing a kaffir lime plant yourself – mine has thrived happily on a conservatory windowsill for years, and guarantees me a year-round supply of fresh leaves. I always shred the leaves finely, removing the tough central stem, for maximum flavour when adding them to liquids or curry sauces.

* Thoroughly rinse leaves from your garden before use. Tearing or shredding them before infusing them in liquid brings out their flavour more fully.

* You can buy banana leaves fresh or frozen from Asian grocers.

* Whole tea leaves are much more flavoursome than tea bags, and carry less bitter tannin. I recommend using loose leaves for all the tea recipes in this book. The quality is infinitely superior and they are actually much better value for money, too, as a little goes a long way and you can steep them multiple times. See page 261 for stockists.

* You can buy lemon verbena plants online, and they are relatively easy to grow. The dried stuff makes a lovely tea, popular in Morocco, but won't have the same taste when used in cooking. Substitute with lemon thyme or a mixture of thyme and lemon zest instead, if you can't find fresh lemon verbena. The fresh leaves also make a glorious tea, with a zingy citrus snap that is lacking in the dried version – simply infuse in boiling water.

* Experiment with some of the more unusual herb varieties, which you can buy online or from good garden centres. You can also grow many of these varieties from seed, which makes them excellent value for money as you'll end up with more plants than you know what to do with.

* Most herbs don't freeze well, so if you want to prolong their life, blitz them into a paste or pesto and freeze in small, ice cube-sized portions. Exceptions are tougher herbs like common thyme and rosemary, which survive the process well.

* However, do freeze the bunches of coriander stalks you are left with after using the leaves in a recipe. They are a key ingredient in curry pastes and soups, and have much more flavour than the leaves alone. Roughly chop them and freeze in a plastic bag, then simply add straight to the blender or pestle and mortar when making a curry paste or soup base. You can also treat parsley stalks in this way, adding them to sauces such as salsa verde.

* Store freshly cut herbs in the fridge. Wrap the bottom of the stalks in moist kitchen paper and keep in the salad drawer. Or treat them like flowers – snip a centimetre off the bottom of a bunch of herbs and put them in a glass of water in the fridge door. However, they do tend to deteriorate more quickly this way than if you keep them in kitchen paper, so make sure you change the water regularly and use the herbs as soon as possible.

Honeyed figs on sourdough
with lemon thyme ricotta

Serves 2 as a main or breakfast, or 4 as a starter or snack

I wasn't sure whether to include this recipe in this book, as it seemed too simple. 'No one wants to be told to make toast,' I said to myself. However, I then remembered that a thick slice of sourdough toast can be a beautiful thing, particularly when it is slathered in clouds of citrus-scented ricotta cheese and topped with sweet, sticky honeyed figs and their purple syrup. I discovered years ago that the fragrant notes of lemon thyme work wonderfully with the bosky depth of figs, and this is my favourite way to combine the two. It makes a good, simple starter or snack, but I like it even more for breakfast.

250g ricotta cheese
6 ripe figs, halved, stalks removed
2 teaspoons runny honey
1 teaspoon lemon zest
3 teaspoons lemon thyme leaves
a generous pinch of sea salt flakes
4 slices of sourdough bread

If your ricotta is a little watery, place it in a sieve lined with clean muslin over a bowl for 20 minutes, to drain, before you begin.

Prepare the figs. Heat the grill to medium. Place the fig halves in a small baking dish, cut sides upwards, so that they sit snugly side by side. Drizzle over the honey.

Place the figs under the grill and cook for 10–15 minutes, until they have softened and are starting to bubble and turn jammy. Set aside. Keep the grill on.

Meanwhile, put the lemon zest and 2 teaspoons of the lemon thyme leaves in a pestle and mortar along with the salt and pound to a rough, green paste. Put the ricotta in a small bowl, then add the paste and mix well with a spoon.

Toast the sourdough slices on each side under the grill (watch them like a hawk so they don't burn).

Divide the slices between two or four plates, then divide the ricotta equally between each slice, spreading it thickly. Top each slice with three fig halves, spooning over the honeyed, purple juices.

Sprinkle the remaining lemon thyme leaves over the top, then serve immediately.

Thai-style pumpkin, kaffir lime & coconut noodle soup

Serves 2

I love all manner of east Asian soups, but *tom kha gai* – Thai coconut milk soup with chicken – is perhaps my favourite for its irresistible blend of the creamy and luxuriant with the fresh, hot and spicy. I wanted to make a vegetarian (even vegan) version of the classic that was just as satisfying. I substitute fudgy chunks of steamed pumpkin for the chicken. They work beautifully, soaking up the rich, coconut liquor. Noodles are not traditional in *tom kha*, but I add them for a more substantial meal, and everyone enjoys a good bowl-slurping session, don't they?

1 teaspoon vegetable or chicken stock powder
400ml full-fat coconut milk
1 lemongrass stick, bruised
8 kaffir lime leaves (fresh, or frozen and defrosted, but not dried), torn
2.5cm piece of galangal

or ginger root, thinly sliced
4 small, hot, red chillies, halved (deseeded if you want less heat)
2 spring onions, roughly chopped
15g coriander, leaves and stalks separated
300g peeled and deseeded pumpkin

or butternut squash (prepared weight), cut into 2.5cm dice
2 teaspoons fish sauce or dark soy sauce, plus extra to taste if necessary
2 teaspoons dark brown or palm sugar, plus extra to taste if necessary

150g button mushrooms, halved
200g baby plum tomatoes, halved
juice of ½ lime, plus extra to taste if necessary, and extra wedges to serve
100g dried rice noodles, cooked according to packet instructions

Place 500ml of water in a large saucepan and bring it to the boil. Add the stock powder and half the coconut milk, along with the lemongrass, kaffir lime leaves, galangal, chillies and spring onions. Roughly chop the coriander stalks and add these too. Lower the heat and simmer gently for 20–45 minutes (the longer you leave it, the more flavoursome it will be).

Place the pumpkin or squash in a metal or bamboo steamer over a large pan or wok full of simmering water. Steam for 10–15 minutes, or until just tender to the point of a knife. Divide between two deep soup bowls and set aside.

Strain the soup liquid through a sieve into a large jug. Discard the aromatics but keep the liquid. Return it to the pan and bring it to the boil. Add the fish sauce, sugar, mushrooms and tomatoes, and cook for 5–10 minutes, until the tomatoes are starting to collapse and the mushrooms have shrunk a little. Lower the heat to a bare simmer, then add the lime juice and the remaining coconut milk and check the seasoning. You may want it a little more sweet/salty/sour, so add sugar/fish sauce/lime juice accordingly.

Divide the rice noodles equally between the two soup bowls, followed by the broth. Roughly chop the coriander leaves and scatter them over the soup. Serve with extra lime wedges to squeeze over.

Pumpkin & ricotta pizza bianca
with brown butter, nutmeg & crispy sage

Leaves

Makes 2 large (about 30cm) pizzas

When I visited Mantova in Italy on a school exchange trip at the age of 14, I was a philistine who hated nearly all foods. My host family served me a plate of pumpkin ravioli to my intense disgust. (I think my 14-year-old self genuinely thought pumpkins were only for Halloween or Cinderella.) My more mature taste buds now consider the classic pumpkin ravioli, in a brown-butter sauce with crispy sage and freshly grated Parmesan (the sweetness of the pumpkin madly but brilliantly paired with a smattering of amaretti crumbs) one of the best dishes of all time. It would certainly be a contender for my last meal on earth. Ravioli, though, is an absolute faff to make, so I've taken all those harmonious flavours and placed them instead on another Italian classic. Sage-scented brown butter and crispy sage leaves, strewn over buttery rounds of dough, glistening with bubbling cheese, take pizza to a whole new level.

For the dough
225g plain flour
75g spelt flour
1 teaspoon caster sugar
7g fast-action dried yeast
1 teaspoon salt
2 tablespoons good-
  quality olive oil
180–200ml lukewarm
  water
2 tablespoons fine
  polenta, for dusting

For the pizza topping
250g ricotta cheese
320g peeled and
  deseeded pumpkin
  or butternut squash
  (prepared weight)
3 tablespoons good-
  quality olive oil
½ teaspoon freshly
  grated nutmeg
¼ teaspoon sweet
  smoked paprika
80g butter
15g sage, leaves picked

First, make the dough. Put the flours in the bowl of an electric mixer fitted with a dough hook, or a large bowl if you plan to make the dough by hand. Put the sugar and yeast on one side of the bowl, and the salt on the other. Make a well in the centre and add the oil, then pour in three-quarters of the water.

Begin to knead using the dough hook or your hands, adding the remaining water gradually until you have a soft dough – you may not need all the water; it shouldn't be sticky, just moist enough to come together. Knead for 10 minutes on an oiled work surface or using the dough hook, until the dough is soft and elastic, then return it to the bowl, cover with a tea towel and leave for 2 hours, or until it has doubled in size.

While the dough is rising, start the topping. Place the ricotta in a sieve lined with muslin over a bowl and allow it to drain (this ensures your ricotta won't be watery).

Slice the pumpkin or squash as thinly as possible into half-moon slices and place them in a medium bowl. Add 1 tablespoon of the olive oil, and the nutmeg and paprika, then season well with salt and pepper and toss with your hands to coat the pumpkin or squash in the oil mixture.

Melt the butter in a small saucepan over a medium-high heat. It will begin to bubble and spit, and separate out into golden liquid and white solids. Keep it on the heat, swirling the pan occasionally, until the white solids start to turn golden brown and the butter starts to smell nutty (about 3–4 minutes altogether). Remove the pan from the heat immediately, then throw the sage leaves into the pan while the butter is hot. They will sizzle and spit. Leave them in the butter for 2–3 minutes, then remove them with a slotted spoon and leave them to drain on kitchen paper. Set both the butter and sage aside.

2 x 125g balls of
mozzarella (drained
weight)
6 tablespoons freshly
grated Parmesan
2 amaretti biscuits,
crushed to fine pieces
(optional)
salt and freshly ground
black pepper

Once the dough has risen, pre-heat the oven as high as it will go (around 240°C/220°C fan/gas mark 9 is ideal). Scatter the polenta evenly over two large baking trays.

On a floured work surface, divide the dough in half and roll out each half so that you have two circles, each about 5mm thick. Place one circle on each baking sheet.

Tear the mozzarella into small chunks and spread these evenly over each circle of dough. Break half the drained ricotta into lumps and scatter these over too. Arrange the pumpkin slices over the top, scatter the remaining ricotta over, then scatter over the Parmesan.

Drizzle the brown butter all over both pizzas, then drizzle them with the remaining olive oil. Season generously with salt and pepper.

Bake for 10–15 minutes (the time will depend on the heat of your oven, so keep checking through the door!), until the dough is golden and slightly crispy around the edges, and the cheese is bubbling. Remove from the oven, then scatter over the crushed amaretti biscuits (if using) and the crispy sage leaves. Serve immediately.

Baked salmon
with a lemon verbena crust & lemon verbena cream sauce

Serves 4

This recipe is a brazen attempt to take my all-time favourite herb and cram as much of its heady citrus aroma into a dish as possible. It was more difficult than I expected. Although very potent when eaten raw or infused into tea, lemon verbena mellows surprisingly when cooked. However, using it both infused in a luxurious cream and blitzed into a vibrant pesto does lend this simple but impressive salmon dish a beautiful, fresh note. Lemon verbena is rarely available in food shops (and the dried leaves won't work here), so I would highly recommend buying a small plant from a garden centre and growing it yourself to ensure a long-lasting supply. The aroma is incomparable. You could, however, substitute with lemon balm or lemon basil.

For the sauce
1 tablespoon olive oil
20g butter
1 small onion or
  1 shallot, finely diced
1 garlic clove, finely
  chopped
5g lemon verbena
  leaves, very finely
  chopped (a few small
  leaves reserved)
100ml white wine
300ml crème fraîche
1 tablespoon lemon juice
salt and freshly ground
  black pepper

For the salmon
4 salmon fillets
finely grated zest of
  1 lemon and
  2 tablespoons juice,
  plus an extra squeeze
3 garlic cloves
10g lemon verbena
  leaves
30g Parmesan or
  pecorino cheese,
  grated
3 tablespoons rapeseed
  or olive oil
50g fresh breadcrumbs

First, make the sauce. Heat the oil and butter in a medium frying pan over a medium heat. Add the onion and sauté, stirring regularly, for about 10 minutes, until soft and golden, but not browned. Add the garlic and lemon verbena and cook for another couple of minutes, then add the white wine, turn up the heat and let it bubble away until the liquid has reduced by two-thirds. Lower the heat, add the crème fraîche and lemon juice, stir well and cook for a couple of minutes, until you have a sauce slightly thicker than double cream. Taste and season, then leave the mixture for the lemon verbena to infuse while you make the salmon.

Use the grill/oven combination setting on your oven, and pre-heat it to 220°C/ 200°C fan/gas mark 7 (or pre-heat a grill to medium-high). Line a small baking dish with baking parchment.

Lay the salmon fillets snugly together along the lined tray. Squeeze over a dash of lemon juice and season well.

Blitz the garlic, the 10g of lemon verbena leaves, cheese, lemon zest and juice, rapeseed or olive oil and breadcrumbs in a food processor until you have a vibrant green crust – don't overdo it, it should be a crust rather than a paste. Spread this over the salmon fillets, pressing it down gently.

Bake (or grill) the coated salmon for 10–12 minutes, or until the salmon is just cooked in the middle (you can check using a sharp knife or temperature probe). Meanwhile, gently warm up the lemon verbena sauce.

Garnish the salmon with a few small lemon verbena leaves and serve it with the warmed sauce, some boiled new potatoes and perhaps some peas.

Cambodian Amok
coconut fish curry, steamed in banana leaves

Serves 2

One of my best memories from a trip to Cambodia several years ago was stopping at a little restaurant stall near one of the most famous Angkor Wat temples. We were sweaty, dusty and exhausted after clambering around temple after temple in sweltering heat, and allowed our tuk-tuk driver to take us to the closest place that served food. Based on my experiences of travelling Europe, where the quality of food is inversely proportional to the restaurant's proximity to a tourist attraction, I was sceptical and resigned myself to the prospect of an overpriced, average lunch. We sat for around half an hour while ominous banging and clattering sounds came from the stove out at the back, only to then be presented with steaming bowls of the most heavenly curry, wafting seductively with brown sugar, coconut, spice and fresh fish. All my reservations immediately disappeared.

Amok means to steam a dish in banana leaves. Doing so lends a wonderful, smoky fragrance to the sauce, lightly set using eggs. Serving in banana leaves (which are widely available in Asian grocers) also looks very impressive, but you can use foil if you can't find them.

This dish is excellent served with sticky or jasmine rice and the stir-fried pineapple, greens and cashews (omit the tofu) on page 101.

For the *kroeung* curry paste

1cm piece of galangal or ginger root, roughly chopped

2cm piece of turmeric root, roughly chopped, or 2 teaspoons ground turmeric

6 garlic cloves

3 lemongrass stalks, tough outer layers removed, very finely sliced

2 banana shallots, roughly chopped

10 kaffir lime leaves (fresh, or frozen and defrosted, but not dried), tough centre stems removed; or finely grated zest of 2 limes

First, make the curry paste. Put everything in a food processor and blitz it to a paste (add a tiny splash of water and keep scraping down the sides to help it blitz). This will make twice the amount you need, so store the excess paste in the fridge (for up to 1 week) or freezer.

To make the curry, in a large frying pan, heat the oil over a medium heat. Add the curry paste and fry for 4–5 minutes until fragrant – stir regularly, so that it doesn't catch and burn. Add the coconut milk, sugar, fish sauce and kaffir lime leaves, then simmer gently for 10 minutes. Turn off the heat. Leave to cool for about 10 minutes, then add the lime juice and taste – you might want a little bit more sugar or fish sauce; the flavour should be deliciously sweet and coconutty. Whisk in the egg thoroughly, then stir in the fish chunks.

Take a banana leaf and fold it over itself a couple of times until you have a large square. Fold the corners of the square together at each side so you have a boat shape that will hold the curry – fix the edges together with cocktail sticks (you can also use staples, as I learned at a cooking class in Malaysia). Repeat with the other leaf. If you're using foil, fold two squares into boat shapes.

Spoon the curry into the leaves or foil (and leave open), then place them in a steamer (preferably a bamboo one, which gives a lovely fragrance) and steam for 20 minutes, or until the fish is opaque and the custard is lightly set. Scatter the chilli and coriander over the top and serve with the lime wedges and some steamed sticky or jasmine rice.

2 whole, hot red chillies,
 stalks removed
1 teaspoon black
 peppercorns, crushed
1 teaspoon sea
 salt flakes
1 teaspoon shrimp paste
 or Thai fish sauce
3 tablespoons flavourless
 oil, such as rapeseed,
 coconut or groundnut

For the curry
1 tablespoon flavourless
 oil, such as rapeseed,
 coconut or groundnut
250ml full-fat
 coconut milk
1 tablespoon palm or
 brown sugar, plus
 extra to taste
 if necessary
1 tablespoon fish sauce,
 plus extra to taste if
 necessary
3 kaffir lime leaves
 (fresh, or frozen and
 defrosted, but not
 dried), shredded (tough
 centre stems discarded)
1 tablespoon lime
 juice, plus lime
 wedges to serve
1 egg
500g thick fillet of
 sustainable white fish,
 such as coley, pollock
 or Pacific cod, cut into
 5cm chunks
2 banana leaves or
 2 large sheets of foil
1 red chilli, deseeded
 and finely sliced
2 tablespoons
 finely chopped
 coriander leaves

Salmon in jasmine tea

Serves 2

A Thai friend of mine, living in Bangkok, scents her refrigerator and bottles of chilled water with jasmine flowers from her garden. I long to have the kind of life where I could do the same. The magical aroma of jasmine is harder to come by in Europe, but jasmine tea – made by layering or mixing tea leaves with jasmine blossoms at night (when the flowers open and exude their fragrance) – is an excellent way to imbue your cooking with it. Jasmine tea bags are usually of very inferior quality, so find loose leaves if you can; preferably jasmine 'pearls', which are made by rolling the scented leaves into tight furls. Poaching salmon in a jasmine tea-scented broth, enriched with some of the deep flavours of a Japanese teriyaki, keeps it beautifully tender and provides a wonderfully delicate sauce. Serve with jasmine rice for an extra hit of this exquisite blossom.

2 tablespoons
  jasmine tea leaves,
  or 4 tea bags
400ml boiling water
2 salmon fillets
2 tablespoons mirin
1 tablespoon sake or
  sherry (or white wine,
  at a push)
2 teaspoons caster sugar
2 teaspoons light
  soy sauce
6 pared strips of
  lime zest
lime wedges, to serve
salt and freshly ground
  black pepper

Put the jasmine tea leaves or bags in a jug and pour over the boiling water. Set aside for 10 minutes to infuse, then remove the leaves or tea bags.

Pre-heat the oven to 200°C/180°C fan/gas mark 6.

Put the salmon fillets in a small baking dish so they fit quite snugly. Whisk together the tea, mirin, sake or sherry, caster sugar, soy sauce and lime zest and pour the mixture over the salmon – it should just about cover both fillets. Set aside for 20 minutes for the flavours to mingle.

Bake the salmon in the oven for 20 minutes, or until the inside of the salmon is cooked and it flakes easily.

Cover the salmon with some foil to keep warm. Strain the liquid from the oven dish through a fine sieve into a small saucepan and set it over a high heat to reduce by half, around 10–15 minutes. Taste and adjust the seasoning as necessary.

Serve the salmon in shallow bowls on a bed of jasmine rice, with the sauce ladled over and lime wedges to squeeze. Serve with some stir-fried or steamed vegetables alongside.

Fried fish
with tangy green mango, lemongrass & peanut salad

Serves 2

This is based on one of my favourite Thai dishes. Fried kingfish with green mango salad is a staple of the famous Bangkok restaurant Krua Apsorn, and one I make a beeline for every time I travel to Bangkok. It was revelatory for me to include very thin slices of fresh lemongrass among the slivers of sharp green mango and the toasted peanuts – a trick I never would have thought of, but the absolute best way to capture the snap of a sliced, fresh lemongrass stalk. You can vary the fish to suit your taste, as long as you use thick fillets or steaks (white fillets are too delicate here). Salmon fillets or swordfish steaks are my favourites. Serve this with steamed or sticky rice, and let the addiction begin.

For the fish
1 tablespoon lime juice
1 teaspoon fish sauce
1 teaspoon caster sugar
2 thick (about 4–5cm) fish fillets or steaks (salmon or swordfish works well)
1 teaspoon rapeseed or olive oil

For the salad
2 small, hot red chillies, roughly chopped (deseeded if you want less heat)
1 small garlic clove, roughly chopped
1 tablespoon palm, coconut or brown sugar, plus extra to taste if necessary
1 tablespoon fish sauce, plus extra to taste if necessary
juice of ½ lime, plus extra to taste if necessary
1 tablespoon rice vinegar
1 banana shallot, very thinly sliced
1 lemongrass stalk, tough outer layers removed, finely sliced
1 unripe mango
50g peanuts, toasted in a dry pan and roughly chopped
4 tablespoons roughly chopped coriander leaves
sticky or steamed rice, to serve

First, prepare the fish. Mix the lime juice, fish sauce and sugar in a small, shallow dish and add the fish fillets, turning to coat in the marinade. Set aside in the fridge while you prepare the salad.

Using a mortar and pestle, pound together the chillies, garlic, sugar, fish sauce, lime juice and rice vinegar. Taste and adjust as necessary – you may want a little more sugar, fish sauce or lime juice. Transfer the mixture to a medium bowl and stir in the shallot and lemongrass.

Peel the mango using a potato peeler, then slice the cheeks off the stone. Cut these into very fine julienne strips and add them to the bowl with the shallots and lemongrass. Stir in the toasted peanuts and coriander and set aside.

Heat a medium non-stick frying pan over a high heat. Add the rapeseed or olive oil. When it starts to smoke, add the marinated fish. Cook for 1 minute on each of the four sides, if using thick fillets, or 2–3 minutes on each flat side if using steaks, until the fish is just cooked in the middle.

Serve the fish on a bed of sticky or steamed rice with the mango salad spooned over the top.

Smoky lapsang souchong braised beef ribs
with honey, prunes & buttered almonds

Serves 4–6

As a teenager, I worked as a waitress in a lovely organic café. Every Saturday I would start my shift with a large pot of lapsang souchong tea. Lapsang souchong is divisive: some adore its pungent smokiness, the product of smoking the tea leaves over pinewood fires, while others say it is like drinking tar. I'm in the former camp, and one day it occurred to me that it would make the perfect cooking liquid for a rich, smoky beef stew. This is somewhere between a Mexican mole and a Moroccan lamb tagine, resulting in meat so tender it melts off the bone.

20g lapsang souchong tea leaves or 6 lapsang souchong tea bags
1 litre boiling water
2 tablespoons rapeseed or olive oil
10 banana shallots, topped and tailed, or 3 onions, roughly sliced
1.8kg beef short ribs or beef shin on the bone
1 teaspoon ground cinnamon or 1 cinnamon stick (8cm)
1 teaspoon ground ginger
1 teaspoon sweet smoked paprika
4 pared strips of orange peel
1 bay leaf
2 garlic cloves, sliced
3 large tomatoes, roughly chopped
1 teaspoon salt, plus extra to season
250g stoned prunes
2 tablespoons runny honey
20g butter
100g blanched almonds
30g roughly chopped coriander
freshly ground black pepper

Pre-heat the oven to 170°C/150°C fan/gas mark 3. Put the lapsang souchong tea leaves or tea bags in a large jug and pour over the boiling water. Set aside for 20 minutes to infuse.

Heat the rapeseed or olive oil in a large, lidded, ovenproof casserole dish over a medium heat. Sauté the shallots or onions for about 5–10 minutes, until the shallots are scorched and burnished, or the onions soft and translucent. Remove from the pan and set aside.

Season the beef ribs well with salt and pepper. Turn up the heat and brown the ribs well, turning occasionally, until a crust forms on each side (don't move them too much). Then, stir in the cinnamon, ginger, paprika, orange peel, bay leaf, garlic and tomatoes and cook for 2 minutes, stirring, until everything is aromatic.

Return the onions or shallots to the pan, then strain the tea through a fine sieve (discard the tea leaves or bags) into the pan and add the salt. Bring to the boil, then reduce the heat to a simmer. Place the lid on the casserole and put it in the oven for 3 hours.

After that time, add the prunes and honey, stir well, then return to the oven for a further 1 hour, until the sauce is thicker and slightly syrupy.

If the sauce is not quite thick enough for your liking by the end of the cooking time, remove the beef and prunes from the dish with a slotted spoon and set aside in a large bowl. Place the casserole on the hob over a high heat and simmer the liquid for 10–15 minutes until reduced and thickened, then return the meat and prunes to the pan. Adjust the seasoning to taste. Set aside to keep warm.

Melt the butter in a small frying pan over a medium heat. Fry the almonds in the butter for about 3–4 minutes, until lightly golden.

Serve the stew with the almonds scattered over and sprinkled with the coriander. This dish is excellent with couscous or bulgur wheat, but rice would also work.

Scarborough fair sausage crumble

Serves 4–6

Forgive the whimsical recipe title, but when I realised this crumble contained parsley, sage, rosemary and thyme, I couldn't give it any other name without it feeling like a missed opportunity. This is a celebration of winter herbs and their astringent notes. Sometimes bordering on the medicinal, these resilient leaves are perfect for cutting through rich ingredients. I've often toyed with the idea of making a savoury crumble, with a rich, meaty sauce on the base and a crumble flecked with cheese and herbs on top. This book finally gave me an excuse to try it out. You can make this recipe your own: add different vegetables to the sauce, vary the types of sausage, and experiment with cheeses. Any version is best served with a green salad or steamed green beans.

For the sausage sauce
1 tablespoon rapeseed
   or olive oil
10 pork sausages
250g chestnut
   mushrooms, chopped
2 onions, finely chopped
3 garlic cloves, crushed
1 teaspoon fennel seeds,
   roughly crushed
a generous pinch of
   chilli flakes
2 x 400g cans of
   chopped tomatoes
1 teaspoon soft light
   brown sugar
100g baby spinach leaves
salt and freshly ground
   black pepper

For the crumble
70g wholemeal flour
130g plain flour
120g cold butter, cubed
1 tablespoon finely
   chopped rosemary
   needles
1 tablespoon finely
   chopped sage leaves
1 tablespoon
   finely chopped
   flat-leaf parsley

Pre-heat the oven to 200°C/180°C fan/gas mark 6.

Make the sausage sauce. Heat the rapeseed or olive oil in a large, heavy-bottomed frying pan over a medium-high heat. Slice open the skins of the sausages and crumble the meat, in rough chunks, into the pan. Cook for about 5–10 minutes, until the sausagemeat is starting to turn golden brown. Do not stir the meat too often – allow it to burnish and caramelise in patches on the base of the pan. Remove the meat from the pan and set it aside.

Add the mushrooms to the pan and cook them over a high heat, stirring regularly, until they have lost most of their liquid and are starting to become slightly sticky and golden – about 5 minutes.

Return the sausagemeat to the pan and add the onions, turning the heat down to medium. Cook the mixture for 10 minutes, stirring regularly, until the onion has softened and turned golden in the fat from the sausages. Add the garlic, fennel seeds and chilli flakes and cook for a couple of minutes more, until the garlic has softened and the fennel smells fragrant.

Add the chopped tomatoes, rinsing out the cans with 200ml of water and adding that to the pan too. Stir well, add the sugar and season with a generous amount of black pepper, then simmer over a medium–low heat for 10–15 minutes, until the sauce has thickened slightly. Leave the sauce on the heat to thicken some more while you make the crumble.

Put the flours and butter in a large bowl and rub the butter into the flour with your fingertips, until the mixture resembles fine breadcrumbs. Stir in the herbs, cheeses and salt and mix well. Add the milk and mix gently so the mixture turns 'pebbly'. Set aside.

When the sausage sauce is rich and thick, taste to check the seasoning. You will probably not need salt, as sausages are naturally salty and the topping will be

1 tablespoon
  dried thyme
60g Gruyère or mature
  Cheddar, grated
40g Parmesan,
  finely grated
¼ teaspoon salt
1 tablespoon whole milk

salty, too, but add a little if you think it necessary. Add the spinach leaves and cook for 1 minute more to wilt them.

Tip the sausage mixture into a medium baking dish, then spread the crumble mixture over the top.

Bake for 30 minutes, until the topping is golden and crunchy, then remove from the oven. Leave for 5–10 minutes to cool slightly before serving.

Spiced tea-scented Christmas cookies

Makes 20

My Greek friend Vana, one of the best cooks I know, first brought these cookies into my life. *Melomakarona*, as they are known in Greece, are a Christmas treat, but in my opinion they are too good to confine to one short period of the year. Both crumbly and sticky at the same time, buttery without being too sweet, they are unbelievably moreish. They are traditionally soaked in a honey syrup, but I have added citrusy Earl Grey tea for an extra hint of flavour. You can experiment with the tea here – any strongly-flavoured tea would work well, particularly something with citrus or floral notes.

For the cookies

350g plain flour
1 teaspoon baking powder
½ teaspoon bicarbonate of soda
⅓ teaspoon salt
100ml extra-virgin olive oil
50g butter, softened at room temperature
60g icing sugar
finely grated zest of 1 orange and 60ml juice
1 teaspoon brandy (optional)
20 walnut halves, to decorate

For the syrup

110g caster sugar
3 tablespoons flavoursome honey
1 heaped tablespoon Earl Grey tea leaves, or other tea leaves of your choice

Pre-heat the oven to 200°C/180°C fan/gas mark 6. Line a baking tray with non-stick silicone or baking parchment.

Sift half of the flour into a bowl and mix well with the baking powder, bicarbonate of soda and salt.

Using an electric mixer or electric hand whisk, in a separate bowl, beat the oil, butter and icing sugar together for 3–5 minutes, until thick and creamy.

Add one-third of the sifted flour mixture, along with one-third of the orange juice, and the brandy (if using) to the butter mixture. Mix briefly, then add another third of the sifted flour mixture and orange juice, mix again, then add the remaining sifted flour mixture and orange juice and mix briefly.

Add the orange zest and the remaining, unsifted flour and mix until just combined. You should have a fluffy, soft dough that is not sticky.

Shape the dough into 20 small balls. Place the balls on the prepared baking tray, spaced well apart, and use a fork to press them down slightly and create an indent in the middle of each ball. Bake for 15 minutes, until the cookies are firm and lightly golden.

While the cookies are baking, make the syrup. Put 120ml of water into a small saucepan and add the sugar, honey and tea. Place over a high heat and bring to the boil, then reduce the heat and simmer for 3–4 minutes, until the liquid becomes slightly syrupy. Strain the mixture through a sieve, discard the tea leaves, and return the syrup to the saucepan. Keep warm.

When the cookies are baked and still hot, place them in the syrup for 30 seconds then flip them over and leave for another 30 seconds so that they have been totally soaked (you will need to do this in batches). Return the soaked cookies to the baking tray and leave them to cool. Place a walnut half on each cookie to decorate. Pour any leftover syrup over the cookies to soak in while they cool.

Rhubarb & ginger rooibos tea loaf

**Makes one loaf,
serving 8**

Rooibos tea is made from the dried leaves of the *Aspalanthus linearis* shrub, native to South Africa. It's not technically a tea, as it does not come from the *Camellia sinensis* plant, but is harvested, treated and prepared as one. Most rooibos is red, owing to the oxidisation of the leaves after picking and cutting, although green varieties also exist (which, like green tea, involve drying the leaves immediately after picking). High in antioxidants, it has a flavour somewhere between wood, caramel, malt and resin. Those deep notes provide the basis for this sticky, low-fat rhubarb tea loaf, punctuated by the snap of ginger. The loaf couldn't be easier to make, and a slice is an excellent afternoon boost with – you guessed it – a cup of rooibos. I also like it toasted for breakfast and spread with ricotta and a drizzle of honey.

2 tablespoons loose-
  leaf rooibos tea, or
  3 tea bags
275ml boiling water
100g raisins or sultanas
150g rhubarb, cut into
  1cm lengths
butter, for greasing
200g plain, wholemeal
  or spelt flour
50g ground almonds
2 teaspoons baking
  powder
1½ teaspoons
  ground ginger
½ teaspoon ground
  cinnamon
1 egg, lightly beaten
50g stem ginger in
  syrup, finely chopped
75g light brown
  soft sugar
1 tablespoon flaked
  almonds
1–2 tablespoons
  demerara sugar

Start your preparation at least 8 hours before you want to make the loaf, preferably the night before.

Put the rooibos tea or tea bags into a jug and add the boiling water. Leave the tea to infuse for 10 minutes, then strain it through a sieve into a bowl, keeping the liquid and discarding the contents of the sieve.

Add the raisins or sultanas and rhubarb to the liquid in the bowl. Soak the fruit for 8 hours, or overnight.

When you're ready to bake, pre-heat the oven to 190°C/170°C fan/gas mark 5. Grease and line a 900g loaf tin.

In a large bowl, mix together the flour, almonds, baking powder, and ground ginger and cinnamon. To the tea and fruit mixture, add the egg, stem ginger and sugar and stir together well. Pour the fruit mixture into the flour mixture, and mix with a large spoon or spatula until evenly combined.

Pour the mixture into the prepared loaf tin, then sprinkle with the flaked almonds and enough demerara sugar to cover evenly. Bake for 55–60 minutes, until the top of the loaf is crusty and golden, but still gives slightly in the middle when pressed, and a skewer inserted in the centre comes out clean. Leave to cool a little in the tin before turning out onto a cooling rack and leaving to cool completely.

The loaf is also very good toasted the following day, and it freezes well.

Kaffir lime & coconut drizzle cake

**Makes one loaf,
serving 8**

Many cooks I know declare they could never be without lemons in
their kitchen. For me, limes are the non-negotiable constant of my fruit
bowl. I sometimes wish I had the temerity to carry one in my handbag
at all times so that I could use it to give inadequate restaurant dishes that
extra rasp of potent, floral astringency that (in my opinion) food often
so desperately needs. There are few dishes that do not benefit from the
zest or juice of a lime. I have often toyed with the idea of using limes in
the classic lemon drizzle cake, and here I've gone one step further by
coupling lime juice and zest with the crisp, citrusy snap of the kaffir lime
leaf, in both its fresh and powdered forms. You can buy powdered kaffir
lime leaf online from Seasoned Pioneers – and I highly recommend
experimenting with this intriguing, deeply flavoured powder in sweet
and savoury recipes – but if you can't find it, simply add the zest of
another lime to the cake batter. You could also use matcha (green tea
powder) instead, for a vibrant colour and slightly different flavour.

For the cake
225g butter, softened
  at room temperature,
  plus extra for greasing
finely grated zest of
  2 limes, plus a few
  pared strips or thin
  slices to decorate
190g caster sugar
4 eggs, lightly beaten
210g plain flour
1 teaspoon baking
  powder
2 teaspoons kaffir
  lime powder
40g desiccated coconut
a pinch of salt
coconut shavings or
  chips, to decorate

For the drizzle
10 kaffir lime leaves
  (fresh, or frozen and
  defrosted, but not
  dried), torn
80g caster sugar
2 tablespoons lime juice

Pre-heat the oven to 190°C/170°C fan/gas mark 5. Grease and line a 900g
loaf tin.

Using an electric mixer or electric hand whisk, cream together the butter,
lime zest and sugar on high speed for about 3–4 minutes, until pale and creamy.
Gradually add the eggs, mixing well between each addition. Sift in the flour,
baking powder and kaffir lime powder, then add the coconut and pinch of salt.
Fold the mixture together with a spoon until just combined. Spoon the mixture
into the loaf tin and bake for 55–60 minutes, until a skewer inserted in the centre
comes out clean.

While the cake is in the oven, make the drizzle. Put 150ml of water into a small
saucepan. Add the lime leaves and place the pan over a high heat. Bring the
liquid to the boil then reduce the heat and simmer for 10 minutes, or until the
water has reduced by just over two-thirds – you want 50ml of liquid left. Turn off
the heat and leave to cool. Remove the kaffir lime leaves using a slotted spoon (or
strain the liquid, discarding the leaves). Once the liquid is cool, stir in the caster
sugar and lime juice.

Remove the cake from the oven and leave to cool a little in the tin. While it's still
warm, prick it all over with a skewer or cocktail stick, then pour over the drizzle.
Decorate with strips of lime zest, or lime slices, and desiccated coconut. Leave to
cool in the tin, then remove to a plate or board to slice and serve.

Blackcurrant leaf ice cream
(and variations)

Makes about 800ml

Crush a delicate, spiky blackcurrant leaf in your hand, hold it to your nose, and you cannot fail to be surprised by the ghost of blackcurrant that lingers there. Those sharp, almost grassy aromas, so bountiful in the ripe fruit, also course through the delicate veins of its leaves. Where the berries have perfume in abundance, the leaves have a fainter, more herbal note, reminiscent of potpourri. It has the zip and tang of a restorative cordial or throat sweet, mellowed by an almost fecund muskiness. The best way to use the leaves is to scrunch them generously into a rich ice cream, the flavour of which is almost impossible to describe: it carries the faintly medicinal note of the blackcurrant leaves, but mellows it with sugar and buttery silkiness. This ice cream is excellent with any dark berry desserts, or simply unadulterated.

300ml whole milk
300ml double cream
40 blackcurrant leaves
4 large egg yolks
100g golden caster sugar

Put the milk and cream in a large saucepan. Wash the blackcurrant leaves thoroughly in cold water, pat them dry with a clean tea towel (they don't have to be completely dry, just not dripping wet), then crush them gently in your hands before adding them to the milk and cream mixture. Place the saucepan over a medium heat. Bring the mixture just to the boil, then remove from the heat, stir well, cover and leave to infuse for 1 hour.

Put the egg yolks in a large bowl or jug and whisk with the sugar until pale and creamy. Warm up the milk and cream mixture over a medium heat until just below boiling again, then strain it through a sieve into the egg-yolk mixture, whisking constantly. Press down on the contents of the sieve with the back of a spoon to extract all the fragrance from the leaves.

Tip the entire mixture (minus the strained leaves) back into the saucepan. Place over a very low heat, whisking constantly, for 15–30 minutes, or until the custard has thickened enough to coat the back of a spoon. Be patient – don't turn the heat up too high, or you'll end up with scrambled eggs. Conversely, if it's not thickening at all after 10–15 minutes, turn the heat up a tiny bit. Keep stirring.

Once the custard has thickened, remove the pan from the heat and pour it into a bowl or jug. Allow to cool, then cover and chill the mixture for at least 6 hours, or preferably overnight.

Once the custard is very cold, churn it in an ice-cream maker until thick (about 15–30 minutes). Decant the ice cream into a freezer-safe container and freeze to firm up for 4 hours before eating.

Also try: herbal variations

Lemon verbena ice cream
Add 10g lemon verbena leaves (also rinsed and dried), lightly crushed in your fist, to the milk and cream instead of the blackcurrant leaves. Make as described. This is beautiful with roasted peaches or poached pears, and is also good with dark berry desserts.

Bay leaf ice cream
Add 4 bay leaves (also rinsed and dried) to the milk and cream instead of the blackcurrant leaves, and make as described. This is excellent for dessert with a fruity crumble such as pear, apple or plum. Try it with the plum crumble on page 49.

Lemon thyme ice cream
Add 10 sprigs of lemon thyme to the milk and cream instead of the blackcurrant leaves, and make as described. This is excellent with any lemon-based desserts, such as lemon tart or a lemon syrup cake.

Lemon balm ice cream
Add 40g lemon balm leaves (also rinsed and dried) to the milk and cream instead of the blackcurrant leaves, and make as described. This is excellent with fresh berries, and also works well with rhubarb.

London Fog ice cream

Makes 1 litre

Leaves

I was first introduced to the 'London Fog', essentially a tea latte made with Earl Grey and a dash of vanilla, during a trip to Canada. It quickly became a morning staple: the perfect hot, fragrant pick-me-up to accompany – of course – a stack of pancakes with maple syrup. It struck me that this luxuriant combination of dairy, Earl Grey and vanilla would also make an excellent ice cream, and I was right. Use the best-quality ingredients you can afford here: it makes all the difference.

500ml double cream
250ml whole milk
160g caster sugar
a generous pinch of salt
1 vanilla pod
3 tablespoons loose-leaf Earl Grey tea, or 3 Earl Grey tea bags
3 pared strips of lemon zest
6 egg yolks

Put half the cream (refrigerate the rest for later), along with the milk, caster sugar and salt in a large saucepan. Split the vanilla pod lengthways with a sharp knife and scrape out as many seeds as possible into the milk mixture, then add the whole pod, too. Add the tea or tea bags and lemon zest, and place over a medium heat. Bring the mixture just to the boil, then remove from the heat, stir well, cover and leave to infuse for 1 hour.

Put the egg yolks in a large bowl or jug with a sieve over the top. Strain the infused milk mixture into the egg yolks through the sieve, pressing down on the tea and vanilla pod with a spatula or wooden spoon to make sure you get every last drop of flavour. Set aside the sieve and its contents for later.

Whisk the milk mixture and egg yolks together, then tip everything back into the saucepan. Place over a low heat, stirring constantly, for 15–30 minutes, or until the custard has thickened enough to coat the back of a spoon. Be patient – don't turn the heat up too high, or you'll end up with scrambled eggs. Conversely, if it's not thickening at all after 10–15 minutes, turn the heat up a tiny bit. Keep stirring.

When the mixture has nearly thickened, put the remaining cream in a large jug. Put the sieve containing the tea and vanilla over the top of the jug.

Once the custard has thickened, pour it into the jug of cream through the sieve, and once more press down to extract all that remaining flavour in the tea leaves and vanilla pod. You can now discard the contents of the sieve.

Whisk the contents of the jug together. Allow to cool, then cover and chill the mixture for at least 6 hours, or preferably overnight.

Once the custard is very cold, churn it in an ice-cream maker until thick (about 15–30 minutes). Decant the ice cream into a freezer-safe container and freeze to firm up for at least 4 hours before eating.

Earl Grey dried fruit compote
with blood orange

Serves 6

I find dried fruit too sweet and cloying on its own, but then I learned to plump it up by cooking it in liquid, which transforms nature's candy into an entirely different beast. The sharpness of blood orange works fantastically well against the slight muskiness of dried prunes and apricots. This dish is particularly good cold from the fridge spooned over hot porridge, but also excellent at room temperature with granola and a dollop of yoghurt, or even served alongside a plain sponge or almond cake. You can also play around with the fruit – try dried figs and cranberries in place of the prunes and raisins. It's good for clearing out all those half-bags of dried fruit that we tend to accumulate in the larder!

2 tablespoons loose-leaf
  Earl Grey tea or 3 Earl
  Grey tea bags
500ml boiling water
150g stoned prunes
150g stoned, dried
  apricots
150g raisins or sultanas,
  or a mixture
2 pared strips of
  orange zest
2 pared strips of
  lemon zest
4 blood oranges

Place the Earl Grey tea leaves or tea bags in a jug and pour over the boiling water. Set the tea aside for 10 minutes to infuse, then strain the liquid into a large saucepan and discard the tea leaves or tea bags.

Add the dried fruit and citrus zests to the saucepan. Place the saucepan over a medium heat and bring to the boil, then cover and reduce the heat to its lowest setting. Simmer for 25 minutes, until the fruit is plump and juicy. Turn off the heat and leave to cool – the compote will thicken as it cools, and its juice will become syrupy.

When the compote is cool, segment the blood oranges over a bowl, reserving any juice. Stir the juice and fruit segments into the compote. Serve at room temperature, or chill and serve cold. The compote will keep in the fridge for a couple of days (or longer if you add the oranges just at the point of serving).

Flowers

There wasn't the slightest sign of life in her eyes. It was as if a strange alchemical process had dissolved her entire being in the rose petal sauce, in the tender flesh of the quails, in the wine, in every one of the meal's aromas.

~ Laura Esquivel, *Like Water for Chocolate*

S UCH ARE the effects of a single meal in Laura Esquivel's captivating magical realist novel, *Like Water for Chocolate*. The protagonist Tita has a 'sixth sense' about everything concerning food, and her preparation of numerous exotic and seductive dishes is interspersed throughout the narrative with the tale of her emotional life and her fraught romance with her lover, Pedro. On this occasion Tita's dish of quail in rose petal sauce is so potent that it causes her sister, Gertrudis, to strip naked and elope on horseback with a visiting soldier, lust leaping 'from her eyes, from her every pore' and rose-scented sweat dripping from her body. What else could you expect from eating a dish that contains twelve red roses, rose essence, a dragon fruit and several tablespoons of honey?

This isn't the only time that floral food has been responsible for a moment of madness on the part of a literary character. C. S. Lewis's Edmund betrays his siblings to the White Witch of Narnia for a taste of Turkish delight, a sweet traditionally flavoured with musk or rose oil. Odysseus's fellow travellers nearly succumb to the soporific and stultifying powers of the lotus blossom, which makes men 'long to stay on forever, browsing on/that native bloom, forgetful of their homeland'. Even Proust's famous madeleines are dipped in a 'decoction of lime-flowers'. Flowers exert a powerful hold over the literary and the culinary imagination, associated with luxury, excess and lasciviousness. Hardly surprising, given their long-standing connection with the tables of royalty and nobility.

Cooking with flowers is perhaps the closest one can get to the imperial palaces of China, the courts of ancient Persia or the banquet tables of medieval England. Chrysanthemum flowers have been used in east Asian cooking for thousands of years, and Japan's Edo period, often cited as a high point for the blossoming of Japanese culture, also saw the blossoming of cherry petals in hot water to make *sakuracha*, cherry blossom tea, believed to bring good fortune. The Romans, Persians, Chinese and Greeks distilled flavoured waters and syrups from the petals of rose, jasmine, geranium, lily, orange and hibiscus flowers. Medieval cooks in England whipped up sweet and savoury dishes using rose and 'blomes of elren' (elderflowers), and Elizabeth I ordered that the royal table should never be without a conserve of lavender. There is something unmistakably regal about scattering fragrant petals into your food, and the dishes we associate with floral flavours today are still those of luxury and decadence: Turkish delight, lavender shortbread, candied violets.

Perhaps the most renowned culinary flower is **saffron**, derived from the stamens of the saffron crocus and famously worth more than its weight in gold. It takes 150,000 crocus flowers to make a kilo of saffron, and the flowers cannot grow wild or reproduce without human nurture, so you can start to understand the fiendishly high price tag. The name saffron derives from the Arabic word for yellow, and it has been valued in both religious and economic terms since at least the Bronze Age. Used as a dye, deodorant, medicine, perfume and cosmetic in addition to its culinary potential, saffron contains the chemicals *safranal* and *picrocrocin* which give it an alluring, subtly metallic taste particularly well suited to seafood dishes and baked goods (consider the Cornish saffron cake, made at Easter and Christmas, which is thought to be a legacy of Phoenician traders). Food writer Niki Segnit describes it perfectly as combining 'the flavours of sea air, sweet dried grass and a hint of rusting metal'. Iranian saffron is some of the best, and most expensive, in the world, but cheaper substitutes are available if you want some of saffron's potent colour and flavour without the price tag: safflower, a type of thistle often called 'bastard saffron', is good at replicating the colour and ferric tang of the real deal, while Norwegian brand Aukrust markets dried calendula flowers as 'the saffron of the North'. I'm not sure how well this marketing would have gone down in the fifteenth century, where traders of fake saffron were often burned alive on funeral pyres built out of sacks of their fraudulent produce, but if these substitutes enable you to get a taste of the musky magic that saffron can bring to both sweet and savoury dishes, I'm all for them. To make the most out of this expensive luxury, steep strands in hot (but not boiling) liquid and add to dishes towards the end of cooking, so as not to damage the liquid's delicate aroma. Cleopatra, who reputedly bathed in saffron-scented mare's milk before sex, used this technique, but I think a good bouillabaisse, braise or bun is probably a better (and more economical) use, if I'm honest.

While there is the very real risk that too much flower power will leave food tasting like your grandmother's bubble bath (or, as Segnit puts it, make you feel like you are 'being pressed to your auntie's perfumed cleavage'), a whisper of floral fragrance goes a long way, and not only when reaching for the sugar bowl. Savoury dishes can benefit from the lightening effect of floral notes: think of the Moroccan habit of including crushed dried **rose** petals in the fiery, chilli paste harissa and the complex spice blend ras el hanout; or the Indian and Persian tendency to enrich layered rice dishes with a handful of rose. The Spanish call **chamomile** *manzanilla*, 'little apple', hinting at its potential for inclusion alongside ingredients such as scallops, pork and herbs, although its mellow earthiness is also well suited to dairy-based desserts such as panna cotta and ice cream. It is most commonly used in tea form, but has yet to emerge as a mainstream culinary ingredient.

The herbal, astringent tang of **lavender** is an excellent counterpoint to stone fruits such as peaches and apricots, but also works well alongside the sweeter meats such as duck and lamb. Its name derives from the Latin *lavare*, to wash, and it remains a staple of the perfume industry. The plant also has a darker side – it is so rich in volatile oils that they can spontaneously combust in the heat of the summer, triggering a heath fire that causes the seeds to germinate. You can add some of this explosive power to your cooking with just a pinch of the intense dried or fresh buds, whose natural partners include rosemary, lemon, thyme and soft cheeses. Incidentally, bees love lavender, so consider adding a couple of plants to your balcony, windowsill or garden. Dry the buds in summer and you will end up with a supply to last you the year round. If you can get your hands on intensely rich lavender honey, it is well worth experimenting with. Less advisable is using lavender as protection against the plague, as grave robbers did during the seventeenth century.

I have included **vanilla** in this chapter because, although technically a seed pod, it comes from *Vanilla planifolia*, the only orchid cultivated for the purpose of flavouring food, and because its status as a highly sought-after and increasingly expensive ingredient is largely to do with the unique properties of its flowers, which are notoriously difficult to pollinate. Outside its native environment (South America), no natural pollinators exist, so the flowers must be meticulously pollinated by hand in its largest growing areas: Mauritius, Tahiti, Madagascar and the Bourbon Islands. Growers can do this only during the 24 hours that the orchid remains in bloom – no wonder vanilla is expensive.

Add to this the need to mature the pods on the vine for six to nine months, to then dry them in the sun and wrap them in blankets to prompt fermentation, and finally to cure them in airtight boxes, and you may also understand why much of the nearly 5.5 million tonnes of vanilla used every year in commercial food production (including ice cream and Coca-Cola) is synthetically derived from coal tar or byproducts of the paper-making process. This *vanillin* is chemically identical to that of the vanilla bean, so although it is often described as 'fake', this is not technically true; however, real vanilla pods contain more than 250 other flavour compounds besides *vanillin*, so have a much richer taste. Don't despair if you have to settle for cheaper vanilla flavourings, though – blind tastings often find people unable to tell the difference in baking recipes (but they are more discerning when it comes to custard, so save your precious pods for special custard occasions like the London Fog ice cream on page 168).

Cooking with flowers is also a way to capture a fleeting moment of high summer. If you can find them, fresh **elderflowers** work astoundingly well with ripe, sweet tomatoes, an unlikely combination introduced to me in a Japanese restaurant. However, for a taste of their perfume throughout the rest of the year, sweet elderflower cordial makes an excellent substitute, a way to experience a taste of medieval England in the tart recipe on page 190. Nasturtium flowers, the beloved garnish of every aspiring Michelin-starred chef, do actually have a practical purpose, contributing a sharp, peppery bite to salads. Violets, recommended for consumption in the seventeenth century because they 'preserveth against Madnesse', make a delightful edible decoration for a variety of desserts, in both fresh and candied form (I cannot vouch for their effect on your sanity). A legacy of medieval culinary practice, flower waters – rose, orange blossom and geranium – work beautifully to perfume the crumb of sponges, cheesecakes and custards, and are an excellent way to introduce floral intrigue to your cooking outside the season for fresh petals. Flowers are also a good example of the intuitive rule that 'what grows together goes together': it simply makes culinary sense to nestle a few bushy sprigs of lavender among a tray of plump baked apricots drizzled with honey, or to perfume an apple compote with a few whiskers of rust-scented saffron.

Just be careful, though, that you don't take it too far, and find yourself being whisked into the sunset by a semi-naked Mexican warrior on horseback.

Tips & tricks

* If using fresh petals, try to grow your own or buy organic, to ensure you are not consuming harmful pesticides.

* Always err on the side of less when using flowers in the kitchen, especially flower waters: you can add more later, if the floral fragrance isn't strong enough for your liking, but once you take your dish into bubble bath (or perfumed cleavage) territory, there is no going back.

* You don't always have to find fresh flowers – although we live in a world of air freighting and mass worldwide agriculture, you are still never going to get fresh elderflowers out of season. Dried petals or flower waters are just as useful in the kitchen: rose, lavender, chamomile and elderflower are all available in dried form, and rose and orange-blossom waters are a convenient way of having those other-worldly perfumes on tap. Just remember that flower waters and dried petals will have a stronger, more concentrated flavour than fresh flowers, so adjust recipes accordingly.

* Nasturtium flowers are very easy to grow in the summer, and you can pickle the seed pods and use them in a similar way to capers.

* Jane Grigson, in her *Fruit Book*, dares to assume that 'everyone keeps a jar of caster sugar with four or more vanilla pods embedded in it. And that as the sugar goes down, it is replenished. That as the pods are used, they are washed, dried and replaced, and renewed from time to time.' I advise you to satisfy her presumption. Storing your expensive pods in this way enables you to maximise their potential. After use infusing ice cream or custard, simply rinse them gently and dry them on kitchen paper before returning to the jar. Waste not, want not. You can use the sugar in baking.

* Dried rose petals are available to buy in Middle Eastern shops, as is rose harissa and ras el hanout, both of which combine spice and petal to delicious effect.

* Leave your own petals on a tray in a warm place to dry, or dry them in a low oven (or the sun, weather permitting). Lavender works particularly well, and you can then store it in an airtight container for later use.

* Steep slit vanilla pods in a small bottle of vodka to make your own vanilla extract. Leave for at least a month before using. I also like to place half a pod in a spice grinder with a good quantity of flaky sea salt and blitz to make a vanilla salt, useful in baking recipes that require 'a pinch of salt' (as nearly all mine do).

* Use fresh elderflowers as quickly as possible after picking, before they start to smell like cat urine (apparently – I have never been unfortunate enough to sample this).

Lavender, lemon & goat's cheese focaccia

Makes one large loaf, serving 8–10

If you can find Persian or Amalfi lemons, available in late winter and early spring in specialist shops, I highly recommend using them for this recipe. This is a Mediterranean or Provençal summer in loaf form, perfect for tearing and sharing with a green salad and some chilled rosé. Use a good-quality olive oil and don't skimp – the oil-drenched crumb is what makes focaccia so irresistible. If you're not a fan of lavender, halve the quantity or leave it out, substituting for fresh thyme or oregano leaves. Feta would also work in place of the goat's cheese, but in that case omit the flaky sea salt at the end.

320ml lukewarm water
1 teaspoon caster sugar
25g fresh yeast, or
  1 x 7g sachet fast-
  action dried yeast
500g plain flour
8g salt
120ml olive oil, plus
  extra for greasing
2 teaspoons
  lavender buds
finely grated zest
  of 2 lemons
  (lemons reserved)
100g soft goat's cheese
½ teaspoon sea
  salt flakes
2 teaspoons thyme
  or lemon thyme leaves,
  to finish

Put the water into a jug and stir in the sugar. If using fresh yeast, crumble in the yeast, stir well to combine, then set aside for 10 minutes. If using dried yeast, don't add the yeast yet.

Put the flour in the bowl of an electric mixer fitted with a dough hook, or a large bowl if kneading by hand. Sprinkle the 8g of salt over the flour on one side of the bowl. Make a well in the middle of the flour and add 40ml of the olive oil and 1½ teaspoons of the lavender. Add the lemon zest. If using dried yeast, sprinkle it into the bowl on the opposite side to the salt.

Pour the water, yeast and sugar mixture into the bowl (or the water and sugar mixture if using dried yeast), on the opposite side to where you put the salt. Using the dough hook or your hands, bring the mixture together into a wet dough. You may need slightly more water – it is supposed to be a wet, sticky dough, so avoid the temptation to add more flour. Knead in the mixer for about 10 minutes, or on an oiled work surface if kneading by hand, until you have an elastic, slightly sticky dough.

Grease a 3-litre plastic container with oil. Tip the dough into it, cover with a tea towel and leave to rise, in a warm place if possible, for around 1–2 hours – it should double in size.

Once the dough has doubled in size, lightly grease an oven dish or tray with high sides (measuring about 35 x 26 x 6cm) with oil and line it with baking parchment. Tip the dough from the plastic box into the centre of the oven dish, trying to keep as much air in it as possible. Gently stretch the dough out to the sides, so it just about covers the bottom of the dish or tray. Again, try to leave as much air in it as possible – don't knock it back.

Top and tail the zested lemons, then slice them as thinly as possible using your sharpest knife. Flick out any seeds from the slices. Cut each slice in half so you have half-moon shapes. Arrange the lemon slices over the surface of the dough in the dish. Cover the dish with a tea towel and leave for a further 1 hour, until the dough has roughly doubled in size again.

Once the dough has risen, pre-heat the oven to 240°C/220°C fan/gas mark 9.

Poke your finger into the dough, all the way to the bottom, to make indentations all over. Crumble the goat's cheese over the dough, sprinkle the remaining lavender over, then drizzle with the remaining olive oil. Sprinkle with the sea salt flakes, then bake for 20 minutes, until the bread is puffed up and golden, with the cheese and lemons becoming slightly charred.

Sprinkle the thyme or lemon thyme leaves over the focaccia once it is out of the oven, and serve warm.

Chicken in rose sauce
with toasted pistachios

Serves 4

In Laura Esquivel's novel *Like Water for Chocolate*, protagonist Tita prepares a dish of quail in rose petal sauce. So powerful are the effects of the meal that she dissolves into a kind of trance, while the aphrodisiac effects of the dish overcome her sister Gertrudis. I can't guarantee this recipe will produce the same results, but its complex flavours are hopefully a reward in themselves.

The original recipe in the novel calls for chestnuts and dragon fruit, but I've adapted it to give it a slightly Persian feel with pomegranate molasses, walnuts and figs, and used chicken rather than the more elusive quail. It is the perfect dish for Valentine's Day, or whenever you need a bit of extra romance in your life.

For the chicken
juice and finely grated zest of 1 lemon
½ teaspoon ground turmeric
½ teaspoon ground allspice
¼ teaspoon ground cinnamon
¼ teaspoon freshly grated nutmeg
a generous pinch of chilli flakes
1 tablespoon rapeseed or olive oil
1 teaspoon rosewater
½ teaspoon salt, plus extra to season
8 skin-on, bone-in chicken thighs
50g shelled pistachio nuts
4 tablespoons roughly chopped coriander

For the sauce
100g walnuts
1 chicken stock cube
5g dried rosebuds (about 12 buds) or petals
500ml boiling water

First, make a marinade by mixing together the lemon zest and juice, along with the spices, chilli flakes, oil, rosewater and salt in a large, non-reactive bowl (a glass bowl is best). Add the chicken thighs and mix well to coat, then cover and refrigerate for at least 30 minutes, ideally overnight.

When you're ready to cook, pre-heat the oven to 200°C/180°C fan/gas mark 6.

Put half the pistachios, along with all the walnuts for the sauce, on separate baking trays (or keep them separate on the same baking tray) and toast them in the oven for 10 minutes, then remove them from the oven and leave to cool.

Once the nuts are cool, mix the toasted pistachios with the remaining (untoasted) pistachios and set them aside. Place the walnuts in a food processor and grind to a fine powder, then set aside until needed.

Make the sauce. Put the stock cube and rosebuds or petals in a medium jug and pour over the boiling water. Set aside for 10–15 minutes while you prepare the rest of the sauce ingredients.

In a medium frying pan, melt the butter over a medium–low heat. Add the onion and sauté for 10 minutes, stirring occasionally, until the onion is soft and translucent – do not allow it to brown. Add the garlic and star anise and cook for a further 2 minutes, stirring, then add the ground walnuts and cook for a further 2 minutes, stirring to coat them in the buttery juices. Add the figs, honey, pomegranate molasses, salt and a good grinding of black pepper, and stir well to mix.

Pour the stock and rosebuds through a sieve into a jug to strain out the flowers, then pour the infused stock into the pan with the walnut mixture (you can discard the rosebuds in the sieve). Stir well to mix. Simmer the mixture vigorously over a medium heat for about 10 minutes, until it has reduced by half.

30g butter
1 onion, very finely
  chopped
2 garlic cloves, crushed
1 star anise, halved
4 figs, finely diced
1 teaspoon runny
  honey, plus extra to
  taste if necessary
3 tablespoons
  pomegranate molasses,
  plus extra to taste if
  necessary
$\frac{1}{2}$ teaspoon salt,
  plus extra to taste
  if necessary
$\frac{1}{2}$–1 teaspoon rosewater
freshly ground
  black pepper

Pour half the walnut sauce into a shallow oven dish, just big enough to fit
all the chicken pieces fairly snugly in a single layer. Place the chicken thighs,
skin-side upwards, on top of the sauce, pressing them down a little into the
sauce. The bottom part of each thigh should be submerged in the sauce, with
the skin remaining exposed. Place the dish in the oven and cook the chicken for
25 minutes, until the skin starts to turn golden and the sauce is thick and
bubbling. Leave the remaining sauce in the frying pan for now, off the heat.

After the 25 minutes, remove the chicken thighs from the dish with a slotted
spoon and place them on a plate. Pour the juices in the oven dish into the
remaining walnut sauce in the frying pan. You can use a gravy separator to skim
off the fat that will have run out from the chicken, if you have one, otherwise you
can skim the sauce towards the end of cooking using a spoon.

Return the chicken to the now empty oven dish, and season the skin with a
grinding of salt. Increase the oven temperature to 220°C/200°C fan/gas mark 7.
Put the chicken back in the oven for 20–25 minutes to allow the skin to crisp up.
The juices should run clear when you pierce the thickest part of the thighs.

Meanwhile, simmer the sauce in the frying pan over a medium heat until fairly
thick (about 5 minutes). Taste and adjust the seasoning as necessary – you may
want a little more honey, salt or pomegranate molasses. Add rosewater, drop by
drop, tasting as you go – it should be noticeable, but fairly subtle. Skim off the
layer of chicken fat that rises to the surface using a spoon, if necessary.

Roughly chop the pistachios. Serve the chicken with the sauce spooned over,
scattered with pistachios and coriander. This is best served with couscous, but
would also be good with brown rice or bulgur wheat. It is also rather nice with
the peach bulgur wheat from page 34, or with a salad of thinly sliced raw fennel.

Slow-cooked lamb

with garlic, lemon & lavender & a toasted pistachio gremolata

Serves 4

Lavender works beautifully with lamb, imbuing the meat with a slightly astringent perfume that seems to bring out its own natural sweetness. It makes sense: lavender is not a far cry, in terms of both appearance and flavour profile, from the rosemary we so often turn naturally to when seasoning our lamb. Lemons, garlic and pistachios complete this beautiful, southern Mediterranean tableau. This recipe is incredibly easy – simply stick it in the oven while you get on with other things – but the result is one of the best ways to eat lamb that I have yet come across. This goes rather well with the couscous tabbouleh on page 59 (but omit the cucumber).

5 garlic cloves
1.2kg shoulder of lamb, on the bone, cut into large chunks (ask your butcher to do this)
½ red onion, very thinly sliced
2 bay leaves
1½ teaspoons lavender buds
zest and juice of 2 lemons (reserve the zest in a covered bowl in the fridge)
2 tablespoons white wine
1 teaspoon sea salt flakes
40g shelled pistachio nuts
4 tablespoons finely chopped flat-leaf parsley
freshly ground black pepper

Pre-heat the oven to 160°C/140°C fan/gas mark 2–3. Slice 4 of the garlic cloves into very fine slices. Leave the fifth whole.

Take a large piece of foil (enough to be able to parcel up the lamb) and lay the lamb pieces on top of it. Using a sharp knife, make small incisions in the pieces of lamb (be careful not to cut into the foil!), and insert a sliver of garlic into each incision.

Place the lamb, on the foil, inside a large, lidded casserole dish so that it fits snugly. Tuck the red onion and bay leaves around the lamb pieces, then sprinkle everything with the lavender.

Bring the sides of the foil up around the lamb to form an open parcel. Pour the lemon juice all over the lamb pieces, along with the wine. Sprinkle over the salt flakes and season with a generous amount of pepper. Gather the edges of the foil together to form a rough, sealed parcel around the meat – try to make sure there are no gaps.

Put the lid on the casserole dish and place the lamb parcel in the oven for 3 hours, until the meat is so tender you can cut it using a spoon.

Remove the lamb from the oven and set aside. Increase the heat to 180°C/160°C fan/gas mark 4. Place the pistachios in a small oven tray and toast in the oven for 8 minutes, until slightly toasted. Remove from the oven and set aside to cool.

Very finely chop the remaining garlic clove on a chopping board, then add the parsley and cooled pistachios. Chop everything finely together, then place in a small bowl and stir in the reserved lemon zest to make a gremolata.

Place the lamb on a large serving platter with any juices, then sprinkle with the pistachio gremolata. Serve with roast potatoes or some hearty grains (barley, bulgur wheat and brown rice all work well) and perhaps a little tzatziki.

Chamomile rice
with teriyaki pork & pickled apple salad

Serves 4

I first came across the idea of combining tea with rice in Japan. *Chazuke*, a popular dish from the Edo period, is made by pouring green tea (or *dashi*) over cooked rice, and then adding a variety of toppings. As with many Japanese tea traditions, this dish was closely bound up with the complex social etiquette of the time: I remember reading that your host or hostess offering you *chazuke* was a subtle yet clear signal that you had outstayed your welcome! Hopefully, this recipe won't have the effect of sending your guests heading for home – in fact, the combination of the delicately floral chamomile rice, tender, umami-rich pork and delightfully crunchy apple salad may well have them hanging around for more.

For the pork
4 tablespoons dark
 soy sauce
1 tablespoon
 caster sugar
2 tablespoons mirin
2 tablespoons sake
2.5cm piece of ginger
 root, grated
a splash of sesame oil,
 plus extra for cooking
600g pork fillet or
 tenderloin, sliced into
 1cm strips

For the chamomile rice
4 chamomile tea bags
700ml boiling water
440g sushi rice

**For the pickled
 apple salad**
1 tablespoon
 caster sugar
80ml rice vinegar
2 tablespoons sesame
 seeds (black, white
 or a mixture)

First, prepare the pork. Mix the soy sauce, sugar, mirin, sake, ginger and sesame oil in a shallow, non-reactive dish or bowl, add the pork strips and toss well to coat. Cover the bowl and marinate the pork in the fridge for at least 2 hours, or even overnight if you want to get ahead with preparation.

Begin the chamomile rice. Put the chamomile tea bags in a jug and pour the boiling water over. Set aside until cool, then remove the tea bags and discard them.

While the tea cools, prepare the salad. Mix the caster sugar and rice vinegar in a medium saucepan over a low heat. Stir continuously until the sugar has dissolved. Remove the pan from the heat and leave the syrup to cool.

Put the sesame seeds in a small frying pan over a medium heat. Toast, shaking the pan occasionally, for 2–3 minutes until they start to smell nutty (and, if using white sesame seeds, they should turn golden). Remove from the heat and set aside to cool.

Slice the cucumber(s) in half lengthways and use a teaspoon to scoop out the seeds. Cut the cucumber into matchsticks and place the matchsticks in a colander. Toss with the teaspoon of salt and set aside (over a bowl or the sink) for 20 minutes, stirring occasionally. (This firms up the cucumber and prevents it from being watery.) After 20 minutes, rinse the cucumber with cold water and pat it dry with kitchen paper. Add it to the rice vinegar and sugar mixture in the pan along with the apple. Peel the mooli and cut this into matchsticks, or, if using regular radishes, top and tail them and slice into thin coins. Add to the cucumber and apple, then add the pickled ginger and toasted sesame seeds and toss well. Set aside for about 30 minutes for the flavours to mingle and the vegetables to soften a little.

…method & ingredients continued on page 185

2 small (Lebanese)
cucumbers or ½
regular cucumber
1 teaspoon salt
1 Granny Smith apple,
cored and sliced into
matchsticks
15cm piece of mooli
(Asian radish), or
1 bunch of regular
radishes
2 tablespoons pickled
(sushi) ginger, roughly
chopped

For the rice, rinse the sushi rice well in cold water until the water runs clear. (I do this in a pan, swishing it around with my hand and pouring off the water. It usually takes around 5–10 changes of water.) Place the rice in a large saucepan and pour the cold chamomile tea over. Place on a high heat and bring to the boil, then immediately reduce the heat to its lowest setting and cover the pan. Cook for 10 minutes, covered, then turn the heat off and leave the pan on the hob for a further 10 minutes. Do not remove the pan lid during this time.

While the rice is cooking, prepare the pork. Heat a splash of sesame oil in a large wok over a high heat. When the oil is hot, use a slotted spoon to remove the pork from its marinade and stir-fry the meat until burnished and slightly caramelised, with no trace of pink in the middle (about 3–5 minutes). It is best to do this in two or three batches (depending on the size of your wok), so the meat fries rather than steams in its own juices. When the pork is just cooked, add any leftover marinade to the pan (it should bubble up immediately) and stir-fry for another couple of minutes to glaze the meat and cook everything through.

Serve the stir-fried pork on a bed of chamomile rice with the salad alongside.

Chamomile panna cotta
with lemon & poppy seed crumble

Serves 4

A couple of years ago I visited San Francisco's famous Bi-Rite Creamery, where I joined its equally famous queue (or 'line', I should say) for a couple of scoops of – perhaps – California's best ice cream. I was pleasantly surprised by a delicate chamomile ice, rippled with buttery pebbles of lemon crumble, which managed to transform and showcase an underrated botanical often used only for unpleasantly musty and 'worthy' herbal tea blends. This dessert gives you the delights of that memorable ice cream, but without the faff of churning and freezing. Honey and vanilla work beautifully with chamomile, accentuating its meadow-sweet fragrance, and the crumble provides the crunch and depth that is so often missing from this dessert. The recipe makes slightly more crumble than you will need, but don't consider this a hardship. Scatter it over the little cherry and almond cakes on page 46 before baking, or use it instead of the crumble topping on the Czech bubble cake on page 251. Or (my recommendation) eat any leftovers with a spoon straight from the bowl while none of your guests are looking.

For the panna cotta
300ml double cream
150ml whole milk
40g caster sugar
1 tablespoon
 flavoursome honey
1 tablespoon loose
 chamomile tea (dried
 chamomile flowers), or
 2 chamomile tea bags
1 vanilla pod, split
neutral-flavoured oil,
 such as groundnut or
 sunflower, for greasing
3 gelatine leaves
 (about 5g)
dried calendula petals or
 other edible flowers, to
 decorate (optional)
fresh berries, to serve

For the crumble
60g plain flour
30g fine polenta
40g cold butter, cubed
2 tablespoons
 poppy seeds

First, prepare the panna cotta. Put the cream, milk, sugar, honey, chamomile and vanilla pod in a medium saucepan over a medium heat and bring the mixture to just below the boil. Take the pan off the heat, cover with a lid and leave the flavours to infuse for 1–2 hours.

After this time, strain the mixture through a fine sieve into a jug, pressing the vanilla pod and chamomile into the sieve with the back of a spoon to extract all of the flavour. (You can rinse the vanilla pod, leave it to dry and use it to scent vanilla sugar – waste not, want not!) Return the mixture to the pan.

Lightly grease four dariole moulds or ramekins with oil.

Fill a small bowl with cold water. Place the gelatine leaves in the water for 2–3 minutes to soften, then gently squeeze the water out of them with your hands. Put them into the pan with the milk and cream mixture, then heat gently, stirring with a wooden spoon, until the gelatine has dissolved (about 1–2 minutes). Divide the mixture equally between the four moulds or ramekins, then place them in the fridge for at least 2 hours, until the panna cotta has set.

While the panna cotta sets, make the crumble. Pre-heat the oven to 180°C/160°C fan/gas mark 4.

Place the flour and polenta in a medium bowl and add the butter. Rub in the butter with your fingertips until the mixture resembles fine breadcrumbs. Stir in the poppy seeds. In a separate, small bowl, rub the lemon zest into the caster sugar with your fingertips until the mixture is moist and fragrant. Stir this into the crumble, too. Tip the mixture onto a small baking tray or dish in a fairly thin

finely grated zest of
  1 lemon
40g golden caster sugar

layer, then bake it in the oven for 20–30 minutes, stirring every 10 minutes or so, until the crumble is lightly golden and crunchy. Remove it from the oven and set it aside to cool.

When you're ready to serve the panna cottas, briefly dip each mould or ramekin into a bowl of hot water (just for 20–30 seconds – you don't want to melt the panna cotta!) to loosen the mixture slightly, then turn out each panna cotta onto its own plate. Scatter a generous helping of crumble over and around each panna cotta, then decorate with a few dried calendula petals or edible flowers (if using). Serve immediately with fresh berries.

Cinnamon & rose shortbread

Makes 12–16

Inspired by the truly exquisite rosebud and cinnamon infusion they serve at Honey & Co. in London, these delicate biscuits will make you feel like you're at the Ritz, daintily nibbling a platter of sweetmeats while sipping tea from wafer-thin bone china with your little finger sticking out. The combination of rose and cinnamon feels like eating a fairytale. Enjoy them as they are, with a pot of rose tea, or with London Fog ice cream or chamomile panna cotta (see pages 168 and 186). For another delightful floral version, swap the rose for a tablespoon of dried lavender buds.

70g caster sugar
1 tablespoon dried
    rosebuds or rose petals
120g butter, softened at
    room temperature
a generous pinch of salt
1 teaspoon ground
    cinnamon
120g plain flour
50g semolina

Pre-heat the oven to 170°C/150°C fan/gas mark 3. Line a baking sheet with baking parchment.

Put the caster sugar in a mini chopper or food processor. If using dried rosebuds, remove the green stalks. Add the buds or petals to the sugar and blitz until flecked evenly with tiny pink rose fragments. Alternatively, you can do this in a mortar and pestle, but it will be a little more time-consuming!

Using an electric mixer or electric hand whisk (or using a bowl, wooden spoon and a lot of muscle power), cream the butter, salt and cinnamon together on high speed for a couple of minutes. Set 1 tablespoon of the rose sugar aside for later, then put the rest in the mixer and beat on high speed to combine with the flavoured butter. Sift in the flour and add the semolina, then mix until just combined and you have a soft dough.

Flour a work surface and roll out the dough to about 5mm thick. Using a scone cutter (or similar cutter; or cut out shapes using a knife – hearts or flowers look lovely), cut rounds out of the dough and place them on the baking sheet with at least 2.5cm between each shortbread. The dough is quite fragile, so move the shortbreads carefully onto the baking sheet.

Bake for 15–20 minutes, until lightly golden, then remove the shortbreads from the oven and place on a cooling rack. While they are still hot, sprinkle them evenly with the remaining rose sugar, then leave to cool completely before eating.

Sambocade (medieval elderflower cheese tart)
with elderflower roasted rhubarb

Serves 8–10

An earlier version of this recipe continues to be the most popular post of all time on my blog. I am pleased to find out that the appetite for medieval confectionery is so great, and more than happy to feed it. This tart is rather loosely based on a fourteenth-century recipe from the court of Richard II, named *sambocade* after the Latin word for elderflower, *sambucus*. The original reads thus: 'Take and make a crust in a trap & take cruddes and wryng out þe wheyze and drawe hem þurgh a straynour and put hit in þe crust. Do þerto sugar the þridde part, & somdel whyte of ayren, & shake þerin blomes of elren; & bake it vp with eurose, & messe it forth.' It was, unsurprisingly, a struggle to adapt this into a modern dessert, so I had to freestyle a little. Although Richard would probably not condone my version, it is a wonderfully unusual dessert and a fabulous showcase for the subtlety of elderflower, particularly when served with a vibrant rhubarb compote.

For the pastry
200g plain flour
120g cold butter, cubed
a pinch of salt
2 teaspoons caster sugar
2–3 tablespoons ice-
    cold water

For the filling
250g ricotta
3 tablespoons double
    cream
6 tablespoons
    elderflower cordial
2 tablespoons
    elderflowers, fresh
    or dried (see stockists,
    page 261)
3 eggs
250g mascarpone
70g golden caster sugar
¼ teaspoon freshly
    grated nutmeg
a pinch of ground cloves
½ teaspoon rosewater
2 tsp lemon juice

First, make the pastry. Put the flour, butter, salt and sugar in a food processor and blitz to fine crumbs. Alternatively, in a bowl, rub the butter into the flour using your fingertips until the mixture resembles fine breadcrumbs, then stir in the salt and sugar.

Gradually add the cold water until the mixture only just starts to clump together. Press the pastry together with your fingers and quickly shape it into a round disc, then wrap in cling film and refrigerate it for 30 minutes.

While the pastry chills, prepare the rhubarb (you could do this a day in advance, if you like). Pre-heat the oven to 180°C/160°C fan/gas mark 4.

Arrange the rhubarb in a single layer in a medium baking dish and toss with the caster sugar and elderflower cordial. Place in the oven and bake for 25 minutes, or until just tender to the point of a knife. Set aside to cool, then refrigerate while you prepare the tart.

After the pastry has chilled for 30 minutes, turn the oven up to 200°C/180°C fan/gas mark 6.

Roll out the pastry to a circle roughly 5mm thick. Tear off a little bit of the pastry to make a small ball. Use the pastry circle to line a 23cm loose-bottomed tart tin (you could also use a 23cm springform cake tin), pressing it up the sides of the tin. It is quite a fragile pastry, but simply patch up any gaps or tears with excess pastry from the sides – you will have a little left over. Use the small ball of pastry to press the case into all the edges of the tin. Run a rolling pin over the top of the

...*method & ingredients continued on page 193*

For the rhubarb
300g rhubarb,
   trimmed and cut
   into 2.5cm lengths
1 tablespoon caster
   sugar
3 tablespoons
   elderflower cordial

tart tin to trim the pastry case (if using a cake tin you can skip this step – it will look slightly more rustic!), then lightly prick the bottom with a fork.

Line the pastry case with a disc of baking parchment (make sure it's large enough to come up the sides as well as cover the base) and fill with baking beans. Blind bake for 15 minutes, then remove the paper and baking beans and bake for a further 12 minutes, until golden. Remove the case from the oven and allow it to cool for a couple of minutes.

Lower the oven temperature to 180°C/160°C fan/gas mark 4.

While the case is baking, make the filling. Put all the filling ingredients in a food processor and blitz until smooth. If you don't have a food processor, whisk everything together vigorously by hand or using an electric hand whisk. Pour the filling into the blind-baked pastry case, then return it to the oven.

Bake for 30 minutes. The best way to check it is done is to use a digital probe thermometer – the inside temperature should be 65°C. If you don't have a thermometer, bake it until the filling is starting to turn very slightly golden, and there is still a generous wobble in the middle if you shake the tin slightly. It will continue to set as it cools.

Turn off the oven with the tart inside, and, using the handle of a wooden spoon, prop open the oven door slightly. Leave the tart to cool for 1–2 hours. Once cool, refrigerate for at least 2 hours before removing (carefully) from the tart tin and serving with the rhubarb compote spooned over the top.

Blueberry & lavender ice cream

Makes 1 litre

Whenever I have found myself in Vienna, I've made a beeline for Veganista: an ice-cream parlour that offers some of the best frozen concoctions I've ever eaten – better even than flavours I've sampled on numerous trips to Italy. I have no idea how they manage to make it vegan, because you'd never know from the taste. I suspect witchcraft. This blueberry and lavender ice cream captivated my heart and taste buds on a recent visit, and I could not rest until I had recreated it (albeit with rather more dairy). It makes sense, if you think about it – we often pair blueberry with lemon, and lemon with lavender, so buds and berries should be natural bedfellows. You could even try making this vegan by using oat cream instead of the double cream. If you're not a lavender addict like I am, use half a teaspoon instead of the full teaspoon.

200g fresh or frozen
   blueberries
1 teaspoon lavender
   buds
a pinch of salt
finely grated zest
   of ½ lemon and
   1 tablespoon juice
150g caster sugar
160ml coconut cream
300ml double cream

Put the berries, lavender, salt, lemon zest and juice and sugar in a saucepan over a high heat and bring to the boil. Lower the heat to medium and simmer for about 10 minutes, until the blueberries have split and released all their juices. Pour the mixture into a large heatproof jug or bowl and stir in the coconut cream. Leave to cool.

Once the berry mixture is cool, use a stick blender or normal blender to blitz it (it will still have some small flecks of fruit in it – it doesn't need to be completely smooth).

Whip the double cream until it is just holding its shape, then whisk it into the blueberry mixture. Cover and chill the mixture for at least 6 hours or preferably overnight, then churn in an ice-cream maker until thick (about 15–30 minutes). Decant the ice cream into a freezer-safe container and freeze for at least 4 hours, or overnight, before eating, to allow it to firm up. The ice cream is great with a piece of lemon shortbread on the side.

Rhubarb, vanilla & cardamom jam

Makes about 4 x 450g

I hate recipes that tell me to scrape the seeds from a vanilla pod and add them to something, because inevitably some seeds always get lost in the process – they stick to the knife, or the bowl, or the spatula, or you just can't get them all out of the pod. Throwing everything – pod and all – into a vat of jam is an excellent way to assuage this guilt and to capture the sought-after aroma of one of the world's most expensive ingredients. The citrus perfume of cardamom works exquisitely with the musky scent of vanilla, and both perform admirably to perk up sour rhubarb stalks. This is best with early forced rhubarb – it will make a delightfully pink jam – but I've also made it successfully with the thicker, greener summer stalks. It's important to use whole cardamom pods and grind them yourself – the flavour is infinitely superior to the pre-ground stuff.

This recipe also works beautifully with fresh apricots – simply swap the rhubarb for 1kg of apricots (weighed before stoning), and chop them into quarters.

1kg rhubarb (trimmed weight), cut into 3cm lengths
1kg jam sugar
1 vanilla pod, split lengthways
seeds from 12 cardamom pods, finely ground
juice of 1 lemon

Put the chopped rhubarb in a large, heavy-based saucepan or preserving pan. Add the sugar and vanilla pod, and heat gently, stirring regularly, until the rhubarb starts to turn juicy and the sugar starts to dissolve. Put a small plate in the freezer (to test for when the jam is set).

Add the ground cardamom and the lemon juice to the rhubarb in the pan, then increase the heat and let the mixture bubble quite vigorously for about 30 minutes, until the jam begins to thicken. (Stir regularly to prevent the mixture catching on the bottom of the pan and burning.)

After 30 minutes, start testing for a set. A sugar thermometer should reach 105°C, or you can test using the plate that you have chilled in the freezer: spoon a small dollop of jam onto it, leave to cool for 1 minute, then run your finger through it – if it wrinkles and parts cleanly, the jam is ready. If not, continue to cook for a few minutes more and test again. As soon as the jam sets, remove it from the heat (don't overcook as the jam can quickly 'turn').

While the jam is cooking, sterilise your jars and lids. I do this by washing them well in soapy water, then putting the jars upside down in an oven at 140°C/120°C fan/gas mark 1 for 20 minutes, adding the lids (also upside down) for the last 10 minutes. Turn off the oven and leave the jars inside until you are ready to bottle the jam. You can alternatively run the jars through a hot dishwasher cycle, then pot the jam while they are still warm.

Decant the jam into the sterilised jars. Cover with wax discs, and seal with the lids. I have kept this jam for several years, unopened, in a cool larder with no problems, but once opened, keep it refrigerated and consume within a month.

Quince, apple & saffron compote

Serves 6

To add saffron to a pot of glowing, poached quince is to gild the lily in the best possible way, heightening the sunrise tones while adding a deep, slightly musky fragrance best described as olfactory gold. Combined with bay leaves and lemon, the saffron prevents the perfumed flesh of the quince and apple from cloying. Serve this warm or at room temperature with ice cream as a dessert, or cold with Greek yoghurt or porridge for breakfast. It is lovely topped with some toasted nuts or granola for a little texture.

juice of ½ a lemon
  (lemon half reserved)
  and 4 pared strips
  of zest
120g caster sugar
2 bay leaves
2 quinces, peeled,
  quartered and cored
3 eating apples
25 saffron strands

Put 700ml of water in a large saucepan with the lemon juice and lemon zest. Throw the juiced lemon half in as well. Add the sugar and bay leaves and place over a high heat. Bring to the boil, stirring to dissolve the sugar, then lower the heat to bring the liquid to a simmer.

Slice each quince quarter in half lengthways, to give you 8 pieces altogether, and add to the pan. Make sure the liquid is only just simmering (it definitely shouldn't be bubbling violently), then leave to simmer, uncovered, for about 1–1½ hours, or until just tender to the point of a knife – keep the heat very low to avoid them collapsing (the time will depend on the age and size of your quinces).

Once the quinces have become tender, peel the apples, quarter and core them, and cut each quarter in half lengthways. Add to the quinces and cook very gently for 30–40 minutes, until the apples are tender.

Using a slotted spoon, remove the fruit from the syrup and place the pieces in a bowl. Measure how much syrup you have – you should have about 200ml, so if you have more than this, bubble the syrup in the pan until reduced to the right amount and it is thick and golden red.

Turn the heat to a very gentle simmer, add the saffron and cook for 5 minutes for the flavour to infuse. Return the fruit to the pan, stir gently, then leave to cool before using.

Apricot, blueberry & lavender breakfast crumble

Serves 2–4, depending on greed

In the way that some women are 'bag ladies', I am an apricot lady. I regularly impulse-buy and hoard these gorgeous fruits, becoming rather obsessive about them during the summer months. It's rare to find me without a punnet in my bag, a spontaneous purchase from some market or shop because the fruit just looked too good. No fruit attracts in my gaze quite like the rosy apricot, with its marigold blush, and no fruit proves so versatile in my kitchen during the warmer part of the year. This recipe ensures I can enjoy apricots even for breakfast. Lavender and apricots look beautiful together, the combination of delicate lilac and marigold orange whispering of Provençal sun. The apricots turn jammy and tart in the oven, while the lavender adds a subtle perfume, heightening the tartness of the fruit without tasting like you've swallowed a bar of soap. Serve with good Greek yoghurt for breakfast or brunch.

For the fruit
8 large, ripe apricots, stoned and cut into 8 wedges
120g blueberries
1 teaspoon dried lavender
¼ teaspoon ground cinnamon
½ teaspoon ground ginger
2 tablespoons runny honey

For the topping
150g jumbo oats
40g rye or spelt flour
½ teaspoon ground cinnamon
½ teaspoon ground ginger
¼ teaspoon freshly grated nutmeg
¼ teaspoon salt
50g flaked almonds
3 tablespoons olive oil
3 tablespoons runny honey
1 teaspoon almond extract

Pre-heat the oven to 190°C/170°C fan/gas mark 5.

Scatter the apricot wedges evenly over the bottom of a medium baking dish, then add the blueberries, lavender, cinnamon, ginger, honey and 2 tablespoons of water and toss together. Set aside.

Next, make the topping. In a small bowl, mix together the oats, flour, cinnamon, ginger, nutmeg, salt and almonds. In a small jug, whisk together the olive oil, honey and almond extract with 2 tablespoons of water.

Pour the liquid mixture into the oats and mix well to combine. Tip this mixture over the apricots, combining with the fruit a little but leaving most of it on top.

Bake the crumble for 40 minutes, until the topping is golden and the fruit is bubbling. Leave the crumble to cool for 5 minutes before serving. I like it with a dollop of Greek yoghurt on the side.

Also try

Peach, blackcurrant & rosemary breakfast crumble
Make the recipe as above, but use 4 peaches, stoned and sliced into eighths, instead of the apricots; and 150g blackcurrants (stalks removed) instead of the blueberries. Omit the spices, lavender and honey in the fruit and instead toss the fruit with 1 tablespoon cornflour, the juice of ½ a lemon, ½ teaspoon ground ginger, 1½ teaspoons finely chopped rosemary needles and 2 tablespoons light brown soft sugar. Use maple syrup instead of honey in the crumble, and vanilla instead of almond extract.

Seeds

Here was the secret of happiness, about which philosophers had disputed for so many ages, at once discovered; happiness might now be bought for a penny, and carried in the waistcoat-pocket; portable ecstasies might be had corked up in a pint-bottle; and peace of mind could be sent down by the mail.

~ Thomas De Quincey, *Confessions of an English Opium-Eater*

S O WROTE Thomas De Quincey in his famous *Confessions* in 1876. Noting that opium-eaters were, at this time, a 'numerous class indeed', De Quincey narrates the tale of his own spiral into opium addiction, and his observations on the properties and effects of this popular drug. Opium, morphine (named after Morpheus, Greek god of dreams), codeine, heroin, laudanum, midnight oil, milk of the poppy: call it what you will, the sap or 'poppy tears' obtained by making careful incisions into the ripe capsules of the poppy flower has been used medicinally for thousands of years. The Sumerians referred to the poppy as *hul gil*, the 'joy plant', while ancient Greek mythology recognised its darker side: the gods Hypnos (Sleep), Nyx (Night) and Thanatos (Death) were all depicted wearing or holding wreaths of poppies. Culturally, it carries contradictory connotations. On the one hand you have the grimy, smoke-hazed fug of the opium den and its languid, incapacitated addicts; on the other, you have glamorous whisperings of opium dreams, artistic visions and papery scarlet petals. Opium can claim partial credit for Chopin's nocturnes, the frenetic paean to artistic madness that is Coleridge's poem 'Kubla Khan', Keats's Odes and even the invention of the stethoscope.

All this seems a far cry from the innocuous crunchy dots that pepper your morning bagel or coffee-shop muffin, but the **poppy seed** has not been entirely divested of its darker side, even today: in 2009 eBay banned the sale of poppy seed-heads after two American students died from drinking *doda* tea brewed from them, which contains opium alkaloids if made correctly. Rumours abound that you can fail a drugs test by eating too many poppy seed baked goods, and Taiwan, China and Saudi Arabia have all placed restrictions or bans on the sale of poppy seeds owing to anxieties about their opiate content. In Singapore, poppy seeds are even classified as prohibited goods by the Central Narcotics Bureau. I advise caution, therefore, if you plan to make and consume some of the recipes in this chapter before a drugs test, or to take them on the plane to Asia.

Poppy seeds don't only straddle the line between gustatory and narcotic pleasure, but also walk that tantalising boundary between the sweet and the savoury. Like all the seeds in this chapter, part of their appeal comes from their versatility. They are as comfortable strewn through the sweet crumb of baked treats as contributing to the carefully layered flavours of an Indian curry. They are commonly used in Eastern European and Baltic desserts, where they are often finely ground and sweetened with sugar to form a thick, irresistibly moreish paste. I have eaten them baked into a tart in my local Polish restaurant, black and glistening between a pastry crust like a seam of coal. On a trip to Austria I saw them peppering the interior of a flaky strudel, and ate them coiled between the folds of a sweet pretzel. There's something deeply satisfying about pulverising the already tiny poppy seed, watching it collapse into a damp rubble that resembles wet sand, offering up an aroma that is almost fecund, and whispers darkly of compost and new rain. The seeds become blacker, denser, glistening like tar and rich with nourishing oils and their own unique fragrance. A warning should always accompany such confections: dental floss is a mandatory requirement when consuming anything punctuated by these fiendishly tenacious little seeds.

The same is true of black **sesame**, East Asia's answer to the poppy seed, which is used both to make a deeply savoury sauce for noodle dishes and to form the soft, black heart at the core of Japan's delicious *mochi*, sweet dumplings made from chewy rice-flour paste. Along with squid ink, black sesame and poppy seeds have the curious accolade of being some of the few wholly black foods we actually want to eat (although I suspect I'm not alone in enjoying the odd overcooked barbecue sausage), offering a slight frisson of intrigue and a little dark glamour.

The famous phrase 'open sesame' originally comes from the story of Ali Baba in the *One Thousand and One Nights*, where it is used to open a cave within which the forty thieves have hidden their treasure. It is thought to refer to the 'pop' emitted by ripe sesame seeds as they split, in many ways making the seed the perfect metaphor for the opening of a grotto laden with riches. It is only by crushing, grinding or splitting seeds that we can reveal their true magic and potential in the kitchen: the quotidian crunch of sesame seeds atop a bun or bagel cannot hold a candle to the seductive, buttery richness of tahini, for example.

Toasting seeds releases the same compounds found in roasted coffee, which perhaps explains how their savoury nuttiness comes to be so moreish, and many recipes involving them will benefit from a quick toast of the seeds (in a dry pan or oven) before you carry on with the instructions. At the courts of medieval England there existed the job of 'Yeoman Powderbeater', who would – under instruction from the 'Clerk of the Spicery' – toast and grind the spices for daily use. I advise you to be your own Yeoman Powderbeater – freshly ground spices are infinitely superior to those bought ready-crushed, so invest in a pestle and mortar or a spice grinder to take your cooking to the next level.

The tapered, dusky-green pods of the **cardamom** plant, the world's third most expensive spice, need at the very least a good bash with a pestle in order to release their perfume, and become a potent force when ground to a powder. Once known as the 'Queen of Spices' to black pepper's 'King', cardamom has been used medicinally for centuries, and is still deployed as a breath freshener the world over – Greeks and Romans would chew the pods whole, a practice that still occurs in India, while Wrigley's chewing gum lists cardamom as one of its ingredients. The pods contain the fragrant compounds *cineol* and *limonene*, which account for their citrus note, and which work so irresistibly in sweet dishes: mango lassi in India, Middle Eastern baklava and, a personal favourite of mine, the various baked goods strewn with cardamom that are so popular in the Nordic countries, thanks to those pesky Vikings raiding Constantinople in the olden days. I've researched comprehensively, by the way, and can report that if you are looking for the best Scandi baked goods, go to Sweden.

Nutmeg offers very little to the cook in its whole, spherical form, but a couple of rasps with a sharp grater sends woody wisps of musky flavour cascading into your rice pudding, custard tart or pumpkin pie, unlocking the potential of this otherwise unassuming little seed. Fashionable Victorians even used to have special nutmeg boxes and graters made, so they could carry the spice around wherever they went. Perhaps you might like to do the same – Charles Dickens and Elizabeth David both approved of this habit. Niki Segnit points out that nutmeg's botanical name, *Myristica fragrans*, 'makes it sound like a Bond girl, appropriately enough for such an exotic, beautiful double-agent of a spice, apt equally to make sweet, creamy dishes less cloying and cruciferous vegetables less bitter'. I couldn't have put it better myself, and you will hopefully find even more novel and exciting uses for this *femme fatale* of the spice cabinet in this book.

The recipes in this chapter explore the addictive complexity (perhaps literally, in the case of the poppy and the nutmeg) of these life-giving seeds. They require us to perform our own 'open sesame' using a few kitchen tools. Try stirring a whisper of crushed cardamom into a banana cake, or folding a handful of poppy seeds into a soda bread to serve with slatherings of lemon curd, in a twist on the classic lemon and poppy seed combination. For savoury inspiration, look east to the noodle dishes of Japan or the myriad uses for tahini in Middle Eastern cuisine, and don't forget the savoury applications of nutmeg, a fabulous enhancement for the silky flesh of roast pumpkin. You may not go so far as to call them 'portable ecstasies', à la De Quincey, but the creativity inspired by these potent powerhouses of flavour shouldn't be reserved only for bohemian artists or Victorian dandies.

Tips & tricks

* Many recipes using seeds benefit from toasting the seeds first in a dry frying pan or the oven: use a medium heat and toss them frequently so they cook evenly. As soon as you start to smell them, remove them from the heat so that they don't burn. It can be tricky to tell when black sesame is toasted, because of the dark colour, so you can add a pinch of white sesame seeds to the pan as an indicator.

* Seeds have a high oil content, which means they can spoil quickly. Use them as quickly as possible after buying, or freeze them, and store items like tahini and seed pastes in the fridge to prevent them from going rancid. Old poppy seeds, especially, take on a horrible dusty flavour when left to languish in the cupboard for too long. Although, once the poppy seed cake on page 222 becomes a staple in your life, you shouldn't have this problem.

* The smaller seeds, like sesame and poppy, can be tricky to grind using a standard food processor. I recommend using a spice grinder or powerful 'bullet' blender. Or, if you want to skip a gym session, use a pestle and mortar.

* Pre-ground cardamom can't compete with the intense flavour of freshly crushed pods, and it takes seconds to grind the pods yourself in a pestle and mortar. However, it is convenient, and I have a jar on hand for recipes where the cardamom provides more of a base note.

* The same goes for nutmeg. Invest in a sharp microplane grater (also useful for ginger, garlic and citrus zesting) and grate the whole seeds from fresh – the flavour is infinitely better, and it's very little faff.

* If you ever manage to find candied nutmeg rind – popular in Malaysia – it is excellent added to a cake batter or enriched bread dough.

* Three nutmegs are apparently the most a person can eat without dying. Luckily, all the recipes in this book use no more than half a teaspoon.

* Should you ever find yourself with a flamingo ready for roasting, the Roman cookbook *Apicius* recommends flavouring it with sesame.

Black sesame cream
& ways to use it

Makes 2 portions

You get several recipes for the price of one here. My love for black sesame parallels my love for poppy seeds, and they have in common an earthy, deeply savoury quality that is as at home with sweet ingredients as it is with savoury. I am borderline obsessed with all the ways in which black sesame manifests itself in Asian desserts, particularly cloud-like steamed buns, whose fluffy exterior conceals a dark, sticky heart of sugared sesame, or glutinous black sesame dumplings served in a fiery ginger broth. This cream is my attempt to extend that addictive flavour to savoury dishes, blending ground black sesame with the creaminess of coconut milk, the tang of lime and rice vinegar and the sweetness of brown sugar. It works gloriously as a dressing for cooked rice noodles, as in the recipe opposite, but functions equally well as a sauce for steamed fish or cooked tofu or vegetables (see opposite for other ways to use it).

35g black sesame seeds, plus a few white for toasting (optional)
1 tablespoon brown rice vinegar
2 teaspoons coconut sugar or light brown soft sugar
1 teaspoon sesame oil
4 tablespoons full-fat coconut milk
¼ teaspoon miso paste
¼ teaspoon dark soy sauce
2 teaspoons lime juice

Pre-heat the oven to 200°C/180°C fan/gas mark 6.

Put the sesame seeds in a baking dish and toast them in the oven for about 5 minutes, until they start to smell nutty. You can put a few white sesame seeds in with the black ones to indicate when they are toasted – the white ones should turn lightly golden. Allow the seeds to cool a little, then tip them into a food processor (a mini one is best) or spice grinder.

Blitz the seeds for about 3–5 minutes, until they start to break down and become slightly oily and paste-like. They should smell very fragrant. You may need to do this in stages so as to not overheat your blender!

In the food processor (or if you used a spice grinder, transfer the sesame paste to a small bowl), add the vinegar, sugar, sesame oil, coconut milk, miso, soy sauce and lime juice. Blend thoroughly (or whisk if using a bowl). Taste and season accordingly – you may want to adjust the balance of sweet/salty/sour to suit your taste. Use immediately or keep the paste in the fridge in an airtight container for 2–3 days.

Other ways to use black sesame cream

* Spoon over steamed fish and vegetables (you may want to add a little more coconut milk to make it more pourable). Serve with steamed rice.

* Spoon over fried tofu and serve with some crunchy Japanese-style pickles, or kimchi.

* Toss with roasted vegetables and serve with brown rice and plenty of lime juice.

Noodles with coconut black sesame cream and ginger & lime-roasted broccoli

Serves 2

For the broccoli
2.5cm piece of ginger root, grated
finely grated zest of 1 lime and juice of ½
½ teaspoon maple syrup or runny honey
1 tablespoon rapeseed or olive oil
½ teaspoon chilli flakes
a pinch of sea salt flakes
1 head of broccoli, cut into small florets

For the noodles
150g edamame beans (podded)
180g rice, udon or soba noodles
2 portions of black sesame cream (see recipe page 208)
2 spring onions, finely chopped
2 tablespoons finely chopped coriander
lime wedges, to serve

Pre-heat the oven to 190°C/170°C fan/gas mark 5.

First, make the broccoli. In a medium bowl, whisk together the ginger, lime zest and juice, maple syrup or honey, rapeseed or olive oil, chilli flakes, and salt. Toss the broccoli florets in the mixture to coat then tip them into a baking dish. Roast the broccoli for 20–25 minutes, until the florets are just tender and slightly crispy.

While the broccoli cooks, blanch the edamame beans in boiling water for 4 minutes, then drain and refresh under cold water.

Cook the noodles according to the packet instructions, then drain and rinse them briefly under cold water before returning them to the pan. Add the black sesame cream, cooked broccoli, edamame beans, spring onions and chopped coriander to the pan and toss everything together. Divide everything equally between two bowls and serve with lime wedges to squeeze over.

Spelt & poppy seed soda bread

Serves 6–8

This, combined with the bergamot curd on page 83, is like eating one of those ubiquitous coffee-shop lemon and poppy seed muffins, but infinitely better (and marginally healthier, too, although perhaps not in the quantities I tend to consume...). The slightly cakey texture of fresh soda bread, hot from the oven, is irresistible when peppered with the crunch of poppy seeds. This is also an excellent way to use up milk that has become too sour to drink or put in tea, as it is an excellent replacement for buttermilk. You can also simply add a good squeeze of lemon juice or a spoonful of vinegar to fresh milk as a substitute for buttermilk, or use runny yoghurt. This loaf, toasted, also works well with any of the jams in this book, or with some hard cheese and fruity chutney.

100g jumbo oats
300g spelt flour
200g white or
  wholemeal plain flour
1 teaspoon salt
1 teaspoon bicarbonate
  of soda
30g cold butter, cubed
100g poppy seeds
500ml buttermilk, sour
  milk, or runny plain
  yoghurt (or a mixture)

Pre-heat the oven to 210°C/190°C fan/gas mark 6–7. Line a baking sheet with baking parchment.

Put the oats, flours, salt and bicarbonate of soda in a large mixing bowl and stir to combine. Rub the butter into the flour with your fingertips until the mixture resembles fine breadcrumbs. Reserve 1 tablespoon of the poppy seeds, then stir in the remainder. Pour in most of the buttermilk (or milk or yoghurt) and mix to a slightly sticky, but firm dough. Add the remaining liquid if you need it.

Shape the dough into a round and place it in the middle of the baking sheet. Using a sharp, serrated knife (a bread knife is good), cut a deep cross in the loaf, cutting nearly all the way to the bottom (this helps it bake evenly – or lets the devil out, if you believe in Irish tradition). Sprinkle with the remaining poppy seeds.

Bake for 35–40 minutes, or until the bottom sounds hollow when tapped. Leave to cool on a wire rack. Eat warm or toasted.

Beetroot, potato, dill & goat's cheese gratin
with toasted seed crumb

Serves 6

Packed full of Scandinavian flavours, this delightful gratin makes the most of seeds: nutritional powerhouses that are so often given merely a supporting role. The buttery, crunchy seed topping in this recipe contrasts beautifully with the layers of soft cheese and tender vegetables. The beetroot and potatoes can, and perhaps should, be prepared in advance, as they can take a long time to cook, depending on their size.

1kg beetroot, all roughly the same size

500g potatoes (not floury), all roughly the same size

25g butter, plus extra for greasing

300ml half-fat crème fraîche

100–200ml whole milk

25g dill, finely chopped, plus extra to garnish

finely grated zest of 1 lemon

1 tablespoon pink peppercorns, lightly crushed

200g soft goat's cheese

60g mixed seeds (I like a mixture of poppy, sunflower, linseed, hemp and pumpkin)

1 teaspoon runny honey

80g fresh breadcrumbs

salt and freshly ground black pepper

Pre-heat the oven to 220°C/200°C fan/gas mark 7.

Put the beetroot on a baking tray lined with foil and roast for 1–2 hours, or until tender to the point of a knife (the time will depend on the size of your beetroot). Once cool enough to handle, peel and cut the beetroot into 5mm slices. (If you're making the gratin straightaway, leave the oven on; otherwise turn it off.)

While the beetroot cook, bring a pan of water to the boil over a high heat, and cook the potatoes whole for 10 minutes. They won't be fully cooked, but that is fine since you are going to cook them further in the oven. Drain and leave to cool, then cut into 5mm slices with a sharp knife. You can remove the skin if you like, but I don't think it's necessary.

Grease a medium baking dish with butter.

In a medium bowl or jug, whisk the crème fraîche and milk (add enough milk to make it fairly runny, the consistency of plain yoghurt) with the dill, lemon zest, pink peppercorns and a generous amount of seasoning. Set aside.

Put half the beetroot and potato slices in the bottom of the baking dish, slightly overlapping, to form a layer. Crumble over half of the goat's cheese, and season generously with salt and pepper. Layer over the remaining potato and beetroot, season well, then crumble over the rest of the goat's cheese. Pour over the crème fraîche mixture, nudging the vegetables slightly so that the creamy mixture gets into the corners of the dish. (If you're making this having cooked the beetroot in advance, pre-heat the oven to 220°C/200°C fan/gas mark 7.)

For the topping, heat half the butter in a small frying pan over a medium heat and add the seeds. Toast until they start to pop, then add the honey and a generous grinding of salt and stir well. Tip the mixture into a small bowl. Add the remaining butter to the pan, then add the breadcrumbs and stir to coat in the butter. Cook for 1–2 minutes, until the breadcrumbs start to toast, then tip them into the bowl with the seeds. Mix well.

Top the gratin with the seed mixture. Bake for 25 minutes, until the topping is golden and everything is bubbling. Sprinkle with dill and serve with a green salad.

Cardamom treacle tart
with poached rhubarb

Serves 8

I've never come across cardamom in a treacle tart before, but in my head it makes complete sense. Some of the sweetest desserts and pastries in existence, namely baklava and other syrup-drenched Middle Eastern confections, use cardamom liberally. Its slightly bitter, citrus perfume is like a breath of fresh air, preventing all that sugar from cloying. Treacle tart – a dessert that, lest we forget, incorporates nearly an entire can of golden syrup – also benefits greatly from this happy marriage, plus a good amount of fiery ginger and sharp lemon for balance. I like to serve it with rhubarb, as the tartness also helps to take some of the edge off that syrupy sweetness, and some ice cream or crème fraîche. See the end of the recipe for some other seasonal pairings.

For the pastry
180g plain flour
100g very cold
  butter, cubed
2–3 tablespoons ice-
  cold water

For the filling
400g golden syrup
90g fresh breadcrumbs
2 eggs, beaten
juice and finely grated
  zest of 1 lemon
1 teaspoon ground
  ginger
seeds of 12 cardamom
  pods, finely ground
a generous pinch of salt
icing sugar, for dusting

For the rhubarb compote
300g rhubarb, sliced
  into 2.5cm lengths
4 tablespoons caster
  sugar, plus extra to
  taste if necessary
1 vanilla pod, split
  lengthways

First, make the pastry. Blitz the flour and butter together in a food processor (or rub together with your fingertips) until it resembles fine breadcrumbs. Add the cold water, 1 tablespoon at a time, until the dough just comes together (you may not need all the water). Bring together gently with your hands to form a flat disc, but do not overwork it.

Roll out the pastry on a floured work surface to a circle roughly 5mm thick and use it to line a 20cm, loose-bottomed tart tin. Run a rolling pin over the rim to trim the edges and cut off the excess pastry. Refrigerate the pastry-lined tin for 30 minutes.

Meanwhile, pre-heat the oven to 210°C/190°C fan/gas mark 6–7.

Prick the base lightly all over with a fork. Line the pastry case with a disc of baking parchment (make sure it's large enough to come up the sides as well as cover the base) and fill with baking beans. Blind bake for 20 minutes, then remove the paper and baking beans and bake for a further 15 minutes, until golden.

Turn down the oven temperature to 200°C/180°C fan/gas mark 6.

For the filling, mix together the syrup, breadcrumbs, eggs, lemon juice and zest, ginger, cardamom and salt. Pour the filling into the baked case, then bake the filled tart for 25–30 minutes, until golden and slightly brown around the edges. It should only have the slightest of wobbles in the centre if you shake it. Leave to cool, then dust with icing sugar.

While the tart is baking, make the compote. Place the rhubarb lengths in a small pan with the sugar and the split vanilla pod and 2 tablespoons of water. Place the pan over a low heat and simmer gently until the rhubarb just starts to disintegrate – about 5–10 minutes. Taste to check the sweetness – you might want a little more sugar if your rhubarb is very acidic. Remove the pan from the heat and set aside to cool.

To serve, slice the tart using a very sharp knife, spoon over a little of the rhubarb compote, and serve with vanilla ice cream or a scoop of crème fraîche.

Other seasonal partners for cardamom treacle tart

*   Segmented blood oranges tossed with a pinch of cinnamon and a couple of drops of orange-blossom water.

*   Fresh apricots roasted with a little fresh orange juice, a little honey and a drop of rosewater.

*   Plums baked with fresh orange juice, star anise and brown sugar.

*   Fresh summer berries tossed with a dash of balsamic vinegar and some lemon verbena, lemon balm or lemon thyme leaves.

*   Honeyed figs (see page 139).

Yorkshire curd tart

Serves 6–8

A classic dessert at Betty's tea room in Yorkshire, and a favourite for both my mother and me, this unusual, buttery confection is somewhere between a cheesecake and a frangipane tart, and makes a fuss out of ingredients usually given only a background role: nutmeg and currants. It is wonderful on its own with a cup of tea, or served warm with some crème fraîche and raspberries as a dessert. You don't have to blitz the cottage cheese in a food processor if you don't have one – the texture of the finished filling will be a little rougher, but I've made it this way, too, and I rather like it.

In summer, you can also try swapping the (dried) currants for fresh redcurrants or blackcurrants.

For the pastry
140g plain flour
90g cold butter, cubed
1 tablespoon
    caster sugar
a pinch of salt
2–3 tablespoons ice-
    cold water

For the filling
60g butter, softened
60g caster sugar
1 egg, beaten
½ teaspoon freshly
    grated nutmeg
¼ teaspoon ground
    ginger
finely grated zest of
    1 lemon
400g cottage cheese,
    blitzed in a food
    processor until smooth
140g ricotta
45g dried currants

To serve
icing sugar

For the pastry, put the flour, butter, sugar and salt in a food processor and pulse until it resembles fine breadcrumbs. Add 1 tablespoon of the cold water, pulse again, then continue to add the remaining water a little at a time, until the mixture just starts to come together. Turn out the pastry onto a floured work surface and knead until it just forms a ball, then wrap it in cling film and chill it for 30 minutes.

When you're ready to bake, pre-heat the oven to 210°C/190°C fan/gas mark 6–7.

Roll out the pastry on a floured surface to a circle roughly 5mm thick. Tear off a little bit of the pastry to make a small ball. Use the pastry circle to line a 20cm tart tin or pie dish (the sides need to be at least 3.5cm high), using the small ball of pastry to press it into all the edges. Run a rolling pin over the top of the tin to trim the pastry case, then lightly prick the bottom with a fork.

Line the pastry case with a disc of baking parchment (make sure it's large enough to come up the sides as well as cover the base) and fill with baking beans. Blind bake for 20 minutes, then remove the paper and baking beans and bake for a further 10 minutes, until golden.

Meanwhile, make the filling. In an electric mixer or with an electric hand whisk, cream the butter and sugar on high speed for 3–4 minutes, until pale and fluffy. Gradually add the egg, whisking well between each addition. Add the nutmeg, ginger and lemon zest, then add the cottage cheese and ricotta. Whisk gently to incorporate everything into the mixture, then fold in the currants.

Turn down the oven to 200°C/180°C fan/gas mark 6. Pour the curd filling into the pastry case, return it to the oven and bake the tart for 50–60 minutes, until the filling is puffy, golden and set with a slight wobble in the centre. Allow the tart to cool, then dust with icing sugar and serve.

Apple, walnut & poppy seed crumble tart

Serves 6–8

Combining the dark savouriness of ground poppy seeds and toasted walnuts with buttery sweet apple, raisin and vanilla, this recipe is my attempt to recreate a number of exquisite poppy seed tarts I have eaten in Austrian and Polish coffee houses. Incorporating a large number of my favourite ingredients, it might be one of the best desserts I've ever made, and is always a hit with dinner guests. Serve the tart warm as a dessert, or cold the following day as a treat with a cup of tea or coffee.

For the dough
300g plain flour
30g ground almonds
75g caster sugar
¼ teaspoon salt
160g cold butter, cubed
3 egg yolks
80g crème fraîche

For the filling
50g walnuts
100g poppy seeds
50g butter
3 eating apples, peeled,
   cored and cut into
   1.5cm dice
90g dark brown
   soft sugar
40g raisins
¼ teaspoon ground
   cinnamon
finely grated zest
   of 1 lemon and
   2 teaspoons juice
1 teaspoon vanilla
   essence or paste
1 tablespoon brandy
   (optional)

Pre-heat the oven to 200°C/180°C fan/gas mark 6.

For the dough, put the flour, almonds, sugar and salt in a food processor. Add the butter and pulse just enough to break up the butter – it should begin to resemble fine breadcrumbs. Add the egg yolks and crème fraîche and pulse again until the mixture just comes together – do not over-mix. Put the dough into a bowl and toss it gently together with your hands – it will be crumbly and slightly sticky. You don't need to bring it together into a ball as you would pastry. Put two-thirds of the crumbly dough mix into a 23cm tart tin. Press the dough gently over the base of the tart tin and up the edges with the back of a spoon – try not to press too hard or compress it too much, just enough to make a rough crust. Set aside.

Put the walnuts for the filling on a small baking tray and place them in the oven for 10 minutes, until toasted. Remove from the oven and set aside.

For the filling, put the poppy seeds in a high-powered food processor (such as a Nutribullet or similar), spice grinder or coffee grinder and grind until they start to smell fragrant, become damp and look like wet sand. Add the walnuts and pulse briefly until they are in small pieces (but not powdered). Set aside.

In a medium frying pan over a medium-high heat, melt the butter and add the apples. Sauté the fruit for about 5 minutes, stirring occasionally, until the apples are starting to shrink and become juicy, then add the sugar. Sauté for another few minutes, stirring, until the apples become golden, sticky and caramelised. Add the raisins and cinnamon and cook for a further 2 minutes, then remove the pan from the heat and add the lemon zest and juice, vanilla and brandy, if using. Add the poppy seed and walnut mixture to the pan and stir well to combine.

Tip the apple and poppy seed mixture into the tart case and level gently with a spoon. Scatter the remaining tart dough, in crumbly pieces, over the top of the filling. It's fine if there are some gaps – you aren't trying to make a pastry lid, but rather a crumble topping, so no need to press it down or make it neat.

Put the tart in the oven and bake for 30–35 minutes, until the dough is golden and the fruit is bubbling. Remove and leave to cool before serving. This is good with vanilla ice cream, or sweetened crème fraîche.

Spiced pumpkin & maple pecan cheesecake

Serves 8

Possibly my all-time favourite cheesecake. Its silky custard blends the buttery notes of roasted pumpkin with the warm woodiness of nutmeg and other autumnal spices, and the caramelised maple topping adds the crunch of pecan pie. To make pumpkin purée, simply roast large chunks of pumpkin in the oven until tender, then remove the skin, blitz the flesh in a food processor and tip it into a muslin-lined sieve to drain over a bowl for a few hours (it can be watery). You may need up to 800g of pumpkin to make 400g of purée, or you can of course use the canned variety. When making this in late summer or early autumn, I like to decorate it with fresh blackberries and edible flowers – red and yellow nasturtiums look fabulously striking on top.

For the cheesecake
70g butter, plus extra
  for greasing
180g digestive biscuits,
  blitzed to fine crumbs
  in a food processor
600g full-fat
  cream cheese
400g pumpkin
  purée (homemade
  or from a can)
130g light brown
  soft sugar
very finely grated zest
  of 1 orange
1 teaspoon vanilla
  extract
¾ teaspoon each
  of ground ginger,
  cinnamon and nutmeg
⅛ teaspoon ground
  cloves
2 eggs

For the topping
35g butter
100g pecan nuts,
  roughly chopped
3 tablespoons maple
  syrup
icing sugar, for dusting

Pre-heat the oven to 200°C/180°C fan/gas mark 6. Grease and line a 20cm springform cake tin.

Melt the butter in a medium saucepan over a medium heat, then stir in the blitzed biscuits. Press the biscuit mixture into the bottom of the cake tin, using the back of a spoon to flatten gently to form a crust. Bake the crust for 10 minutes, until golden, then remove from the oven and set aside to cool while you make the filling.

Turn down the oven temperature to 180°C/160°C fan/gas mark 4.

Meanwhile, using an electric hand whisk, mix together the cream cheese and pumpkin purée. Add the sugar, orange zest, vanilla and spices, then finally add the eggs and beat to incorporate. Pour into the tin over the biscuit base.

Place an oven tray of water at the bottom of the oven, then put the cheesecake into the oven (on a shelf, not in the tray of water!). Bake for about 1 hour, until the cheesecake has just set on top, but still has a generous wobble in the middle if you shake it gently – it will continue to set as it cools. Turn off the oven with the cake inside, and, using the handle of a wooden spoon, prop open the oven door slightly. Leave the cake to cool in the oven for 1–2 hours (this helps to prevent it from cracking). Once cool, take it out of the tin and transfer it to a serving plate.

For the topping, melt the butter in a frying pan over a medium heat. Add the chopped pecans to the butter. Fry for 1 minute, then add the maple syrup. Fry for another couple of minutes, until the pecans are sticky and fragrant. Tip them over the top of the cheesecake. Refrigerate for at least 4 hours before dusting with icing sugar and serving.

Austrian poppy seed cake
with lemon glaze

Makes one 20cm cake

Only true poppy seed lovers need apply for this cake. It is deeply dark and nutty, a texture and flavour achieved from grinding these already tiny seeds in a blender or spice grinder to release their potent flavour. Naturally gluten-free, this cake gets its moist, buttery texture from the seed oils, which release as the seeds are ground. The inspiration for this recipe is a delicious poppy seed and lingonberry cake that I ate for breakfast (yes, for breakfast; I have no regrets) in a beautiful café in Salzburg several years ago. Ensure your poppy seeds are as fresh as possible: they tend to turn rancid and musty very quickly, so buy them shortly before you plan to use them.

For the cake
250g poppy seeds
150g butter, at room temperature, plus extra for greasing
180g light brown soft sugar
5 eggs, separated
2 teaspoons vanilla extract
125g full-fat plain or Greek yoghurt
a pinch of salt

For the glaze
2 tablespoons lemon juice
100g icing sugar
lemon slices, to decorate (optional)

First, prepare the poppy seeds. Using a spice grinder or powerful blender (a Nutribullet or similar), grind the seeds briefly until they start to break up, turn darker, smell fragrant and resemble wet sand. Set aside.

Pre-heat the oven to 195°C/175°C fan/gas mark 5–6. Grease and line a 20cm cake tin.

In an electric mixer or with an electric hand whisk, cream the butter and sugar on high speed for 3–4 minutes, until pale and creamy. One at a time, add the egg yolks, whisking well after each addition, then whisk for a couple of minutes more until everything is light and fluffy. Whisk in the vanilla, yoghurt and salt, then fold in the ground poppy seeds until just combined.

In a separate, clean bowl, with a clean whisk, whisk the egg whites to stiff peaks. Use a spatula or large spoon to fold one-third of the whites into the butter and seed mixture to loosen it, then carefully fold in the remaining egg white using a circular, scooping motion, trying to keep as much air in the mixture as possible.

Spoon the mixture gently into the tin, level the top, and bake for 40 minutes, or until the cake springs back when pressed in the centre. Leave to cool in the tin for 5 minutes, then turn out on to a wire rack. Leave to cool completely before adding the glaze.

Whisk the lemon juice and icing sugar together to make the glaze. Spoon the glaze over the cake, allowing a little to run down the sides. Allow to set before eating. I sometimes place a couple of slices of lemon in the middle, to decorate.

Banana, tahini & white chocolate muffins

Makes 12

These are inspired by the tahini and white chocolate *babka* from Honey & Spice in London. To be frank, that *babka* is probably the best thing I have ever eaten. Its oozing core of molten tahini and white chocolate surrounded by a buttery brioche crust sees me making ridiculous detours every time I visit London just so I can pass by the deli and grab one (OK, three) pieces. As I don't live near London and I don't always have time to make bread, I had to come up with an alternative so I could get my fix on a regular basis. Introducing banana and cardamom to that already indulgent mixture of ingredients proved an excellent idea, resulting in a highly addictive sweet–savoury combination. These muffins are an excellent way to use up overripe bananas – the blacker the better.

For the muffins
200g plain flour
1 teaspoon baking
   powder
1 teaspoon bicarbonate
   of soda
seeds from 8 cardamom
   pods, finely ground
¼ teaspoon sea
   salt flakes
100g white chocolate
   chips, or 1cm pieces
   of white chocolate
3 large bananas,
   mashed
70g light brown
   soft sugar
1 egg
50g butter, melted
   and cooled
1 teaspoon vanilla
   extract
60g tahini

For the tahini glaze
2 tablespoons tahini
100g icing sugar
1 teaspoon lemon juice
1 tablespoon sesame
   seeds (a mixture of
   black and white
   looks nice)

Pre-heat the oven to 200°C/180°C fan/gas mark 6. Line a 12-hole muffin tray with paper cases (or grease thoroughly with some extra butter if you don't have paper cases).

Sift together the flour, baking powder and bicarbonate of soda, then stir in the cardamom and salt. Stir in the white chocolate.

In a separate bowl, mash together the bananas, sugar, egg, melted butter, vanilla and tahini.

Mix the wet ingredients into the dry, being careful not to over-mix – this is the key to a light muffin. Divide between the 12 cases and bake the muffins for 20–25 minutes, until they spring back when pressed lightly with a finger.

Transfer the muffins in their cases to a wire rack to cool.

Make the glaze. In a small bowl, whisk together the tahini, icing sugar, lemon juice and 2 tablespoons of water. When the muffins are cool, spoon the glaze over the top. Sprinkle with the sesame seeds and leave for an hour or so for the glaze to set before eating (if you can wait!).

Pear, nutmeg, cranberry & maple porridge
(& other seasonal porridge ideas)

Serves 1 or 2, depending on greed

I know – you probably don't need to be told how to make porridge. Consider this less of an instruction, then, and more of a suggestion for how to brighten up your morning bowlful in ways you might not have considered before. (Apologies to any die-hard fans of the Spartan, Scottish way to eat porridge – these ideas may well seem sacrilegious in your eyes.) These are my go-to recipes for jazzing up my porridge with the changing seasons, based on old favourites that I make countless times every year. I come back to this pear version time and time again, and it is probably the recipe I cook most, on average, over the year. I even eat it on Christmas morning – it feels that much of a treat.

An important note about quantities: I am an absolute porridge fiend, and can eat an astonishing amount of the stuff for breakfast (an old boyfriend of mine used to refer to my breakfast as a 'porridge mountain'). These recipes serve 1 if you are like me, or 2 if you have a more restrained appetite for the stuff.

100g jumbo oats
200ml whole milk
a generous pinch of salt
40g dried cranberries
¼ teaspoon freshly
   grated nutmeg, plus
   extra to finish
1 ripe, juicy pear
   (Conference or Comice
   works well), cored and
   cut into 1.5cm dice
2 tablespoons
   maple syrup

Put the oats in a medium saucepan with the milk, salt, cranberries, nutmeg and 300ml of water. Place over a medium-high heat and bring to the boil, stirring, then lower the heat to a simmer and cook for 5–8 minutes, stirring regularly, until the porridge thickens and the oats soften. You may need to add a splash more water to reach the correct consistency.

When the porridge is nearly ready, set aside a few pieces of pear to garnish, then stir the remainder into the porridge. Pour the porridge into a bowl (or two), and scatter over the reserved cubes of pear. Grate over a generous few shavings of nutmeg, then drizzle over the maple syrup. Serve immediately.

Other seasonal ideas

Apple and honey
Swap the cranberries for sultanas, the pear for one grated eating
apple (discard the core), the nutmeg for ½ teaspoon ground cinnamon
and the maple syrup for honey (the more flavoursome the better). Cook
as page 226.

Banana and coconut
Swap the pear for a roughly chopped banana, the nutmeg for ½ teaspoon
ground cinnamon and the cranberries for dried blueberries. Cook as page
226, then drizzle with maple or coconut syrup and sprinkle with a couple
of tablespoons of toasted, desiccated coconut, sunflower seeds or sesame
seeds (or a mixture).

Blackcurrant and elderflower
Place 200g blackcurrants in a small saucepan with 3 tablespoons
elderflower cordial. Bring to the boil, then simmer gently until the fruit
has burst and become juicy. Set aside to cool, then refrigerate. Spoon
over hot porridge (this makes enough for several servings), perhaps with
a grated apple stirred into the oats.

Roasted stone fruit
Halve and stone 500g apricots or plums, and place in a medium oven
dish in a single layer. Sprinkle over 4 tablespoons light brown soft sugar.
If using plums, add the juice of an orange and a star anise, broken into
pieces. If using apricots, add 4 crushed cardamom pods and 1 tablespoon
orange-blossom water, plus a splash of water. Cover the dish tightly with
foil and bake at 190°C/170°C fan/gas mark 5 for about 30 minutes, or
until the fruit is completely tender. Serve warm or cold on porridge made
with cinnamon and sultanas. (This makes enough for several servings.)

Roasted rhubarb and vanilla
Cut 400g rhubarb into 2.5cm lengths and place them in a medium
baking dish. Add a vanilla pod, split lengthways and seeds scraped out
into the dish, and 6 tablespoons caster sugar. Cover tightly with foil and
bake at 190°C/170°C fan/gas mark 5 for 15–30 minutes, until completely
tender. Serve warm or cold on porridge made with dried cranberries and
cinnamon. (This makes enough for several servings.)

Berries & Currants

> 'I have heard all this before,' said Mr. Bounderby. 'She took to drinking, left off working, sold the furniture, pawned the clothes, and played old Gooseberry.'

~ Charles Dickens, *Hard Times*

Such was the journey of Stephen Blackpool's wife to moral ruin in Charles Dickens's *Hard Times*. Francis Grose, in his *Classical Dictionary of the Vulgar Tongue* from 1796 (what a title!), defines 'playing old gooseberry' as using violence or threats to put an end to a disturbance, drawing on a medieval name for the Devil. In modern parlance, though, we tend to use the phrase 'playing gooseberry' to mean being the socially awkward third party in the presence of an amorous couple. This has its origins in the nineteenth century, and is seemingly derived from the idea that a discreet chaperone, tasked with supervising a couple against social impropriety, would go off to pick gooseberries or watch butterflies, thus allowing the pair to steal a moment or two together. To me this makes rather a lot of sense: identifying oneself with a fruit that is as culinarily awkward as one feels socially at that moment in time. The **gooseberry** remains a sadly underrated ingredient in the kitchen, making it the perfect metaphor for uncomfortable isolation or even devilry.

Unlike its more obvious berry cousins, the gooseberry cannot simply be plucked off a vine and enjoyed, but requires the sweet tempering treatment of sugar and gentle heat. The berries are like miniature jade crystal balls, their translucent skins revealing the faintest misty white blooms beneath the surface. Hazardous to harvest – watch out for the thorns – they generously give forth clouds of muscat perfume when cooked, having a particular affinity with other floral flavours. The awkward reputation of the gooseberry is undeserved, as it couples beautifully and harmoniously with many other ingredients: elderflower is the classic pairing, or mackerel (the French actually call gooseberries *groseilles à maquereau*, or 'mackerel currants'), or anything heavy with dairy. It also, for me, encapsulates one of the most interesting aspects of this branch of the fruit family. We may think we know our berries, but there is a whole world of novelty and potential beyond the supermarket punnet.

'Never, ever cook a **strawberry**', I once read in a recipe book during my early years of learning to cook. The stern, authoritative warning stuck with me, and I remember dutifully removing the squashed, misshapen strawberries from those economical supermarket packs of frozen berries before baking with them, fearing what hideous result might occur were one of them to slip through the net. (The irony there being that if there is one thing worse than cooking a strawberry, it is freezing one.) I still remember the tragic moment on one episode of *The Great*

British Bake Off where a contestant made the grave and fatal error of attempting to put a layer of strawberries in his steamed pudding. They collapsed into a sad puddle of despair, as did his dreams of winning the contest. A trip to Prague a couple of years after watching this brought about a small revelation, when I discovered strawberries nestled into the crumb of delicious little *bublanina*, or 'bubble cakes', sold at an Easter market stall (you can find the recipe on page 251). Folding strawberries through a vanilla-scented cake batter, or mixing them with other fruits beneath the buttery topping of a crumble or pie, can in fact yield excellent results: their juices mingle deliciously with other fruits, and soak beautifully into the crumb (judicious use of cornflour is advised, though – strawberries produce a lot of juice when cooked).

It pays, therefore, to be a bit experimental with ingredients we tend to take for granted, or for which we have a stockpile of traditional, failsafe uses. We may think the only home for strawberries is alongside a bowl of cream or, at the most, topping a French-style fruit tart, but they are surprisingly good alongside salty or ripe soft cheeses when given a little lift with black pepper and treacly balsamic vinegar. **Blueberries** tend to be reserved for breakfast muffins, waffles or compote, but try stirring them through earthy grain salads, where they provide a pop of sharpness and colour comparable to that of the now ubiquitous pomegranate seed. Of course, there is no point in experimenting for the sake of it: many of the recipes in this chapter take established, approved flavour combinations and add the tiniest modicum of adventure: a raspberry and white chocolate cheesecake with the grassy tang of goat's cheese, for example, or a gamey reindeer dish given interest with a whisper of juniper and a tart blackcurrant sauce.

The candy-sweet strawberry aside, I often think of berries as 'grown-up fruits'. You have to work to get the most out of a gooseberry or currant, and even the tart **raspberry** proves too sour for some tastes. If you want proper **blackberries**, as nature intended them, you must wait patiently for them to ripen in hedgerows before heading out with an ice-cream tub or two, ready to come back slightly bloodied and sticky, sore from standing on your tiptoes to reach a particularly juicy specimen. Yet your efforts will be rewarded many times over, as you return clutching a crop infinitely more flavoursome than the tastelessly juicy varieties often shipped in from Mexico, which resemble towering beehive hairdos and are juicily vapid. **Blackcurrants**, when treated properly, have a gloriously complex bouquet of flavours ranging from floral to grassy and herbal. Over ninety-five per cent of Britain's blackcurrants go into producing Ribena, which seems to me a colossal waste. With a little kitchen creativity, I hope we can at least put the remaining five per cent to delicious uses, exploiting their particular affinity with dairy and herbs. Whitecurrants, if you can find them, are perhaps the most beautiful of the lot, resembling strings of vintage pearls, while **redcurrants** have a versatility that goes well beyond jelly – try them as a substitute for pomegranate seeds in Middle Eastern dishes.

The Nordic countries are, to my mind, rulers of the berry world. Their temperate climes provide excellent growing conditions for wild blueberries or bilberries, which are much more flavoursome than the swollen, tasteless imports we often find on our supermarket shelves, and guaranteed to turn your tongue purple after a couple of mouthfuls. Up to a fifth of the entire land area of Sweden contains bilberry bushes, but don't despair if you can't make it over there for late summer – I have foraged for them on the North York Moors with delicious results. You can also buy them frozen or preserved in jars in many parts of Europe and some supermarkets: try them in place of blueberries when baking.

The northern regions also give forth wild raspberries, tiny alpine strawberries and a few other sought-after fruits that still seem rather exotic to our British tastes. Lingonberries have something of the tang and colour of cranberries, and similar savoury uses: they are popular served with elk and reindeer in Norway, Finland and Sweden, but are also used in cordials, syrups and desserts. If you are lucky enough to find some, they freeze well, and you can use them in the baked Brie or reindeer recipes on pages 236 and 245, respectively.

Sea buckthorn, as its name suggests, is often found close to the coast. Its fragile berries are tricky to harvest – I remember attempting to pinch a few off the thorny vine in northern Denmark and just ending up with splattered orange fingers – but their sourness and high vitamin content sees them used in a variety of jams, lotions, syrups and juices throughout the Nordic countries, and they are becoming more widespread in British fine-dining, perhaps owing to their dramatic saffron hue. Even more significant in the world of orange berries is the cloudberry, which you'll find growing wild only in marshland, and whose fragility also makes it tricky to harvest. Secret knowledge of good cloudberry spots is often handed down throughout the generations – there is an urban legend of a woman in Finnmark, northern Norway, who broke her leg while picking cloudberries and staggered several kilometres away before she would call an ambulance, lest she risk giving away her prized location. Resembling peachy-orange raspberries, these fruits are high in nutrients and intriguing in flavour, with a tart, musky taste popularly used to adorn cakes and waffles. They are rippled through whipped cream and eaten in delicate wafers as part of the Norwegian Christmas meal, and can be bought year-round in frozen or preserved form, albeit with a high price tag (a kilo tub of frozen cloudberries currently sells in my local shop in Oslo for £30). Should you ever be lucky enough to get your hands on them, I recommend trying them out instead of the blackcurrant compote in the cheesecake on page 248.

As the elusive cloudberry illustrates, berries are also some of the few fruits that remain immune to the perils of foreign cultivation and air-freighting, and thus require us to put a little effort into sourcing and utilizing them. Try as you might, you will not find gooseberries or blackcurrants in the shops outside an all-too-brief window around June and July, and in my masochistic eyes this just makes them even more special. They are jewels to be hoarded, celebrated, and consumed in abundance for a tiny period of the year, reminding us of just how much we take for granted in modern food production.

Tips & tricks

* Fresh berries can be expensive, especially out of season. For recipes involving cooked berries, frozen packets from the supermarket are often much better value (and you now know that you don't have to pick out the strawberries – you're welcome).

* If you end up with a glut of fresh berries in the summer, freeze them for use later – you can rinse the firmer berries like gooseberries and blackcurrants and leave them to dry before freezing, but don't attempt to wash ripe raspberries or you'll end up with mush. You can freeze strawberries, but they will be fit only for blitzing into a smoothie (they're very good with blood orange juice and a drop of orange-blossom water) or for making cakes, jams or compotes. Gooseberries are actually easier to top and tail when slightly frozen, so don't bother doing this before freezing.

* Transform disappointing strawberries into a palatable dessert using a trickle of balsamic vinegar, a couple of teaspoons of sugar and a drop of lemon juice. Leave the fruit to macerate for a few minutes – the difference in flavour is astounding. If you're feeling adventurous, add a grinding of black pepper to the mixture, too.

* The best berries come from pick-your-own farms, farm shops and farmers' markets during the summer. I defy you to get them all home without snacking on a few. The best blackberries are nature's gift to us in early autumn – all you need is a bag or a box, and perhaps a pair of gloves to guard against the thorns.

* For a useful guide to some of the more unusual berries, Hugh Fearnley-Whittingstall's *Fruit* book contains a brief overview of mulberries, Worcesterberries, loganberries, tayberries, bilberries, blueberries and whortleberries.

Baked Brie

with blackcurrants, toasted pecans, honey & herbs

Serves 4–6

Here it is: your new go-to dinner party starter. It looks incredibly impressive but takes about two minutes to prepare, and the combination of molten, honeyed cheese with tangy blackcurrant, buttery pecan and fragrant herbs is both unusual and utterly addictive. Simply bring it to the table in its oven dish and let your guests dive in. I like to serve it with Scandinavian-style rye crackers, but a good, crusty baguette is also an excellent vehicle for transporting cheese to mouth. I highly recommend seeking out blackcurrant vinegar (I get it from demijohn.co.uk), but you could replace it with the more common raspberry vinegar, or a good, syrupy balsamic. Feel free to double the recipe to use a 500g wheel of Brie (or a Camembert), but adjust the cooking time to make it slightly longer. Redcurrants or whitecurrants would also work here.

45g pecan nuts
250g wedge of Brie
70g fresh or frozen
  blackcurrants
2 teaspoons thyme
  leaves or finely
  chopped rosemary
  needles
3 teaspoons
  blackcurrant vinegar
  or balsamic vinegar
3–4 teaspoons
  runny honey

Pre-heat the oven to 190°C/170°C fan/gas mark 5.

Put the pecans in a small oven dish and place in the oven for 8 minutes, until toasted. Remove (leave the oven on), set aside to cool, then roughly chop.

Take a small baking dish, the right size to fit the piece of Brie snugly. Slice the Brie horizontally in half (so you have two flat triangles). Put one half in the dish, cut side up. Take half the toasted pecans and press them gently into the cheese. Do the same with the blackcurrants (some will fall off the sides into the dish – that's fine, but try to get as many as possible on the cheese). Sprinkle over half the thyme or rosemary, then drizzle over half the vinegar and half the honey.

Put the other piece of Brie on top, rind side upwards (so you have essentially sandwiched the cheese back together as the wedge it was). Press the remaining pecans and blackcurrants onto the top of the cheese (again, some will fall off). Drizzle over the remaining vinegar and honey and sprinkle with the remaining thyme or rosemary.

Bake for 10–15 minutes, or until the cheese has melted and spread out a little in the dish. Remove from the oven, leave for 5 minutes, then dive in with crackers or good crusty bread.

Smoky aubergine salad
with redcurrants

Serves 6

Somewhere between a salad and a dip, this is best served with slices of grilled halloumi (or crumbled feta) and some flatbread for scooping it up. It is perfect for outdoor cooking – you can grill the aubergines on the barbecue – and goes well as a side with all manner of meat and cheese dishes, and even oily fish. Redcurrants and aubergines are obviously not natural bedfellows, but pomegranate seeds are often paired with aubergines and it occurred to me that redcurrants have a very similar jewel-like appearance and burst sharply on the tongue in the same way. The combination works well, but you can use pomegranate seeds as a substitute for redcurrants outside of the currant season.

6 aubergines
100g walnuts
2 tablespoons rapeseed or olive oil
5 red onions, finely sliced
a pinch of salt, plus extra to season if necessary
2 tablespoons balsamic vinegar
2 tablespoons lemon juice, plus extra to taste if necessary
3 tablespoons pomegranate molasses, plus extra to taste if necessary
2 tablespoons good-quality olive oil
a large handful of mint leaves, roughly chopped or torn
75g watercress
150g redcurrants, stripped from their stalks
freshly ground black pepper

Pre-heat the grill to high. Line an oven tray with foil and lay the aubergines on top, side by side. Place under the grill and cook, turning occasionally, for 25–45 minutes (depending on the size of your aubergines), until the skin is blackened and crispy and the flesh inside is completely soft and smoky. Alternatively, you can do this on a barbecue. Set the aubergines aside to cool.

Meanwhile, turn the oven to 200°C/180°C fan/gas mark 6, place the walnuts in a small oven tray and bake them for 10 minutes, until toasted. Set aside to cool, then roughly chop.

Heat the rapeseed or olive oil in a large frying pan over a medium-high heat. Add the onions and the pinch of salt and cook, stirring regularly, for 5–10 minutes, until they start to soften and turn slightly golden. Lower the heat and cook for 15–20 minutes, until totally soft and caramelised – you may need to add a drop of water to stop them sticking. Stir in the balsamic vinegar and set aside to cool slightly.

When the aubergines are ready, scoop out the flesh, discarding the skin and stalks. Place the flesh in a large bowl and add the caramelised onions, along with the lemon juice, pomegranate molasses and good-quality olive oil. Mash everything together gently with a fork. Season well with salt and pepper, then taste, adjusting with a little more lemon juice or molasses accordingly.

Stir in the toasted walnuts, along with the mint leaves and watercress, then gently fold in the redcurrants. Serve warm or at room temperature.

Blueberry & quinoa salad
with feta & toasted almonds

Serves 2 (or 3–4 depending on greed)

Blueberries are one of those fruits that seem destined to be used only for baking muffins or scattering atop a bowl of muesli, but their sharp juiciness actually makes them perfect in hearty salads, in the same way you might use pomegranate seeds. I learned from Niki Segnit's invaluable *Flavour Thesaurus* that coriander seeds contain a flavour compound called linalool, which is also a key component of synthetic blueberry flavour. The woody, citrus notes of the seeds add greater depth to this salad, packed with good-for-you nuts and grains.

For the salad
½ red onion, peeled and very thinly sliced
2 teaspoons lemon juice
a generous pinch of salt
a generous pinch of sugar
150g quinoa
250ml hot vegetable stock
1 celery stalk, finely diced

10g butter
1 heaped teaspoon coriander seeds, crushed in a mortar and pestle
½ teaspoon sweet smoked paprika
60g blanched almonds
140g blueberries
10g parsley leaves,
roughly chopped
a large handful of baby spinach leaves
100g feta, crumbled

For the dressing
finely grated zest of ½ lemon and
1 tablespoon juice, plus extra to taste

3 tablespoons good-quality olive oil
1 teaspoon Dijon mustard
1 tablespoon maple syrup, plus extra to taste if necessary
1 tablespoon cider vinegar
salt and freshly ground black pepper

Put the red onion in a large bowl with the lemon juice and pinches of salt and sugar. Toss well and leave while you prepare the rest of the salad.

Meanwhile, put the quinoa in a medium saucepan and place over a medium heat. Toss the pan occasionally to toast the quinoa evenly. When it starts to pop (about 5 minutes), add the hot vegetable stock, bring to the boil, then lower the heat to a simmer. Cover the pan and cook for 12 minutes, until nearly all the water has been absorbed. Turn off the heat and leave the quinoa to steam for another 5 minutes, then fluff up with a fork and set aside to cool while making the dressing.

Whisk all the dressing ingredients together, adjusting with a little more lemon juice or maple syrup, and seasoning to suit your taste. The dressing should be quite assertive, as quinoa can take a lot of flavour. Pour the dressing over the cooked quinoa, then add the celery and prepared red onion and mix well.

In a small saucepan or frying pan, melt the butter over a medium heat. Add the coriander seeds, paprika and almonds. Cook for about 5 minutes, stirring regularly, until the almonds are golden and smelling wonderful. Season with salt and pepper, turn off the heat and leave to cool.

Add the blueberries, parsley and baby spinach to the quinoa and toss gently. Divide the salad between two plates and top with the crumbled feta and the almonds. Serve immediately.

Raspberry, white chocolate & goat's cheese cheesecake

Serves 10–12

This is rather different to your standard cheesecake – the addition of goat's cheese gives it a gentle tang and slightly crumbly texture, setting off the fragrant juice of the berries and resulting in a complex flavour that is not overly sweet. Blueberries or blackberries also work in place of raspberries. I recommend serving this with some passionfruit coulis and a few extra fresh berries. If you don't like the taste of goat's cheese – though it is very subtle here – simply replace it with the same amount of cream cheese (though I feel that is rather missing the point!).

80g butter, plus extra
  for greasing
140g digestive or
  gingernut biscuits,
  blitzed to crumbs in
  a food processor
50g jumbo oats
300g white chocolate
150g soured cream
200g full-fat
  cream cheese
200g soft, mild, rindless
  goat's cheese
4 eggs
finely grated zest of
  1 lemon
200g raspberries

Pre-heat the oven to 200°C/180°C fan/gas mark 6. Grease and line a 23cm springform cake tin.

Melt the butter in a medium saucepan over a medium heat, then stir in the blitzed biscuits and the oats. Press the biscuit mixture into the bottom of the cake tin, using the back of a spoon to flatten gently – don't press too hard – to form a crust. Bake the crust for 12 minutes, until golden, then remove from the oven and set aside to cool while you make the filling.

Turn down the oven temperature to 170°C/150°C fan/gas mark 3.

Melt the white chocolate in a heatproof bowl suspended over a pan of simmering water (don't let the base of the bowl touch the water), stirring regularly to help the chocolate melt. Remove the bowl from the heat and leave to cool slightly, then whisk in the soured cream.

Using a food processor or electric hand whisk, combine the white chocolate and soured cream mixture with the cream cheese, goat's cheese, eggs and lemon zest. Gently fold in the berries using a spatula or large spoon. Pour the mixture into the cake tin over the biscuit base.

Bake the cheesecake for 40–45 minutes. The best way to tell when it is done is to use a digital probe thermometer – the centre should reach 65°C. If you don't have a thermometer, watch for the point where the cake is lightly golden around the edges and just set on top, but still has a generous wobble in the middle if you shake it gently – it will continue to set as it cools. Turn the oven off with the cake inside, and, using the handle of a wooden spoon, prop open the oven door slightly. Leave the cake to cool in the oven for 1–2 hours (this helps to prevent it from cracking). Once cool, refrigerate for at least 2 hours before serving.

Rosemary pork chops
with mushroom & goat's cheese cream & blackberry walnut salsa

Serves 2

An ode to autumn if ever there was one: creamy mushrooms, resinous rosemary and the musky sharpness of blackberries. This makes an unusual and impressive main course – you can make the blackberry salsa in advance to speed up the process. If you can find some wild mushrooms, such as chanterelles, they would make this even more special. You could also use chicken breasts instead of pork, although they will take slightly longer to cook.

For the salsa
½ small red onion,
  very finely chopped
1 teaspoon caster sugar
½ teaspoon salt
1 teaspoon balsamic
  vinegar
1 teaspoon red
  wine vinegar or
  raspberry vinegar
a good squeeze of
  lemon juice
50g walnuts
125g blackberries,
  roughly chopped
½ teaspoon
  runny honey
1 tablespoon very
  finely chopped flat-
  leaf parsley

For the pork & sauce
zest of 1 lemon and
  juice of ½
2 garlic cloves, crushed
1 tablespoon finely
  chopped rosemary
  needles, plus 2 sprigs
400g pork chops
  or escalopes
2 tablespoons rapeseed
  or olive oil
150g button
  mushrooms,
  thinly sliced
1 shallot, finely sliced

First, get started with the salsa. Put the red onion in a medium bowl with the sugar, salt, vinegars and lemon juice. Stir well to mix and set aside for 1 hour, stirring occasionally.

Next, marinate the pork. Put the lemon zest and juice, garlic and chopped rosemary, along with a generous seasoning of salt and pepper, in a shallow, non-reactive dish or bowl. Add the pork chops or escalopes and rub the marinade over them using a spoon or your hands. Refrigerate for about 30 minutes.

Pre-heat the oven to 200°C/180°C fan/gas mark 6.

Tip the walnuts for the salsa into a small baking dish and toast in the oven for 10 minutes, until slightly darker and fragrant. Set aside to cool. Turn down the oven to a low heat (about 90°C/70°C fan/gas mark ¼). Once the walnuts are cool, finely chop.

When the red onion has been macerating for 1 hour, add the walnuts, along with the blackberries, honey and parsley. Stir well and set aside.

Finish the pork. Heat half the rapeseed or olive oil in a medium frying pan over a medium-high heat. Add the pork, then cook for about 5 minutes (depending on thickness) on each side, until fully cooked through (the chops or escalopes should reach 70°C on a meat thermometer). Once cooked, place the pork on a baking sheet and keep warm in the low oven while you make the sauce.

In the same pan in which you cooked the pork, heat the remaining rapeseed or olive oil over a high heat. Remove any very burnt bits of pork marinade from the pan (a few sticky brown bits are fine – they will add flavour). Add the mushrooms and the rosemary sprigs and sauté, stirring regularly, for about 5 minutes, until the mushrooms have shrunk and turned golden and almost sticky. Lower the heat slightly, add the shallots and cook for another couple of minutes.

Pour the white wine into the pan and let it bubble away until reduced by slightly over half. Add the goat's cheese or curd and crème fraîche and stir well,

100ml white wine
90g soft goat's
  cheese, crumbled,
  or goat's curd
2 tablespoons
  crème fraîche
salt and freshly ground
  black pepper

simmering gently for 1–2 minutes, until you have a creamy sauce. Taste, and adjust the seasoning, if necessary.

Serve the pork with the cream sauce and a spoonful of the salsa alongside. I like to serve this with boiled new potatoes.

Reindeer steaks
with blackcurrant & juniper

Serves 2

Living in Norway, I have fairly easy access to reindeer meat (which I highly recommend for its deep, ferrous richness), but venison makes a good substitute, or even some very good, aged beef. The cleansing freshness of juniper perfectly accentuates the grassy notes in blackcurrants, and together they make a powerful, sharp sauce that cuts through the bosky richness of game. I add a little double cream to soften the sourness, but if you like your sauces very tangy, leave it out. This dish is excellent with buttery mash for those slightly chillier, late-summer evenings.

1 tablespoon plain flour
2 reindeer or venison steaks (about 150–200g each)
25g salted butter
1 bay leaf
3 tablespoons white wine
130g fresh or frozen blackcurrants
200ml beef stock
7 juniper berries, lightly crushed
2 teaspoons quince or redcurrant jelly, plus extra to taste if necessary
3 tablespoons double cream (optional)
2 tablespoons finely chopped flat-leaf parsley
salt and freshly ground black pepper

Spread out the flour on a plate and season well with salt and pepper. Lay the steaks on the flour to coat on one side, then flip over to coat the other.

In a medium frying pan, melt the butter over a medium-high heat. Cook the steaks for about 5 minutes on each side, depending on their thickness and how rare you want the meat (I recommend serving it rare, as reindeer and venison are very lean). A meat thermometer should read 52°C.

Once the steaks are cooked to your liking, set them aside on a plate under some foil to keep warm. Throw the bay leaf into the frying pan and add the white wine. Let the wine bubble and reduce, scraping the pan with a wooden spoon to release any sticky bits, then once it has reduced by about half, add the blackcurrants, beef stock, juniper berries and quince or redcurrant jelly. Let the whole thing simmer vigorously for about 3–4 minutes, until reduced and slightly syrupy, then taste to check the seasoning – add a little more jelly if you want it sweeter. Lower the heat, then stir in the double cream, if using.

Thickly slice the steaks and serve with the sauce poured over and the parsley sprinkled on the top. Buttery mashed potato, or Dauphinoise potatoes if you are feeling extravagant, are the best accompaniments.

Pear, gooseberry, elderflower & almond breakfast oat crumble

Serves 2–4, depending on greed

This recipe is the reason I hoard kilos of gooseberries in my freezer, stocking up in huge quantities during their very fleeting season. Their musky sourness and hint of floral perfume marry perfectly with the buttery flesh of ripe pear and the sweetness of elderflower. The combination works as a normal dessert crumble, too, but I like to make this slightly healthier oat-based variation, so I can justify enjoying it for breakfast. Fragrant syrup, spiced oats and a big scoop of thick, Greek yoghurt make this my desert-island morning meal. Start making room in your freezer: once you try this recipe, you too will obsessively stockpile those elusive, fuzzy berries. Incidentally, this keeps well in the fridge for a few days and reheats excellently in a microwave or oven, so you can enjoy taking time over it at the weekend and still have some left for the weekday breakfast rush.

300g fresh or frozen gooseberries, topped and tailed

3 tablespoons elderflower cordial

3 ripe pears (Conference or Comice works well), cored, quartered and cut into 2.5cm dice

1 tablespoon cornflour

150g jumbo oats

40g spelt flour

1 teaspoon ground ginger

½ teaspoon mixed spice

¼ teaspoon salt

40g flaked almonds

3 tablespoons olive oil

3 tablespoons maple syrup

1 teaspoon almond extract

Pre-heat the oven to 200°C/180°C fan/gas mark 6.

Put the gooseberries in a medium baking dish with the elderflower cordial and toss together. Add the pears and cornflour and mix to combine.

In a small bowl, mix together the oats, flour, ginger, mixed spice, salt and flaked almonds. In a measuring jug or mug, whisk together the olive oil, maple syrup and almond extract, along with 2 tablespoons of water. Stir this into the oat mixture until the mixture is moist and starts to clump together.

Tip the oat mixture over the gooseberries and pears, then give it a couple of nudges with a wooden spoon to roughly combine with the fruit – you still want most of it over the top, though.

Bake for 40 minutes, until the oats have turned crunchy and golden and the fruit has softened. (Check it halfway through cooking, and if it looks like it's a bit dry, add a splash of water to the dish.) Allow the oat crumble to rest for a couple of minutes, then serve with a scoop of thick, Greek yoghurt and perhaps some fresh raspberries or blackberries alongside.

Floral blackcurrant curd

Makes about 3 x 450g jars

The combination of berries, flowers and a good amount of butter and sugar makes for a truly elegant preserve. You could use almost any berries here but I love the grassy sharpness of blackcurrant. It takes a little patience to keep whisking the curd, but the results are worth it. Try to use the best butter and eggs you can afford – with so few ingredients, quality makes all the difference. I love this curd simply slathered over toast (or, to be really decadent, brioche). However, it also makes a glorious filling for a Victoria sponge, a fabulous topping for a scone, or a delightful breakfast rippled through Greek yoghurt with granola.

3 large lemons
500g fresh or frozen blackcurrants
1 tablespoon lavender buds, crushed rose petals or finely shredded lemon verbena (optional)
130g butter
400g granulated or caster sugar
5 large eggs, beaten

First, sterilise your jars. I do this by washing them well in soapy water, then putting the jars upside down in an oven at 140°C/120°C fan/gas mark 1 for 25 minutes, adding the lids (also upside down) for the last 10 minutes. Turn off the oven and leave the jars inside until you are ready to bottle the curd. You can alternatively run the jars through a hot dishwasher cycle, then pot the curd while they are still warm.

Zest two of the lemons and place the zest in a large saucepan. Juice all three lemons into the saucepan.

Next, make a berry purée. Put the blackcurrants and the flowers or herbs (if using) into the saucepan with the lemon zest and juice over a medium-high heat. Bring to the boil, then lower the heat and simmer for 10 minutes or so, until the fruit starts to collapse and everything is juicy and fragrant.

Pour this mixture into a sieve set over a heatproof bowl, then use a stiff spatula or ladle to push the mixture through the sieve until only the seeds and pulp remain (this takes a few minutes and a bit of muscle). Discard the contents of the sieve.

Add the butter and sugar to the berry purée. Suspend the bowl over a pan of simmering water (the water shouldn't touch the base of the bowl), and whisk until the butter has melted. Remove the bowl from the heat and let the mixture cool for a few minutes before adding the eggs (if it is too hot, they will scramble).

Put the bowl back over the simmering water and whisk the mixture as it heats up until it thickens and reaches the 'ribbon stage' (when a dollop dropped from the whisk forms a ribbon on the surface of the mixture). The temperature should reach 76°C on a sugar thermometer. For this curd, the process can take anything from 20 minutes to over 1 hour. Have patience – it will thicken eventually; and remember to keep whisking so you don't end up with scrambled eggs.

When the curd is thick, allow it to cool a little in the bowl, whisking occasionally, then pour into the warm jars and seal. The curd will keep in the fridge for about 1 month, and freezes well, too.

Blackcurrant & lemon verbena cheesecake

Serves 8–10

Having ordered a delightful-sounding blackcurrant and lemon verbena cheesecake in a London restaurant a couple of years ago, I was not thrilled when eventually presented with a bowl containing a dollop of cream cheese, a glossy trickle of blackcurrant compote and a disc of buttery pastry perched vertiginously on top, as if provocatively celebrating the anarchic deconstruction of this traditional dessert. The flavours were remarkable, the herbal tang of the lemon verbena bringing out the intense, grassy sourness of fresh blackcurrant, but I maintain that prising the elements of a cheesecake apart makes the whole thing too clinical. So, here is my improved version of a truly astounding flavour combination. It's a simple ode to the bold flavours of late summer, its colour reminiscent of lavender and peppered with curling wisps of aromatic verbena. There is no gelatine, simply the thickness of the yoghurt and cheese to hold the cake together, so it slices messily and eats in a hedonistic, creamy, tangy frenzy. This is best eaten on the day it is made, as the base can become soggy after more than a day in the fridge.

You'll need to make the strained yoghurt the night before you intend to make the cheesecake.

1kg thick, full-fat plain or Greek yoghurt

250g fresh or frozen blackcurrants

2 tablespoons caster sugar

50g butter, plus extra for greasing

150g gingernut or digestive biscuits, blitzed to crumbs in a food processor

400g full-fat cream cheese

150g icing sugar

1 teaspoon vanilla paste

4 sprigs lemon verbena (the top sprigs with the smallest leaves), leaves picked

The night before you intend to make the cheesecake, line a colander or sieve with muslin or cheesecloth and pour the yoghurt into it. Put the sieve or colander over a bowl, giving at least 5cm between the bowl and the bottom of the sieve, then leave overnight in the fridge or a cool place. The liquid will drain from the yoghurt and leave a thick, cheese-like consistency in the muslin.

Make the blackcurrant compote. Put the blackcurrants in a small saucepan with the caster sugar and 1 tablespoon of water. Place over a high heat and bring to the boil, then reduce the heat to low and simmer very gently until the berries start to burst and release their juice. Remove the pan from the heat and leave the compote to cool.

Pre-heat the oven to 200°C/180°C fan/gas mark 6. Grease and line a 20cm springform cake tin.

Make the cheesecake base. Melt the butter in a small saucepan over a low heat, then stir in the biscuit crumbs. Spread the biscuit mixture evenly over the bottom of the cake tin, pressing it down with the back of a spoon. Bake for 10 minutes, until golden, then set aside to cool.

When the base is cool, rub a little butter (or flavourless oil) around the inside of the tin without dislodging the biscuit base (this will help to release the cheesecake later).

In a large mixing bowl, whisk together the cream cheese, icing sugar, vanilla paste and strained yoghurt (discard its liquid, or use to make the soda bread on page 211). Add three-quarters of the blackcurrant compote to the cheese mixture and swirl it through with a spoon, but don't mix it in completely. Pour the mixture into the cake tin and put it in the fridge for at least 8 hours to set. Chill the remaining blackcurrant compote.

When you're ready to serve, dollop the remaining blackcurrant compote over the surface of the cheesecake, then scatter over the lemon verbena leaves. Run a knife around the edge of the cake to loosen it, then release the sides of the tin (leave the cheesecake on the tin base for stability). Slice and serve – this can be a little messy, as the set isn't very firm, but it will taste great!

Czech bubble cake
with berries

Makes one 20cm cake

I discovered this cake at a food market in Prague. The Czech name is *bublanina*, probably because of the way the batter bubbles up around the fruit. It is wonderfully versatile – you can make it with any mixture of berries, even strawberries, which we are typically told not to bake with as they turn watery. A few strawberries in the mixture of berries won't hurt here, though; in fact, they perfume the crumb delightfully. This makes it a very economical cake, as you can use those handy bags of frozen mixed berries available in supermarkets. Cherries or plums (stoned and sliced) work well, too.

This is best as a pudding cake, served warm on the day it is baked.

For the topping
30g cold butter, cubed
60g plain flour
30g golden caster or
  demerara sugar

For the cake
150g golden caster sugar
90g butter, softened at
  room temperature
2 eggs, lightly beaten
½ teaspoon almond
  extract
200g plain yoghurt
200g plain flour
1 teaspoon baking
  powder
a pinch of salt
300g fresh or frozen
  mixed berries, plus
  extra to decorate

Pre-heat the oven to 190°C/170°C fan/gas mark 5. Grease and line a 20cm springform cake tin.

Make the topping. In a small bowl, rub the cold butter into the flour with your fingertips until the mixture resembles fine breadcrumbs. Stir in the sugar and set aside.

Next, make the cake. Using a stand mixer or an electric hand whisk, beat the sugar and butter at a high speed until fluffy and pale. Add the eggs a little at a time, mixing well between each addition. Stir in the almond extract and the yoghurt.

In a small bowl, mix together the flour, baking powder and salt and then fold it gently into the egg and butter mixture until you have a thick batter.

Pour the batter into the tin. Scatter the berries over the top and press down gently. Tip the crumble topping evenly over the berries. Bake the cake for 50–60 minutes, or until a skewer inserted into the centre comes out clean. Serve warm, topped with a few berries and a scoop of crème fraîche, Greek yoghurt or ice cream.

Gooseberry, elderflower & ginger crumble cheesecake

Serves 8

This is a variation on a cheesecake I made for a cooking TV show, *Food Glorious Food*, several years ago. After the stress of the competition – low points included having to transport two cheesecakes in a giant coolbag on a six-hour journey across the country, negotiating three changes of train and two taxis, and having to re-bake said cheesecakes at 4am that morning because I'd forgotten a crucial ingredient the first time around – it took many years before I could bring myself to make it again. I'm glad I did, though, because this mash-up of my two favourite desserts, incorporating one of my favourite underrated berries, is certainly worth bringing to a wider audience, and encapsulates everything that is wonderful about British puddings. The original version used rhubarb, which is also definitely worth trying – see the variation at the end of the recipe.

For the filling

600g gooseberries, topped and tailed
3 tablespoons elderflower cordial
1½ tablespoons caster sugar
1 teaspoon arrowroot powder
70g butter, plus extra for greasing
180g gingernut or digestive biscuits, blitzed to crumbs in a food processor
375g ricotta
300g full-fat crème fraîche
1 tablespoon runny honey
120g caster sugar
3 large eggs
seeds from 1 vanilla pod, or 1 teaspoon vanilla extract

Put the gooseberries, elderflower and sugar in a small saucepan over a medium heat, and heat gently for 5–10 minutes, until the berries start to burst and release their juice. Bring to a simmer and allow to simmer gently for a couple of minutes, until the gooseberries have softened and become juicy but are mostly still holding their shape. Remove the pan from the heat.

Set aside about a third of this gooseberry mixture in a bowl. Allow to cool, then place in the fridge to chill. Leave the remaining gooseberries in the pan. Mix the arrowroot with 1–2 teaspoons water to form a loose paste, then stir the paste into the gooseberries in the pan to thicken them. Set the pan aside to cool.

Pre-heat the oven to 190°C/170°C fan/gas mark 5. Grease and line a 20cm springform cake tin.

Melt the butter in a small saucepan over a medium heat, then stir in the blitzed biscuits. Press the biscuit mixture gently into the bottom of the cake tin, using the back of a spoon to flatten gently – don't press too hard – to form a crust. Bake the crust for 10 minutes, until golden, then remove from the oven and set aside to cool while you make the filling.

Turn down the oven temperature to 180°C/160°C fan/gas mark 4.

In a large bowl, whisk together the ricotta, crème fraîche, honey, sugar, eggs and vanilla. Add the gooseberry and arrowroot mixture from the pan and fold in gently with a spatula or large spoon, but don't over-mix – you should still see pale streaks of green. Pour the mixture into the cake tin over the biscuit base. Bake for 35 minutes, until the edges of the cake start to set but there is still a lot of wobble in the centre.

For the crumble

30g cold butter, cubed

60g spelt or wholemeal
flour

30g demerara sugar

1 teaspoon ground
ginger

½ teaspoon freshly
grated nutmeg

25g blanched almonds,
roughly chopped

1 tablespoon cold water

To serve

icing sugar, for dusting

mint sprigs or edible
flowers, to decorate

While the cheesecake is baking, prepare the crumble. Put the butter and flour into a mixing bowl or food processor and rub them together using your fingertips, or use a processor, until the mixture resembles fine breadcrumbs. Stir in the sugar, ginger, nutmeg and almonds. Add the water and mix gently so the mixture turns 'pebbly'.

Remove the cheesecake from the oven after 35 minutes. Scatter the crumble mixture evenly over the top (gently, so as not to mess up the cake, which is still only partially cooked). Return the cheesecake to the oven and increase the temperature to 190°C/170°C fan/gas mark 5. Bake for a further 20–25 minutes, until the crumble is golden and the cheesecake is mostly set, with a generous wobble in the centre. The best way to check that the cheesecake is done is to use a digital thermometer – the inside should reach 65°C.

Turn off the oven with the cheesecake inside, and, using the handle of a wooden spoon, prop open the oven door slightly. Leave the cake to cool for 1–2 hours. Once cool, refrigerate for at least 4 hours (it will firm up as it chills), before serving dusted with icing sugar with spoonfuls of the chilled gooseberry compote. I also like to decorate the cake with mint sprigs and/or edible flowers.

Rhubarb variation

You can also make this with early season forced rhubarb – the pink looks beautiful. Chop 400g rhubarb into 2.5cm pieces, then place it in a baking tray with 2 tablespoons of water and 50g caster sugar. Bake at 200°C/180°C fan/gas mark 6 for about 20–30 minutes, until the rhubarb is completely tender. Mash it to a purée with a fork, then tip it into a sieve suspended in a bowl and leave it for 10 minutes to allow any excess liquid in the purée to run off (you can discard it once it has). Put the drained purée in a small bowl and mix it with the arrowroot as above, then leave it to cool. Fold all of this mixture into the cheesecake filling, as with the gooseberry-arrowroot mixture above.

Strawberry shortcake tart
with basil sugar

Serves 6

This is a deceptively easy dessert, but one with a substantial wow factor from the fragrant basil sugar strewn across the top. If you haven't yet tried strawberries with basil, I urge you to take the plunge: rather like a tomato-and-basil combo, they bring out the best in each other. This is the perfect make-ahead dessert for high summer, when the fresh ingredients are both at their best (although the basil sugar will liven up even lacklustre berries at other times of year, too).

For the crust
120g butter, softened at room temperature
50g caster sugar
¼ teaspoon ground cinnamon
150g plain flour
25g ground almonds
40g semolina
a generous pinch of salt

For the filling
250g mascarpone
½ teaspoon vanilla extract or paste
2 tablespoons icing sugar

For the strawberries and the basil sugar
350g strawberries, at room temperature
1 tablespoon lemon juice
40g granulated sugar
5 large basil leaves, plus extra to decorate

Make the crust. Using an electric mixer or electric hand whisk, cream the butter, sugar and cinnamon together on high speed for about 3–4 minutes, until pale and creamy. Add the flour, ground almonds, semolina and salt and mix briefly with a wooden spoon to make a soft, crumbly dough.

Tip the dough into a loose-bottomed tart tin (20–23cm in diameter – the smaller the tin, the thicker the crust). Press the dough up the sides of the tin and evenly along the bottom using your fingers or the back of a spoon. Once done, put the tin in the fridge for 30 minutes. Meanwhile, pre-heat the oven to 180°C/160°C fan/gas mark 4.

Bake the crust for 20–30 minutes, until lightly golden, then remove it and leave it to cool completely.

Meanwhile, whisk together the mascarpone, vanilla and icing sugar. Chill the mixture until needed.

When the crust is completely cool, and when you're ready to serve, spoon the mascarpone filling into it and level it roughly with the back of a spoon.

Hull and quarter the strawberries. Place them in a bowl with the lemon juice and toss together (do this at the last minute, or the strawberries will turn soggy).

Put the sugar and basil leaves in a mini food processor or blender and pulse briefly, until the sugar becomes light green and flecked with basil – don't overprocess, or you will end up with something more like pesto! You could also use a mortar and pestle, but be careful not to over-mix.

Arrange the strawberries over the mascarpone, then sprinkle the basil sugar over the top. Decorate the tart with basil leaves (the small ones look best) and serve immediately.

Rhubarb, blueberry & almond baked oatmeal

Serves 4–6, depending on greed

I have the wonderful Heidi Swanson to thank for this. The baked oatmeal with blueberries and banana from her book *Super Natural Every Day* has become almost legendary among food bloggers, and although I've made the original countless times, I've also experimented over the seasons with different fruits and flavours. This is a perfect way to celebrate early season forced rhubarb, with its candy-pink stalks and sweet tanginess – I wanted to find a way to incorporate it into every meal, not just dessert. This recipe makes a wonderfully nourishing and unusual breakfast or brunch – one for lazy weekend mornings, although it also reheats well in the oven or microwave for slightly more frenetic breakfasting. Do try the rhubarb, strawberry and coconut version below, too – strawberries and rhubarb complement each other perfectly, and their colours can't fail to cheer you up as you wait for spring to come.

350g forced rhubarb,
    cut into 2.5cm lengths
30g caster sugar
1 heaped teaspoon
    cornflour
200g blueberries
200g jumbo oats
60g flaked almonds
40g light brown
    soft sugar
1 teaspoon baking
    powder
1½ teaspoons ground
    cinnamon
½ teaspoon ground
    cardamom
½ teaspoon salt
3 tablespoons melted
    butter, plus extra
    for greasing
475ml whole milk
1 large egg
1 teaspoon almond
    extract
1 teaspoon vanilla
    extract

Pre-heat the oven to 210°C/190°C fan/gas mark 6–7. Grease a medium baking dish with butter. Scatter the rhubarb pieces evenly over the bottom and add the caster sugar and the cornflour. Toss to coat the rhubarb. Add 130g of the blueberries and mix gently.

In a medium bowl, mix together the oats and 40g of the almonds, along with the brown sugar, baking powder, cinnamon, cardamom and salt.

In a large jug, whisk together the melted butter, milk, egg and the almond and vanilla extracts.

Sprinkle the oat mixture on top of the rhubarb and spread it out so it forms an even layer. Pour the milk mixture evenly over the oats, and give the dish a couple of (gentle!) bashes on the worktop to make sure the milk is evenly distributed. Sprinkle the reserved blueberries and flaked almonds over. Bake for 40 minutes, until the oat mixture has set and turned crunchy on top and the fruit is bubbling up around it. Leave to cool for 5 minutes before serving.

Also try

Rhubarb, strawberry & coconut baked oatmeal
Make the recipe as above, but start with 250g rhubarb (in 2.5cm lengths) and 250g strawberries, hulled and quartered, in the baking dish. Increase the quantity of cornflour to 3 teaspoons. Swap the flaked almonds for desiccated coconut, use melted coconut oil instead of butter and omit the almond extract. Top with a couple of extra strawberries, sliced lengthways, before baking as above.

Stockists & Index

Stockists

For fresh bergamot and blood orange, other citrus and unusual seasonal fruit

    Natoora (natoora.co.uk)
    Ocado (ocado.com)

For dried herbs, spices, seeds, grains, salts and other dry goods (including dried elderflowers)

    JustIngredients (justingredients.co.uk)
    Seasoned Pioneers (seasonedpioneers.co.uk)
    Sous Chef (souschef.co.uk)
    Spice Mountain (spicemountain.co.uk)

For Middle Eastern ingredients and flavourings, such as preserved lemons, dried rose petals, date molasses and pomegranate molasses

    Honey & Spice (52 Warren Street, London)
    Ottolenghi shop (ottolenghi.co.uk/shop-online)

For Japanese and other east-Asian ingredients including yuzu, tea and noodles

    The Wasabi Company (thewasabicompany.co.uk)

For high-quality, loose-leaf tea

    Bird & Blend Tea Co. (birdandblendtea.com)
    Good & Proper Tea (goodandpropertea.com)
    Palais Des Thés (palaisdesthes.com)
    Postcard Teas (postcardteas.com)
    Whittard (whittard.co.uk)

For growing your own unusual botanicals

    James Wong plant collection @Suttons (suttons.co.uk/james-wong-seeds-plants.htm)

For infused olive oils, including basil, bergamot, lemon and rosemary flavours

    Olio Italia (olioitalia.eu)

Index

almonds
  blueberry & quinoa salad 240
  braised beef ribs 157
  cherry cakes 46
  chickpea, orange & kale salad 74
  pear, gooseberry & elderflower oat breakfast
     crumble 246
  rhubarb & blueberry baked oatmeal 259
apples 17–18, 21
  date jam 48
  fennel slaw 40
  goat's cheese, honey & hazelnut tarts 27
  honey porridge 227
  pickled salad 183
  quince & saffron compote 198
  walnut & poppy seed crumble tart 218
apricots 52–3, 56
  blueberry & lavender breakfast crumble 201
  giant couscous tabbouleh 59
  pistachio clafoutis 77
  porridge 227
  steamed dumplings 79
aubergine
  burgers with feta, walnuts, sour cherries
     & tahini sauce 32
  pineapple & coconut curry 104
  smoky salad 239
Austrian poppy seed cake 222
avocado
  crab, pomelo, yuzu & noodles 118
  papaya & feta salad 108
  salmon ceviche 70
  salmon salad 117
  salsa with sesame tuna rice bowl 113

Baked Brie with blackcurrants, toasted pecans,
  honey & herbs 236
Baked salmon with lemon verbena crust & cream
  sauce 147
Bali banana pancakes 121
banana 94
  Bali pancakes 121
  coconut drømmekage 122
  coconut porridge 227

  coffee & caramel upside-down cake 125
  tahini & white chocolate muffins 225
banana leaves 133, 136
  coconut fish curry 148
barley *see* black barley
basil
  goat's cheese stuffed chicken 37
  peach salsa 23
  sugar 256
bay leaves ice cream 167
beef braised ribs with lapsang souchong 157
beetroot
  black barley, orange, olives & smoked fish 73
  potato, dill & goat's cheese gratin 212
bergamot 54
  curd 83
  olive oil syrup cake 85
  salmon ceviche 70
  Tunisian citrus cake 87
berries 230–5
  cranberry, pear, nutmeg & maple porridge 226
  Czech bubble cake 251
  juniper with reindeer steaks 245
  see also blackberries; blueberries; gooseberries;
     raspberries; strawberries
biscuits
  cinnamon & rose shortbread 189
  spiced tea-scented Christmas 161
Black barley with beetroot, blood orange, olives
  & smoked fish 73
Black sesame cream 208
blackberries 231
  walnut salsa 242
blackcurrant leaves 132–3
  ice cream 166
blackcurrants 231
  baked Brie, pecans, honey & herbs 236
  elderflower porridge 227
  floral curd 247
  lemon verbena cheesecake 248
  peach & rosemary breakfast crumble 201
  with reindeer steaks 245
blood oranges *see* oranges
blue cheese
  crusted pork escalopes 40
  risotto with pine nuts & balsamic pears 24

blueberries 231
  apricot & lavender breakfast crumble 201
  lavender ice cream 194
  quinoa salad with feta & almonds 240
  rhubarb & almond baked oatmeal 259
bread
  halloumi flatbreads 23
  lavender, lemon & goat's cheese focaccia 176
  rhubarb & ginger rooibos tea loaf 162
  sourdough and honeyed figs 139
  spelt & poppy seed soda 211
  see also buns
broccoli ginger & lime roasted 209
bulgur wheat peach with harissa chicken 34
buns chestnut, maple, pear & vanilla cinnamon 43
butter brown 142

cake
  Austrian poppy seed 222
  banana & coconut drømmekage 122
  banana, coffee & caramel upside-down 125
  cherry & almond 46
  Czech bubble 251
  fig, hazelnut & raspberry 82
  kaffir lime & coconut 165
  olive oil & bergamot syrup 85
  Tunisian citrus 87
  see also muffins
Cambodian amok (coconut fish curry) 148
caramel banana & coffee upside-down cake 125
cardamom 205, 207
  mango & coconut cheesecake 126
  mango & lime frozen yoghurt 98
  rhubarb & vanilla jam 197
  treacle tart 214
cashew nuts
  salmon salad 117
  toasted with pineapple, tofu & greens 101
cauliflower date & preserved lemon dumplings 65
chamomile
  panna cotta with lemon & poppy seed
    crumble 186
  rice with teriyaki pork & pickled apple salad 183
cheese
  baked Brie with blackcurrants, pecans, honey
    & herbs 236
  sweet cheese & quince pastries 28
  Yorkshire curd tart 217
  see also blue cheese; feta cheese; goat's cheese;
    halloumi; ricotta cheese

cheesecake
  blackcurrant & lemon verbena 248
  gooseberry, elderflower & ginger crumble 252
  mango, coconut & cardamom 126
  raspberry, white chocolate & goat's cheese 241
  spiced pumpkin & maple pecan 221
cherries 19
  almond cakes 46
  pickled & spelt salad 37
  see also sour cherries
Chestnut, maple, pear & vanilla cinnamon buns 43
chicken
  basil and goat's cheese stuffed 37
  grilled harissa with peach bulgur wheat &
    cucumber yoghurt 34
  in rose sauce 180
  smoky chargrilled 74
chickpeas
  blood orange, kale & almond salad 74
  spinach & mango curry 99
chocolate *see* white chocolate
Cinnamon & rose shortbread 189
coconut
  banana drømmekage 122
  banana porridge 227
  fish curry in banana leaves 148
  kaffir lime drizzle cake 165
  mango & cardamom cheesecake 126
  noodles with black sesame cream 209
  pineapple & aubergine curry 104
  pineapple, vanilla & pepper crumble 129
  pumpkin & kaffir lime noodle soup 140
  rhubarb & strawberry baked oatmeal 259
coffee banana & caramel upside-down cake 125
compotes
  Earl Grey dried fruit 169
  quince, apple & saffron 198
cookies *see* biscuits
coriander 136
  salmon ceviche 70
corn blackened with papaya, avocado & feta
  salad 108
couscous giant tabbouleh 59
crab noodles, pomelo, yuzu & avocado 118
cranberries pear, nutmeg & maple porridge 226
Crispy mackerel with tahini sauce & toasted pine
  nuts, date & blood orange salsa 67
cucumber yoghurt 34
curd
  bergamot 83
  floral blackcurrant 247

Stockists & Index

currants 230–5
    redcurrants and smoky aubergine salad 239
    see also blackcurrants
curries
    chickpea, spinach & mango 99
    coconut fish (Cambodian amok) 148
    pineapple, aubergine & coconut 104
    roast duck Thai red 111
Czech bubble cake 251

dates 53, 56
    apple jam 48
    blood orange salsa 67
    cauliflower & preserved lemon dumplings 65
desserts
    apricot & pistachio clafoutis 77
    chamomile panna cotta 186
    pineapple, vanilla, pepper & coconut crumble 129
    ultimate crumble 49
    see also cheesecake; ice cream; tarts (sweet)
dill beetroot, potato & goat's cheese gratin 212
dried fruit Earl Grey compote 169
duck roast Thai red curry 111
dumplings
    cauliflower, date & preserved lemon 65
    steamed apricot 79

Earl Grey dried fruit compote 169
elderflower 174, 175
    blackcurrant porridge 227
    gooseberry & ginger crumble cheesecake 252
    pear, gooseberry & almond breakfast oat
        crumble 246
    sambocade 190

fennel and apple slaw 40
feta cheese
    aubergine burgers, walnuts, sour cherries &
        tahini sauce 32
    blueberry & quinoa salad 240
    papaya & avocado salad 108
figs 52, 56
    hazelnut & raspberry pudding cake 82
    honeyed on sourdough 139
    pumpkin & goat's cheese tart 60

fish
    crab, noodles, pomelo, yuzu & avocado 118
    coconut curry, steamed in banana leaves 148
    fried with mango, lemongrass & peanut salad 153
    mackerel with tahini sauce, pine nuts, date &
        orange salsa 67
    smoked with barley, beetroot, orange & olives 73
    sesame tuna crusted rice bowl 113
    see also salmon
Floral blackcurrant curd 247
flowers 172–5; *see also* chamomile; elderflower;
    lavender; rose; saffron; vanilla
Fried fish with green mango, lemongrass & peanut
    salad 153
fruit *see* berries; currants; Mediterranean fruits;
    orchard fruits; tropical fruits

garlic
    slow-cooked lamb with lemon & lavender 182
    tahini sauce 32
Giant couscous tabbouleh 59
ginger
    crumble with plums, brown sugar & marzipan 49
    gooseberry & elderflower crumble cheesecake 252
    lime-roasted broccoli 209
    rhubarb rooibos tea loaf 162
goat's cheese
    apple, honey & hazelnut tarts 27
    basil stuffed chicken 37
    beetroot, potato & dill gratin 212
    lavender & lemon focaccia 176
    mushroom cream with pork chops 242
    pumpkin & fig tart 60
    raspberry & white chocolate cheesecake 241
gooseberries 230
    elderflower & ginger crumble cheesecake 252
    pear, elderflower & almond breakfast oat
        crumble 246
grapefruit 94–5
    quinoa, pistachios & halloumi 102
    Tunisian citrus cake 87
greengages 18–19, 21
greens with pineapple, tofu & cashews 101; *see also*
    kale; spinach
Grilled harissa chicken with griddled peach bulgur
    wheat & cucumber yoghurt 34

halloumi
  flatbreads with spicy chipotle peach & basil
    salsa 23
  quinoa, grapefruit & pistachios 102
hazelnuts
  apple, goat's cheese & honey tarts 27
  fig & raspberry pudding cake 82
herbs 133–4, 136
  baked Brie, blackcurrants & pecans 236
  dill, beetroot, potato & goat's cheese gratin 212
  lemon balm ice cream 167
  lemon thyme ice cream 167
  Scarborough fair sausage crumble 158
  see also basil; lemon verbena; rosemary; sage
honey
  apple, goat's cheese & hazelnut tarts 27
  apple porridge 227
  baked Brie, blackcurrants, pecans & herbs 236
  braised beef ribs 157
  figs on sourdough 139
  mango, coconut & cardamom cheesecake 126
  quince & sweet cheese pastries 28
  spiced Christmas cookies 161

ice cream 167
  blackcurrant leaf 166
  blueberry & lavender 194
  London Fog 168

jam
  rhubarb, vanilla & cardamom 197
  spiced apple & date 48
  see also curd
jasmine tea with salmon 152
juniper with reindeer steaks 245

kaffir lime leaves 134, 136
  coconut drizzle cake 165
  pumpkin & coconut noodle soup 140
kale with chickpea, orange & almond salad 74

lamb slow-cooked with garlic, lemon &
  lavender 182

lavender 173–4
  apricot & blueberry breakfast crumble 201
  blueberry ice cream 194
  lemon & goat's cheese focaccia 176
  slow-cooked lamb with garlic & lemon 182
leaves 132–7
  bay leaf ice cream 167
  see also banana leaves; blackcurrant leaves; herbs;
    kaffir lime leaves; tea leaves
lemon balm ice cream 167
lemon thyme ice cream 167
lemon verbena 136
  with baked salmon 147
  blackcurrant cheesecake 248
  ice cream 167
lemongrass mango & peanut salad 153
lemons 53–4, 56
  lavender & goat's cheese focaccia 176
  slow-cooked lamb with garlic & lavender 182
  Tunisian citrus cake 87
  see also preserved lemons
limes
  ginger-roasted broccoli 209
  mango & cardamom frozen yoghurt 98
  see also kaffir lime leaves
Little cherry & almond cakes 46
London Fog ice cream 168
lychees with duck Thai red curry 111

mackerel with tahini sauce, pine nuts, date & blood
  orange salsa 67
Malaysian pineapple, aubergine & coconut
  curry 104
mangoes 92–3, 96
  chickpea & spinach curry 99
  coconut & cardamom cheesecake 126
  lemongrass & peanut salad 153
  lime & cardamom frozen yoghurt 98
maple syrup
  chestnut, pear & vanilla cinnamon buns 43
  pear, nutmeg & cranberry porridge 226
  spiced pumpkin & pecan cheesecake 221
marzipan crumble with plum, brown sugar &
  ginger 49
meat
  braised beef ribs 157
  reindeer steaks with blackcurrant & juniper 245
  roast duck Thai red curry 111

slow-cooked lamb with garlic, lemon &
    lavender 182
  see also chicken; pork
Mediterranean fruits 52–7
  pomegranate and tahini dipping sauce 65
  see also apricots; bergamot; dates; figs; lemons;
    limes; oranges
muffins banana, tahini & white chocolate 225
mushrooms goat's cheese cream with pork
  chops 242

noodles
  coconut black sesame cream 209
  crab, pomelo, yuzu & avocado 118
  pumpkin, kaffir lime & coconut soup 140
nutmeg 142, 205–6, 207
  pear, cranberry & maple porridge 226
nuts
  chestnut, maple, pear & vanilla cinnamon
    buns 43
  peanut, mango & lemongrass salad 153
  see also almonds; cashew nuts; hazelnuts; pecan
    nuts; pine nuts; pistachios; walnuts

oats
  apricot, blueberry & lavender breakfast
    crumble 201
  pear, gooseberry, elderflower & almond breakfast
    crumble 246
  porridge 226–7
  rhubarb, blueberry & almond baked 259
  ultimate crumble 49
olive oil candied bergamot syrup cake 85
olives barley, beetroot, orange & smoked fish 73
oranges 53, 56
  barley, beetroot, olives & smoked fish 73
  chickpea, kale & almond salad 74
  date salsa 67
  Earl Grey dried fruit compote 169
  Tunisian citrus cake 87
orchard fruits 16–21; *see also* apples; cherries;
  peaches; pears; plums; quince

pancakes Bali banana 121
papaya 93–4, 96
  avocado & feta salad 108

pastries honey quince & sweet cheese 28; *see also*
  tarts (savoury); tarts (sweet)
peaches 17
  basil salsa 23
  blackcurrant & rosemary breakfast crumble 201
  bulgur wheat with harissa chicken 34
peanuts mango & lemongrass salad 153
pears 18, 21
  chestnut, maple & vanilla cinnamon buns 43
  gooseberry, elderflower & almond breakfast oat
    crumble 246
  nutmeg, cranberry & maple porridge 226
  sweet balsamic with blue cheese risotto 24
pecan nuts
  baked Brie, blackcurrants, honey & herbs 236
  spiced pumpkin & maple cheesecake 221
persimmon 94
  gingered with sesame tuna rice bowl 113
pine nuts
  crispy mackerel and tahini 67
  salmon ceviche 70
  toasted with blue cheese risotto 24
pineapple 93, 96
  aubergine & coconut curry 104
  stir-fried with tofu, greens & cashews 101
  vanilla, pepper & coconut crumble 129
pistachios
  apricot clafoutis 77
  quinoa, grapefruit & halloumi 102
  toasted gremolata 182
  toasted with chicken in rose sauce 180
pizza pumpkin & ricotta 142
plums 18, 21
  crumble with brown sugar, ginger & marzipan 49
  porridge 227
pomegranate and tahini dipping sauce 65
pomelos 95, 96
  crab, yuzu, avocado & noodles 118
  salmon salad 117
poppy seeds 204–5, 207
  apple & walnut crumble tart 218
  Austrian cake 222
  butter sauce 79
  spelt soda bread 211
pork
  blue cheese crusted escalopes 40
  rosemary chops with mushroom & goat's cheese
    cream 242
  teriyaki with chamomile rice 183
  see also sausages
porridge 226–7
potatoes beetroot, dill & goat's cheese gratin 212

preserved lemons cauliflower & date
    dumplings 65
prunes with braised beef ribs 157
pumpkin
    fig & goat's cheese tart 60
    kaffir lime & coconut noodle soup 140
    ricotta pizza bianca 142
    spiced maple pecan cheesecake 221
pumpkin seeds candied 60

quince 16–17, 21
    apple & saffron compote 198
    sweet cheese pastries 28
quinoa
    blueberry salad with feta & almonds 240
    grapefruit, pistachios & halloumi 102

raspberries 231
    fig & hazelnut pudding cake 82
    white chocolate & goat's cheese cheesecake 241
redcurrants smoky aubergine salad 239
Reindeer steaks with blackcurrant & juniper 245
rhubarb
    blueberry & almond baked oatmeal 259
    cheesecake 253
    elderflower roasted 190
    ginger rooibos tea loaf 162
    poached 214
    roasted & vanilla porridge 227
    vanilla & cardamom jam 197
rice
    blue cheese risotto 24
    chamomile with teriyaki pork 183
    sesame-crusted tuna bowl 113
ricotta cheese
    lemon thyme with figs and sourdough 139
    pumpkin pizza bianca 142
    sambocade 190
Roast duck Thai red curry 111
rose 175
    cinnamon shortbread 189
sauce with chicken 180
rosemary
    peach & blackcurrant breakfast crumble 201
    pork chops with mushroom & goat's cheese cream
      & blackberry walnut salsa 242

saffron 173
    and quince & apple compote 198
sage
    candied 77
    crispy with pizza bianca 142
salads
    blueberry & quinoa 240
    chickpea, blood orange, kale & almond 74
    fennel & apple slaw 40
    mango, lemongrass & peanut 153
    papaya, avocado & feta 108
    pickled apple 183
    pickled cherry & spelt 37
    seared salmon 117
    smoky aubergine 239
salmon
    baked with lemon verbena crust & cream sauce
      147
    ceviche with bergamot, avocado, coriander &
      toasted pine nuts 70
    in jasmine tea 152
    seared salad with pomelo, avocado & cashews 117
salsas
    avocado 113
    blackberry walnut 242
    date & blood orange 67
    peach & basil 23
Sambocade 190
sauces
    black sesame cream 208
    garlic tahini 32
    pomegranate & tahini 65
    poppy seed butter 79
    tahini 67
sausages Scarborough fair crumble 158
Scarborough fair sausage crumble 158
Seared salmon salad with pomelo, avocado & toasted
    cashews 117
seeds 204–7
    candied pumpkin seeds 60
    see also cardamom; nutmeg; poppy seeds; sesame
sesame 205, 207
    black cream 208
    black cream with coconut noodles 209
    crusted tuna rice bowl with persimmon, avocado
      salsa & sesame cream 113
Slow-cooked lamb with garlic, lemon & lavender &
    toasted pistachio gremolata 182
Smoky aubergine salad 239
Smoky lapsang souchong braised beef ribs with
    honey, prunes & buttered almonds 157

Stockists & Index

Soba noodles with crab, pomelo, yuzu & avocado 118
soups pumpkin, kaffir lime & coconut 140
sour cherries aubergine burgers, feta, walnuts & tahini sauce 32
spelt
 pickled cherry salad 37
 poppy seed soda bread 211
Spiced apple & date jam 48
Spiced pumpkin & maple pecan cheesecake 221
Spiced tea-scented Christmas cookies 161
spinach and chickpea & mango curry 99
Steamed apricot dumplings 79
Stir-fried pineapple with tofu, greens & toasted cashews 101
strawberries 230–1, 235
 rhubarb & coconut baked oatmeal 259
 shortcake tart 256

tahini
 banana & white chocolate muffins 225
 crispy mackerel 67
 garlic sauce 32
 pomegranate dipping sauce 65
tarts (savoury)
 apple, goat's cheese, honey & hazelnut 27
 pumpkin, fig & goat's cheese 60
tarts (sweet)
 apple, walnut & poppy seed crumble 218
 cardamom treacle 214
 sambocade 190
 strawberry shortcake 256
 Yorkshire curd 217
tea leaves 136
 Earl Grey dried fruit compote 169
 jasmine tea with salmon 152
 lapsang souchong braised beef ribs 157
 London Fog ice cream 168
 rhubarb & ginger rooibos loaf 162
 spiced Christmas cookies 161
Thai-style pumpkin, kaffir lime & coconut noodle soup 140
tofu with pineapple, greens & cashews 101
tropical fruits 92–7
 lychees with duck Thai red curry 111
 see also banana; grapefruit; mangoes; papaya; persimmon; pineapple; pomelos
tuna sesame-crusted rice bowl 113
Tunisian citrus cake 87

Ultimate crumble 49

vanilla 174, 175
 pineapple, pepper & coconut crumble 129
 rhubarb & cardamom jam 197
 rhubarb porridge 227
vegetables
 cauliflower, date & preserved lemon dumplings 65
 fennel & apple slaw 40
 ginger & lime roasted broccoli 209
 kale, chickpea, orange & almond salad 74
 mushroom & goat's cheese cream with pork chops 242
 spinach, chickpea & mango curry 99
 see also aubergine; beetroot; pumpkin; rhubarb
Very green quinoa with grapefruit, maple pistachios & pan-fried halloumi 102

walnuts
 apple & poppy seed crumble tart 218
 aubergine burgers, feta, sour cherries & tahini sauce 32
 blackberry salsa 242
white chocolate
 banana & tahini muffins 225
 raspberry & goat's cheese cheesecake 241

yoghurt
 cucumber 34
 frozen with mango, lime & cardamom 98
Yorkshire curd tart 217
yuzu crab, pomelo, avocado & noodles 118

About the Author

Elly McCausland is a food writer, keen cook, gardener, tea collector and traveller. When not pottering around the kitchen, she works as a Senior Lecturer in English Literature at the University of Oslo. In 2016 her food blog, 'Nutmegs, seven', won Food Blog of the Year at the Guild of Food Writers Awards. This is her first cookbook, which won the 2019 Jane Grigson Trust Award.

@nutmegs_seven

Acknowledgements

A gigantic cake-filled thank you to all of my recipe testers, who saved my sanity when the task seemed just too enormous. An especial thanks to Laura, my best friend, chief recipe tester and the wittiest person I know, who somehow managed to try out more of my recipes than anyone else while simultaneously navigating the challenges of new motherhood. Also to Oliver, whom I am sure helped in some small way, if only by eating up any surplus raw cake mixture. If baby Joshua's first words aren't 'please bake me something from *The Botanical Kitchen*', then I will be sorely disappointed. I should also thank Annis and Michael, my chief vegan recipe testers, for their enthusiasm and dedication in testing everything I threw at them (not literally). Thanks to my mother, for tirelessly baking strawberry and curd tarts until the recipe was just right and for providing moral support in times of crisis (food-related and otherwise), and my father and brother, who did absolutely zero recipe testing but made appreciative noises at the correct times when eating the results. Thank you to my wonderful Granny, whose shortbread remains the best I have ever tasted and whose cooking was a high point of my childhood. Also Kate, Diane, Merlin, Emma, Adrienne, Emily, Amy, Randolph, Sarah, Vana, Annie, Suzy, Holly, Katherine, Natasha, Erin, Miruna, Eleanor, Grace, Henry and Patrick (you two probably win the award for 'most precise recipe feedback'), Hannah (you win the award for 'most thoroughly documented with photo evidence') – I cannot tell you what joy I found in you telling me that you had enjoyed my food, and your feedback was invaluable. Tore, Norrun, Anna Ma and Johannes: a huge thank you for letting me install myself in your delightfully *koselig* kitchen and offering yourselves up as my guinea pigs. Danny: for willingly consuming everything I put in front of you and tolerating the hours I spend in the kitchen when I could be staring at a wall with you instead. I would also like to thank every random stranger and friend who ever uttered the words, 'You really should write a cookbook.' Here it is. Please buy it.

Thank you also to the Guild of Food Writers, without whose generous award back in 2016 this journey would probably never have happened. My agent, Charlie, for his encyclopaedic knowledge of the London food scene, good company and invaluable help in taking this book from vague dream to actual reality. The fabulous team at Absolute: Jon, Emily, Marie and Anika, for bringing this book to life and for all your creative input, and Adam, Siân and Polly, for making my food look like something out of a fairytale – your talent knows no bounds. The Jane Grigson Trust, for believing in this book from the beginning and honouring it with your wonderful award in 2019. I hope Jane would be pleased with it.

Finally, thank you to Jack Van Praag, who many years ago inspired a love of food and cooking that has taken me places I never imagined. Not bad for a girl who lived off cheese sandwiches and fish fingers until she was seventeen.

Publisher
Jon Croft
Commissioning Editor
Meg Boas
Senior Editor
Emily North
Art Director and Designer
Marie O'Shepherd
Junior Designer
Anika Schulze
Photography
Polly Webster
Food Styling and Home Economy
Adam O'Shepherd
Food Styling Assistant
Siân Williams
Copyeditor
Judy Barratt
Proofreader
Rachel Malig
Indexer
Zoe Ross

Typefaces
Set in Suranna, Baskerville and Futura

BLOOMSBURY ABSOLUTE

Bloomsbury Publishing Plc
50 Bedford Square, London, WC1B 3DP, UK

BLOOMSBURY, BLOOMSBURY ABSOLUTE, the Diana logo and the Absolute Press logo are trademarks of Bloomsbury Publishing Plc.

First published in Great Britain 2020

A catalogue record for this book is available from the British Library.

Library of Congress Cataloguing-in-Publication data has been applied for.

HB: 9781472969453
ePUB: 9781472969446
ePDF: 9781472969439

2 4 6 8 10 9 7 5 3 1

Printed and bound in China by Toppan Leefung Printing.

Bloomsbury Publishing Plc makes every effort to ensure that the papers used in the manufacture of our books are natural, recyclable products made from wood grown in well-managed forests. Our manufacturing processes conform to the environmental regulations of the country of origin.

To find out more about our authors and books visit www.bloomsbury.com and sign up for our newsletters.